A basic handbook
of American drama

A STUDENT'S GUIDE TO 50 AMERICAN PLAYS provides concise and readable information on the characters, themes, and styles of the most important works of the American theater.

For each play:

- An annotated cast of characters
- A summary of the essential action
- A digest of critical opinion
- A biography of the playwright
- Evaluation of the play in the context of the playwright's career and the development of American drama

Plus:

How to Read a Play
An index of titles, authors, and major characters

ABRAHAM H. LASS, a well-known teacher, school administrator, and writer, is principal of Abraham Lincoln High School in Brooklyn, New York. He is the author of *How to Prepare for College, The College Student's Handbook* (with Eugene S. Wilson), *The Way to Write* (with Rudolf Flesch), and many other works.

MILTON LEVIN is a member of the English Department at Trenton State College. He has worked as both actor and director with college and community theaters. His writings on drama include a book on Noel Coward and short articles on modern plays and playwrights.

A Student's Guide to
50 American Plays
edited by Abraham H. Lass
Principal, Abraham Lincoln High School, Brooklyn, New York
and Milton Levin
Professor of English, Trenton State College

 WASHINGTON SQUARE PRESS · NEW YORK

A STUDENT'S GUIDE TO 50 AMERICAN PLAYS

A *Washington Square Press* edition
1st printing.......................August, 1969

L

Published by Washington Square Press,
a division of Simon & Schuster, Inc., 630 Fifth Avenue, New York, N.Y.

WASHINGTON SQUARE PRESS *editions are distributed in the U.S. by Simon & Schuster, Inc., 630 Fifth Avenue, New York, N.Y. 10020 and in Canada by Simon & Schuster of Canada, Ltd., Richmond Hill, Ontario, Canada.*

Standard Book Number: 671-46873-1.

To

*Betty, Janet, and Paul
and Mimi and Melissa*

Preface

A hundred years ago, a collection like this would have been impossible. A decade from now, it will probably be inadequate. Right now we believe it serves a purpose.

In mid-nineteenth-century America, in a volume which was a predecessor of *Life* and *Look* magazines—Gleason's *Pictorial Drawing-Room Companion*—there appeared an illustration captioned "The Lecture-Room of the American Museum, New York, 1853." Actually it is a picture of a theater, complete with proscenium, forestage, tiered galleries, and boxes. But to the puritanical ladies and gentlemen crowding the house, "lecture room" and "museum" were respectable and "theater" was not.

Today, of course, any news service can obtain a shot of a "hip" Off Broadway audience removing its clothes in happy collaboration with the actors, and a microphone planted in any little theater in the land can pick up words which people of a certain age never used to hear spoken even in private.

Have we emerged from the Dark Ages, or are we just entering them? Are we, in Hamlet's phrase, "crawling between earth and heaven" still?

This collection of fifty American plays, spanning more than one generation if not more than a century, offers the reader an opportunity to gain perspective on today's theater. He can see for himself how we have come to the content and style of the present; he can also decide for himself what is worth preserving in our dramatic repertory.

Reading a book of plays is important, because drama passes from the scene—literally and figuratively—all too soon. We do not have a memory of plays if we have been prevented by the accidents of birth, economics, or geography from seeing major productions.

Is there a tradition, a cultural foundation, of American drama? No editor could make a selection of fifty plays that would satisfy every reader, but in this book we have tried to include many that still live, not only in the memory of play-goers but in active production, both in revival and in repertory.

We hope to reach a number of readers: those who have seen some of the best American plays and wish to know about others; those who have still to discover any American plays earlier than last season's hits; those who have seen or read many American plays and need to refresh their memory. Meeting and understanding—on the printed page—the characters, themes, and styles of these plays, the student can go on to experiencing them—in production—much more richly.

For each play, as introduction or as review, we offer the following:

1. An annotated cast of characters.
2. A summary of the action of the play.
3. A digest of contemporary critical opinion of the play, placing it in its proper context in the playwright's career and in the development of American drama.
4. A biography of the playwright.

If the plays in this collection have anything in common despite their differences in age and quality, it is their ability to give both pleasure and insight to the reader as well as to the spectator.

Pleasure will come from keeping your eye on the ball—or, as that celebrated non-American playwright Anton Chekhov once said, on the pistol. Writing to a would-be dramatist, Chekhov observed, "If in the first act you hang a pistol on the wall, then in the last act it must be shot off. Otherwise you do not hang it there." The playreader can enjoy more kinds of suspense than Hitchcock ever dreamed of.

On the matter of insight into the special quality which differentiates one playwright from another, Chekhov was also illuminating. It is not, after all, a matter of style. In *The Sea Gull*, Trepleff, settling himself to write, and discarding one phrase after another, says:

> . . . It's agonizing (*a pause*). I come more and more to the conviction that it is not a question of new and old

forms, but what matters is that a man should write without thinking about forms at all, write because it springs freely from his soul.

It may seem strange that we come down to such a word as "soul" in summing up what may be gained from studying fifty American plays; yet even today, or especially today, a backward glance at the work of our dramatists may help us understand American goals, American humor, American people, and American ways.

A. H. L.
M. L.

Contents

How to Read a Play

A play in a book is only a shadow of a play . . . an architect's blueprint of a house not yet built . . .
                    —Tennessee Williams, in the Afterword
                         to his play *Camino Real*

This is an invitation to find the substance behind the shadow, to build the house from the blueprint.

Of course, we'd all prefer to experience these plays in performance, not in print: to know the "special alchemy composed of words, sounds, gestures, colors, lines, movements, rhythms, and silences," as the great French actor-manager Louis Jouvet once put it.

But in every good reader of plays there potentially sits a good actor-manager: he interprets the dramatist's clues to bring the words to life. As his own producer and director, he distributes the roles to actors of his own choice; designs the sets and costumes; visualizes the exits and entrances; blocks out the positions of the actors on stage; determines the pace of the action; regulates offstage music, sound effects, and lighting.

And how is the reader to do all this? The secret lies not so much in *how* as in *when*. For the playreader has one enormous advantage over the playgoer: the curtain rises and falls only when *he* wants it to.

A good stage performance is like heightened living; it's over before we realize, before we've really absorbed some of the lines and some of the action. The reading of a play, on the other hand, is as leisurely, as deliberate, as we want to make it. We're like the comfortable and unhurried mother of the protagonist in Elmer Rice's *Counsellor-at-Law:* we have *plenty* of time—time to turn back a page and reread a scene or an act, time to make a note, time to reread the whole play.

Yes, plays should be read at least twice. In every play, as in an iceberg, what's on the surface is often nothing to what's beneath it.

At first reading—a quick, light reading—we read for narrative, for plot outcome, for first impressions of character. The second time around, we know enough about these people to understand much, much more: the inner action, "the motive and the cue to passion."

When we read novels and short stories, we sometimes learn as much about the characters from the author's comments as from the characters' speech and action. When we read a play, however, we have at best the fragmentary stage directions and single-line descriptions of the characters that the dramatist chooses to provide; most of the time, we must understand what makes these people tick by listening to their words and looking at their actions: "looking" with the mind's eye; "listening" with the mind's ear. What makes the problem —an exciting problem to solve—is that the words on the page are only half the story. The text is deceptive; we must (on that second reading) translate the _sub_text and the _sub_plot.

In real life we are always aware that what people say and do is not necessarily what they think and feel. At any given moment, we may be saying A, doing B, thinking C, and feeling XYZ. (A) We say, "I'll enjoy driving out to see Uncle Richie and Aunt Liz today." (B) We take two aspirins to assuage a slight headache that has unaccountably come up at the thought of the Merritt Parkway on a holiday. (C) "I wonder why Ellen insists on wearing that color green." (XYZ) We feel a sudden desire to go upstairs and play our latest Casals recording while we eat peanut brittle and read the book-review section.

If we understand the subtext of a scene, we can imagine the rhythm, tempo, and pitch it would have in performance. Changes of thought are indicated by actors through changes in voice (inflection, tone, pitch, pause) as well as through changes in position and through gesture and movement.

One of the most remarkable actresses of the American theater was the late Laurette Taylor, whose incandescent portrait of the mother in Tennessee Williams' _The Glass Menagerie_, in 1945, was unforgettable. When Miss Taylor was appearing at the Westport Country Playhouse, Lawrence Langner said of her:

She would come on stage doing three things at once: carrying a remembrance of whence she came; recognizing the other characters on stage, and bringing in her main motivation in the play; and she could project all these feelings to the audience as she entered.*

To bring to life on the stage of our mind the characters we are reading about, we must become wholly involved with them. Who is each person, where does he come from, where is he going, whom is he expecting to meet, what is he expecting to find?

Writing about the drama, George Bernard Shaw said, "It is no mere setting up of the camera to nature: it is the presentation in parable of the conflict between Man's will and his environment: in a word, of problems."

In discovering the subplot, the playreader sees the climax in the life of the main character. And it is in the play's climax, it is in the crisis that the character comes to grips with the conflict and the problems of which Shaw spoke. (The conflict may be between two sides of his own self as well as between his will and his environment.) In coming to grips with the conflict, he makes an important discovery about himself or about others which changes the way he thinks or feels, and this discovery alters his direction. The reader, in suspense, asks, Which way will he go?

In drama, to understand people in the context of their lives we must pick up clues of mood, tone, and style in the dialogue. To see that Willy Loman in Arthur Miller's *Death of a Salesman* is something of a poet, we need only listen to his cry "The woods are burning!"—the symbol of his personal tragedy. To understand Peter's undercurrent of hatred for his father and for the stifling environment of the farm in Eugene O'Neill's *Desire Under the Elms*, we must read again the bitter words "Here—it's stones atop o' the ground—stones atop o' stones—makin' stone walls—year atop o' year—him 'n' yew 'n' me 'n' then Eben—makin' stone walls fur him to fence us in!"

Almost as important as the speech given to a character by the dramatist is the *pause* that is indicated. The reader of the play sees the lines of dialogue marching down the page. Does he also see the stops, the breaks, the silences? Interwoven

* *The Magic Curtain* (New York: E. P. Dutton, 1951).

into the speeches are the meaningful pauses: people look up (without speaking) in a certain way when a door opens to admit another character; people (interminably!) light cigarettes, without speaking, while they gather some inner force for the next line. The critic Harold Clurman praised Marlon Brando's performance as Stanley Kowalski in Tennessee Williams' *A Streetcar Named Desire* by saying, "He has what someone once called 'high visibility' on the stage. His silences, even more than his speech, are arresting."

To recreate living characters, the reader does well to remember that *gesture* often speaks louder than words. The way we say something reveals more, sometimes, than what we say. In John Van Druten's *I Remember Mama*, when Mama is in the hospital trying to slip past the guard in order to see her sick little girl, the line is: MAMA (*quickly, lowering her head*): "Floors need cleaning." By lowering her head, Mama is not just trying to escape detection; being a thoroughly honest woman, she is unable to look somebody in the eye when she is lying about being a cleaning woman.

"I write quite visually," the playwright Harold Pinter has said. "I watch the invisible faces quite closely. The characters take on a physical shape. I watch the faces as closely as I can. And the bodies."

Good advice for the playreader! Watch the faces. And— equally good advice—watch the setting. In Elmer Rice's *Street Scene*, the tenement facade is one of the characters; in Archibald MacLeish's *J. B.*, the circus top is one of the play's symbols; in Hecht and MacArthur's *The Front Page*, the roll-top desk in the reporters' room is one of the most important devices of the plot.

Most of us are better at seeing with the mind's eye than listening with the mind's ear; yet some of the most effective clues the playwright gives us are found in music or sound effects. In Carson McCullers' *The Member of the Wedding*, during Act II, a piano is being tuned in a house nearby: the sound heightens effectively the dreaminess and the melancholy of the action. In Garson Kanin's *Born Yesterday*, during the famous card-playing scene, the *slap! slap!* with which that wonderful blonde deals the cards is completely eloquent about her relationship to the man with whom she is playing.

When one is rereading a play, it is easier to know why the dramatist felt he had to write this particular play, at this particular moment, in this particular way. *Born Yesterday,* on first reading, is a bright and superficial comedy; on rereading, it is a satire that reflects postwar American revulsion against profiteering and political corruption.

A second glance at the fifty plays in this collection can in the same way lead the reader to make certain observations about where our drama has been and where it seems to be going. To take only one example—a very funny example—of the "pointing with alarm" (or pointing with pride) that is possible, here is James Thurber writing in 1960 on the decline of comedy:

> . . . the nightmares and matineemares that now afflict the drama . . . Once, last summer, when the robin woke me with his Gershwin tune, I lay there retitling certain plays to fit the temper and trend of the present day and came up with these: Abie's Irish Neurosis—The Bitter and Ache Man—Ned Macabre's Daughter—I Disremember Mama—They Slew What They Wanted—Toys in the Psychomatic—The Glands Menagerie—The Manic Who Came to Dinner—and a title calculated to pop you out of bed and into a cold tub. Oklahomosexual.

More seriously, reading a play involves more than imaginative looking and listening. It can be an exercise in human relationships. Brooks Atkinson once reported an incident after a performance of *Death of a Salesman* that echoes this: it shows how close to ourselves is every experience of drama. Going down to the lounge during intermission, Atkinson saw a middle-aged man who had been shaken by his meeting with Willy Loman, the play's defeated, tired protagonist. The man was muttering, "That New England territory never was any darn good."

What can drama give us? What do we want of the theater? There have always been almost as many answers as there have been playreaders and playgoers. In these days, we are perhaps seeing the beginning of a critical reaction against the so-called theater of the absurd and its related theater of the sordid and the trivial. In 1964, shortly before his death, the great Irish playwright Sean O'Casey, writing in *The Atlantic* about "The Bald Primaqueera," said magnificently what many readers (and audiences) have felt for some time:

The future is to have the inheritance of the theater of the ridiculous, of the absurd, of rape, of murder and sudden death, of incest, of futility, of violence, and of a basilisk pot of sexual distortions, and the land of Hope and Glory will disappear beneath the mud of a dull inferno. . . .

Ah, to hell with the loutish lust of Primaqueera. There are still many red threads of courage, many golden threads of nobility woven into the tingling fibers of our common humanity. No one passes through life scatheless. The world has many sour noises; the body is an open target for many invisible enemies, all hurtful, some venomous . . . It is full of disappointments . . . a world that aches bitterly till our time here ends. Yet, even so, each of us, one time or another, can ride a white horse, can have rings on our fingers and bells on our toes, and if we keep our senses open to the scents, sounds and sights all around us, we shall have music wherever we go.

A. H. L.

M. L.

A Student's Guide to 50 American Plays

Craig's Wife

by

GEORGE KELLY (1887–   )

The Characters

Walter Craig—a well-to-do businessman, romantic and honest, who assumes that others share his ideals.

Harriet Craig—his wife. She believes that she is practical, and that the end justifies any means. She also believes that what she wants is security, but her real drive is for complete possession and domination of her husband and her home.

Miss Austen—Walter's aunt; a good-hearted, perceptive old lady.

Ethel Landreth—Harriet's niece; a sweet, idealistic girl.

Mrs. Frazier—a neighbor.

Billy Birkmire—one of Walter's friends.

Eugene Fredericks—a young college professor, in love with Ethel.

Mrs. Harold—the housekeeper.

Mazie—the maid.

1

The Setting

The living room of the Craig home, in New York, is elegantly furnished but chilling in its orderliness. Everything is precisely arranged, as if set for a photograph. Nonetheless, when Mrs. Craig is on stage, she spends much of her time straightening, smoothing, checking for dust, or making readjustments in the furnishings.

The Story

Returning from a trip to her ailing sister in Albany, Mrs. Craig is disturbed to find that Mrs. Frazier, whom she has scrupulously avoided, is in the house visiting Miss Austen. To make matters worse, the neighbor has brought some of her roses. Roses, to Mrs. Craig, are a nuisance, dropping petals and destroying the look of the room. She orders them removed.

Her niece has returned with her, and is concerned about leaving her mother. Mrs. Craig, bored with her sister's history of illness, insists that this was a sensible move. Ethel confides in her aunt that she is tentatively engaged to a professor at Smith College, where she is a student. Harriet disapproves. A girl should not approach marriage romantically, but practically. Ethel's young man is poor, hence unacceptable. Harriet explains that her own marriage, in which she has been carefully developing her control over her husband, should be a model for Ethel.

Alone for a moment, Mrs. Craig phones "Information" to discover the name of the person whose number her husband left with the housekeeper the evening before, but the operator will not give her this information. When Mr. Craig comes home, he explains that the number belongs to Fergus Passmore, at whose house he had been playing cards.

When Mrs. Frazier leaves, Harriet continues her attack by scolding Miss Austen for letting the woman come in and feed her vulgar curiosity. Exasperated, Walter's aunt decides she must tell her nephew what is wrong with his wife. Harriet leaves the room in a huff; she has no time for an old maid's fantasies. Miss Austen tells Craig that she is leaving. Trying to explain, she points out Harriet's excessive concern about her furniture, the fact that all of Walter's old friends have stopped visiting, and her belief that he missed a promotion because Harriet had antagonized one of the bank directors. Walter finds it difficult to believe that his wife is scheming to isolate them from the outside world so she can devote herself to the worship of her house.

Birkmire arrives with news that Passmore and Mrs. Passmore have been found dead and that Walter may be a murder suspect. The newspaper reports refer to a man seen leaving Passmore's house about midnight. Craig and Birkmire decide to go to Passmore's house to observe conditions at first hand, and then, if it seems desirable, go to the police. Harriet has seen the newspapers and realizes that Walter may be the man the police are looking for. When two detectives arrive, she suspects the worst; but they are only interested in tracing the call made that afternoon to discover the address that went with Passmore's number (Harriet's call). She claims complete ignorance. Walter returns moments after the police leave, and she tells him the detectives have been looking for him. She has no doubt of his innocence, but is terrified about scandal. However, in developing her story she lets slip enough so that Walter guesses the matter of the phone call. He charges her with checking up on him. She justifies her actions by calling him a romantic fool who must be protected from his own lack of common sense. His aunt's warnings begin to assume a clearer meaning. Harriet, when he questions her, does not really deny what Miss Austen said, but she cannot see why Craig is angry about her sensible arrangement.

Their quarrel is interrupted by Mrs. Craig's discovery of a letter Mazie had left on the mantelpiece. Such disobedience of her rules means more to her than her husband's concern. She angrily calls the girl in and fires her. After Mrs. Craig goes upstairs, Walter thinks for a moment, then walks to the fireplace and deliberately drops Harriet's favorite ornament on the hearth where it smashes to pieces. He settles down to smoke, something Harriet never permits him to do in the living room.

The next morning, after having spent the night asleep in the armchair, Walter realizes that his little acts of defiance have been foolish. The morning paper brings news that Passmore had written a suicide note, so the search for the murderer is over. Mrs. Craig is delighted that she kept her husband from becoming involved. Walter tries to explain why he smashed the ornament, but Harriet is amused, still confident of her hold over him.

Ethel comes down determined to return to Albany to see her mother. She is also worried because her fiancé has not called. (He had called the night before, but Harriet had abruptly hung up on him, and now says nothing about it to her niece.) Miss Austen also prepares to leave, and Mrs. Harold is going with her. She tells Mrs. Craig not to bother to call the employment agency which will not send any more servants.

Disturbed about not hearing from Ethel, Mr. Fredericks arrives. Again Mrs. Craig coolly dismisses the inconvenient facts, doing her best to explain away her failure to tell Ethel about the phone call. Walter offers to drive the young couple to the station.

Craig tells his wife he is leaving her. He agrees that he is a romantic fool, but he cannot put up with Harriet's dishonesty. She denies that she is dishonest, really convinced that she has only been practical. After Walter has gone, she starts cleaning the hearth, but is interrupted by the arrival of a telegram. Her sister has died. This truly shocks her. She weeps, realizing that she is now truly alone.

Critical Opinion

In 1925 *Craig's Wife* won the Pulitzer Prize and was hailed by critics as a penetrating character study. Harriet Craig was so novel a character in the popular theater that George Kelly felt it necessary to provide an explanation for her behavior. Her mother had been, she says, "one of those 'I will follow thee, my husband' women," while her father impoverished the family to support another woman. After her mother's death, the other woman became her stepmother and quickly gained control of her husband and got rid of the daughters as soon as possible. Though she hated her stepmother, Harriet accepted her principles.

In his portrayal of Harriet, Kelly provides us with a fully developed demonstration of her neurosis, which takes the form of compulsive straightening and cleaning. Part of the effect of the play derives from the fact that the fussy housewife who won't let her husband smoke in the living room or have his friends visit is usually the subject matter of comedy. Here she is a somewhat tragic character.

Kelly carefully chooses the details that firmly underline his theme: Harriet hates nature because it is messy (she even wants the housekeeper to dust the leaves on the bushes outside the dining-room window), but even more because it is beyond control; she dresses in colors and fabrics that blend well with the furnishings, as if she were a priestess to the things she worships.

Today the psychological insights in *Craig's Wife* seem less impressive. Compared to such characters as Emma Bovary or Hedda Gabler, Harriet Craig is one-dimensional. Although Flaubert and Ibsen wrote long before the discoveries of modern psychology were formulated, their sensitive awareness of human complexity gave depth and dimension to their characters. The broader contexts of their work focused on society and its values.

Kelly writes from the outside in, explaining Harriet in order to make her behavior plausible, rather than beginning with the character and examining its implications. *Craig's Wife* is not so much a psychological portrait as it is an extremely skillful example of what might be called the "comeuppance" theme.

Kelly's skill is impressive. Few playwrights have his ability to construct such a foolproof plot. Every bit of detail is carefully worked into the pattern at the end. The playwright succeeds in destroying Mrs. Craig's world in a single evening, and part of the audience's pleasure comes from observing the challenge he sets himself—to build the circumstances in which the heroine almost attains her goal, only to have every one of her actions turned back on her. All of this is done almost unobtrusively, but with just enough directness to permit the audience to enjoy the display of craftsmanship as well as the triumph of justice.

The Author

George Kelly, a member of the prosperous Kelly family of Philadelphia, began his theater career by following his older brother Walter onto the vaudeville stage. Walter Kelly had developed a very popular comic role, "The Virginia Judge."

George began as an actor in vaudeville playlets, and was soon writing one-acters, in many of which he appeared. His great skill in dramatic construction owes much to these early experiences. Some of the characters and themes that he later developed in his full-length plays first appeared in these vaudeville sketches.

Kelly first impressed the public as a writer of comedy. *The Torchbearers* (1922), a satire on amateur theatricals, captures much of the foolishness and pretentiousness of an ambitious but untalented group of actors. *The Show-Off* (1924) is also a farce, but with an undercurrent of social criticism. The hero is a parody on the back-slapping, Babbitt-type businessman. *Craig's Wife* (1925), Kelly's first serious play, established him as a dramatist of skill and scope. His subsequent work, however, failed to add to his laurels.

In general, Kelly's plays have a serious cast. As in *Craig's Wife*, he has analyzed and condemned his central character, usually a woman, for a damning flaw. The tone of his work grew increasingly puritanical. In *Daisy Mayme* (1926) another scheming woman is defeated. In *Behold the Bridegroom* (1927) the hero rejects a girl for her impure past. *Maggie the Magnificent* (1929) has a heroine the author admires, but he cannot avoid making her seem self-righteous and unpleasant. In his last play, *The Fatal Weakness* (1946), he attempted a return to a comic mode, but with little effect.

Kelly's strong moral attitude combined with his skillful dramaturgy creates only cold parables. In *Craig's Wife* the combination succeeded because the methodical dismantling of the heroine's carefully constructed world has a sense of appropriateness and inevitability. However, when the subject demands more anger than distaste, and a fuller sense of the complexity of life, Kelly's mechanical formulae seem old-fashioned and artificial.

Desire Under the Elms

by

EUGENE O'NEILL (1888–1953)

The Characters

Ephraim Cabot—a New England farmer, still tough and vigorous at 75. He measures himself and his family by the stern demands of a wrathful God who requires man to be hard, to struggle uncomplainingly with the reluctant, stony land. The softer urgings he restrains in his own nature he condemns in others.

Peter) his sons by his first wife, both in their late thirties.
Simeon) They are physically strong but mentally dull.

Eben—his son by his second wife, about 25. Hatred of his father, dedication to his dead mother, and unsatisfied sexuality make him tense, savage, often irrational.

Abbie Putnam—Ephraim's third wife, 35. She tries to be calculating and coldly determined, but she finds it difficult to control her passions.

The Setting

The Cabot farmhouse in 1850 is sturdy and plain. The parlor has a few pieces of elegant furniture, but it is closed and shuttered. Only the kitchen and the bedrooms, furnished with simple, worn pieces, are in use.

Over the roof bend two enormous elms. "There is a sinister maternity in their aspect, a crushing, jealous absorption."

The Story

The beauties of the sunset set the older brothers to dreaming briefly about the gold in California. Yet, reluctant to leave their years of labor behind, they determine to stay until their father dies. They wonder where he could have gone since he left the farm two months ago. Eben, who takes care of the house, brags about praying for his father's death. He insists the farm legally belonged to his mother. Ephraim not only stole it from her but worked her to death. The young man is determined to avenge her. In a burst of self-confidence, he prepares to visit Min, the town tart. He is driven to fury when his brothers tell him they have all had her, Ephraim first.

Later that night, Eben returns and roughly wakens his brothers to inform them their father has remarried. Simeon and Peter realize their inheritance is now a dead hope, and they decide to leave for California, walking if necessary. Eben offers to pay their way if they sign over to him their claims on the farm. They agree, if their father really has married. When the couple is sighted, they sign and Eben pays them with his father's savings, which he has found hidden beneath the floor. Simeon and Peter rudely greet their stepmother and father; then, whooping and dancing wildly, they start off for the West.

Abbie is not sorry to see them go. She frankly wants the house for herself and makes little effort to conceal her aversion to her husband. She is, however, immediately drawn to Eben and tries to make friends with him. He scorns and reviles her, charging her with harlotry and stealing the farm. Confidently she dismisses his threats.

Two months later, Abbie has grown even more passionately attracted to her stepson, but he infuriates her by insulting her and bragging of his visits to Min. She complains to Ephraim that Eben has tried to make love to her, then tries to use her husband's anger by suggesting his best revenge would be to exploit the young man's labor but disinherit him. When Ephraim rejects the idea of leaving the farm to a woman,

Abbie suggests that they might have a son. He rapturously promises her anything if she can give him a new heir.

That night, still enthralled by the thought of a new son, Ephraim cannot sleep. He tells Abbie about his life, about his other wives, and especially about his trip west in search of an easier life. But his wives did not understand him, and the easy life he rejected as worthless. God demands hardship before He considers man's work valuable. So Ephraim came back to the stony land of New England. Still, nothing is right because he is lonesome and his sons have failed him. Abbie is hardly listening as she thinks of Eben in the next room. Disgusted with her inattention, Ephraim decides to sleep in the barn with the placid, warm cows.

Abbie goes to Eben's room and for a moment he seems ready to succumb. Sensing that his dedication to his mother stands between them, Abbie invites the young man to court her in the parlor. There she identifies herself with his mother, protecting him and sharing his resentments against his father. His struggle against her is transformed into passionate desire when he feels that loving Abbie will be his mother's vengeance.

A son is born to Abbie, but Ephraim does not realize that he is not the father. He dances exuberantly and triumphantly at the party he gives for the baby.

Later that night, contemptuous of Eben, the old man taunts him with Abbie's success in getting the farm for herself. He tells his son that his wife had once complained that Eben had tried to use her for his purposes. Enraged, Eben tries to kill his father, but the old man is too strong for him. When Abbie comes out, Eben turns on her and curses her. She frantically tries to convince him that the scheme was planned before they fell in love, but Eben is near hysteria and will not listen. He damns her and the child, wishing the baby dead, and announces he is leaving in the morning. He promises to stay, however, if Abbie can prove that she was not just scheming to take the farm from him.

Struck by her lover's wish for the child's death, Abbie smothers her son. Triumphantly, she announces her act to Eben. He is appalled and rushes off to tell the sheriff.

When she tells Ephraim what has happened, he is not too surprised, for his sense of imminent evil has been strong. He is disgusted by his son's latest display of weakness in going for the sheriff. However, Eben tells the sheriff that he, too, is responsible and will share the punishment. For once Ephraim is impressed.

This latest blow has discouraged the old man, and he decides to abandon the unrewarding life and join his other sons in California. He looks for his hoarded money, but that, of course, is gone. Bitterly confirmed in his belief that man was not meant for a life of ease, he consoles himself with his new conclusion that, like God, man was meant to be lonely.

Critical Opinion

The origins of *Desire Under the Elms* stretch back to Euripides' *Hippolytus,* the tragedy of Phaedra's doomed love for her stepson. The murder of the baby has parallels in Euripides' *Medea.* Like his great Greek predecessor, O'Neill sees in the story the disasters wrought by uncontrolled passions, but he brings to his play an awareness of modern psychology and a preoccupation with the American conflict between two gods.

Euripides bases his tragedy on a struggle between Aphrodite and Artemis, goddesses of love and chastity. O'Neill turns to Freud for his explanations. Abbie's love for Eben is an unstable mixture of maternal protectiveness and unrestrained sexuality, and the latter wins out in the murder of the baby as well as in the seduction of Eben. The young man is almost a textbook demonstration of the Oedipus complex. He is competing with his father for his mother's love and for masculine dominance. After a night with Min, he returns triumphantly to announce that she is *his,* no longer his father's. When Abbie seduces him, it is in his mother's parlor while she plays the mother's role. Hope for his father's death runs in Eben's mind throughout the play. Only when he can accept his relationship with Abbie as a mutual love can he also accept some responsibility for his actions.

While these psychological elements were strikingly novel when the play appeared in 1924, they now seem less significant than the contrast between Ephraim's puritanical, Old Testament philosophy and the lovers' discovery of a less abrasive belief. The play owes much of its power to the unresolved tension between the playwright's assertion that Eben and Abbie are redeemed and transfigured by love and self-sacrifice, and his allegiance to Ephraim's grimmer view that the world is a harsh and lonely place. Though Eben is meant to be the tragic hero who grows and learns through severe testing, it is Ephraim who is more likely to be remembered as he staunchly goes about remaking his world, bereft of wife or child or hope. Similar ironies surround the dramatization of other desires: for property, for security, for peace. In each instance, the ending points toward a rejection of worldly, material greed and to an uplifting spiritual view, while the dark tone of the play as a whole throws doubt on optimistic conclusions.

Desire Under the Elms is the most enduring of O'Neill's non-autobiographical plays. The struggle with the father is a pattern borrowed from the author's own life, appearing in play after play, rising to the surface most honestly in *Long Day's Journey into Night*. From the start *Desire Under the Elms* was described as sordid and sensational, condemned for its crude and clumsy plot maneuverings and dully repetitious dialogue, and ridiculed as a sophomoric attempt to give tragic stature to lumpish, bestial characters. Yet it has never failed to grip audiences, and more than forty years of disparagement have left it undamaged. Despite, or perhaps because of, all its crudities, O'Neill somehow created a dramatic metaphor that is far greater than the sum of its parts. The persistence of critical discussion is itself a sign of the play's vitality. Many of the author's works that raised fewer critical problems have been nearly forgotten. Another sign of its vitality is the eagerness with which performers approach the three major roles, for each is profoundly challenging and satisfying.

Mourning Becomes Electra
(A Trilogy)

by

EUGENE O'NEILL (1888–1953)

The Characters

Brigadier General Ezra Mannon—about 50. A stern, cold, commanding figure, he is the richest man in town and the most respected, but he has always kept his distance from everyone.

Christine—his wife, ten years younger; a beautiful woman whose dark, voluptuous looks and passionate nature seem exotic in the austere society of New England.

Lavinia—their daughter, 23. Her adoration of her father is matched by her hatred of her mother. Rigid and unattractive, she controls the singeing fury within her.

Orin—their son, 20. The war has only superficially masked the weak boy who lives only for his mother's love and protection.

Captain Adam Brant—commander of a clipper ship, in his 30's. A handsome, virile gallant and seducer, he is by no means as decisive and ruthless as he pretends to be.

Peter Niles } neighbors; Peter is in love with Lavinia; his sister
Hazel Niles { Hazel is in love with Orin.

Seth Beckwith—the Mannons' gardener, about 75. His knowledge of the Mannon family history and his understanding of Mannon psychology make him an explanatory chorus and an oracle.

All the Mannons, including Brant, have faces which are masklike in repose.

The Setting

Except for one scene aboard Adam Brant's ship, all the action of the three plays takes place near the front portico of the Mannon house, in the living room, or in the library. The house as first built by Ezra's father is big, gloomy, and oppressive despite the Greek Revival facade with white pillars and broad steps. The contrast between the cold, formal public face and the dark rooms dominated by grim portraits of the Mannon ancestors parallels the contrast between controlled appearance and inner turmoil in the characters. The house is frequently referred to as a tomb or sepulcher.

The Story

Aeschylus' *Oresteia* consists of three plays. In *Agamemnon* the great general returns victorious from the Trojan War, but on his first night home his wife, Clytemnestra, and her lover, Aegisthus, murder him. In *Choephoroe (The Libation Bearers)* Orestes, Agamemnon's son, arrives in Mycenae seven years later from concealment abroad, and with the encouragement and help of his sister, Electra, he murders his mother and her paramour. In *The Eumenides (The Furies)* Orestes, near madness with guilt and pursued by the Furies, seeks the protection of the gods, who turn the matter over to a court of Athenian citizens. They recognize the necessity for Orestes' crime and the fullness of his expiation. They decree an end to murder and revenge. The Furies are appeased, and the trilogy ends with a hymn to peace.

O'Neill followed this sequence of events but made profound changes in emphasis and theme.

PART I: "HOMECOMING"

The townspeople are excited by rumors of General Lee's surrender and the end of the Civil War. At the Mannon mansion, Lavinia, eager for news of the war's end, awaits the return of her father and brother. She is tense about matters at home. Seth, who has been puzzled by something familiar about Captain Brant's appearance, suggests that their frequent visitor may be the son of Ezra's Uncle David, who had fallen in love with a Canuck nursemaid and run off with her. When Brant comes to call, pretending that he is in love with her, Lavinia tricks him into admitting that Seth's guess is right. Angrily, he denounces his Mannon father, who had become an alcoholic and later hanged himself, and he savagely curses Ezra, who had refused to help Brant's mother when she was destitute. He has sworn to get his revenge.

Lavinia faces her mother with this information, but the older woman is already familiar with the facts. Then the daughter, whose hatred for her mother is almost beyond control, tells Christine that she, too, had been in New York the day before and knows that Christine and Brant are lovers. Determined to protect her father, she promises to keep her mother's secret if the affair is ended at once.

The adulterers consider how they can defeat Lavinia, but they know she has them in her power. Desperate, Christine reveals a plan that now seems their only hope. Since Ezra had written of some heart trouble, she has spread rumors suggesting that his physical condition is much worse than it is. She tells Brant of a drug which will poison her husband while simulating a heart seizure.

A week later, Mannon returns. Lavinia, obsessed with love for her father, greets him rapturously, and reluctantly leaves him alone with his wife. Ezra tells Christine that in the years of war he has become more aware of human pain and loneliness and wants to reawaken the love he knows he has destroyed. Knowing that anger and tension can bring on a heart attack, she scorns his overtures, pours out her contempt for his coldness, and tells him of her affair with Brant. In pain, he asks for his medicine. Christine gives him the poison.

Ezra dies in his daughter's arms. Before the end he manages

to gasp out enough to indicate to Lavinia that her mother has poisoned him.

PART II: "THE HUNTED"

Two days later, Orin returns. The war has produced in him a grim acceptance of death. His sister is upset at how calmly he reacts to his father's end. She warns him against their mother, hinting at dark disclosures to come, but he is as deeply attached to Christine as Lavinia was to their father, and he does not listen. Christine welcomes him as if he were her lover as well as her baby.

Though she knows her power over him, Christine is eager to dispel his doubts as quickly as possible. She tells him all of Lavinia's suspicions, but explains them so that the girl seems to be insane. He tells her that he is glad his father is dead, for he hated him both as a father and as a soldier. He suggests that his mother go with him on a voyage to the South Seas, to the paradisaical islands he has read about, a trip that Brant has also planned. Only one small detail disturbs Orin: his mother's letters had been few and cool during the last months. His sister's hints about Brant are not entirely erased.

Lavinia gets Orin alone and repeats her story. At first he rejects everything she says, but he can hardly believe she is mad. The suggestion that his mother is in love with Brant makes Orin furious. She tells him they can easily trick their mother into going to her lover.

A few days after the funeral, Lavinia and Orin tell their mother they are going to visit friends for a few days. Christine rushes off to Boston, and the children follow her there as she meets her lover. After she leaves, Orin shoots Brant.

Returning home, the brother and sister confront their mother with the news of Brant's death, and Orin boasts of the murder. Carried away by his love for his mother, he assures her that he blames only Brant for Ezra's death, and now they are free to go on a long voyage together. Crushed by her daughter's victory and by the vision of an empty life before her, Christine rushes into the house and shoots herself. Orin hysterically berates himself for the loss of his beloved mother.

Part III: "The Haunted"

Immediately following Christine's funeral, Lavinia takes Orin on a Pacific voyage. They return a year later. Lavinia has changed, becoming very like her mother, passionate and domineering. Orin, on the other hand, is tormented by guilt despite his sister's reiteration that the death of Christine was just. She is eager to marry Peter and at first agrees that Orin can marry Hazel.

It is soon apparent that the return to the Mannon house has intensified Orin's bitterness and melancholia. He begins writing a history of the family. In it he suggests that the disasters that have befallen the Mannons are due directly or indirectly to Adam Brant's attempts to avenge his mother, the Canuck nursemaid. He has also grown strangely attached to his sister, whom he resents for stealing his mother's identity yet loves because she is now a mother substitute. She lives in terror that Orin will be driven by guilt to tell their story. He accuses Lavinia of having been in love with Brant. On their trip they had spent a month on one of the islands Brant described, and Orin was shocked by the ease with which Lavinia accepted the amoral behavior of the natives. He even suspects that she had given herself to a handsome young man, and she says she did, then immediately says she is joking.

Growing more dictatorial, Lavinia does not permit Orin to see anyone alone. However, he does see Hazel for a few minutes and gives her his manuscript with instructions to have Peter read it before he marries Lavinia. Discovering them together, Lavinia asks for the return of the manuscript. Orin agrees if his sister will do whatever he asks. She says she will not marry Peter. Orin suggests an incestuous union to symbolize their guilt and their new identity as Christine and Ezra. Repelled, Lavinia calls her brother a miserable coward and wishes him dead. When Peter enters, Orin says he is going to his room to clean his pistol. Peter is disturbed by Orin's incoherence and erratic behavior, but Lavinia keeps him from going into the other room until it is too late.

With Orin gone, Lavinia tries to persuade herself that she is free to marry Peter and escape the Mannon doom. Hazel comes to plead with her to release her brother, whom Lavinia will destroy. Peter, too, is disturbed, not quite able to accept

Lavinia's assurance that Orin's manuscript contained nothing important. Desperate, Lavinia asks Peter to marry her at once, or even to take her physically without marriage. She embraces him passionately, calling him "Adam." She knows that her love for Brant and the whole burden of the past cannot be set aside. To drive Peter away, she admits to her adultery with the Polynesian boy, crying out in anguish. Like her mother, she finds no outlet for her passion in the cold, severe New England society.

Lavinia accepts a future of self-punishment. She will live alone in the ugly old house for the rest of her life.

Critical Opinion

As he had done with *Desire Under the Elms* five years earlier, O'Neill took a Greek tragic legend and reworked it in American terms. Again he chose a New England setting, a mid-nineteenth-century date, and a conflict between the flesh and the spirit. However, in writing his version of the *Oresteia,* O'Neill did not conceal his source (consider the title!). Actually, a knowledge of Aeschylus' trilogy is almost a prerequisite to grasping the full meaning of O'Neill's plays.

The characters are once more approached through the insights of Freudian psychology. Orin's Oedipus complex and Lavinia's Electra complex are responsible not only for the depth of their attachment to their parents but also for their later assumption of the parents' roles. More important, O'Neill employs psychological dynamics as the source of the tragic inevitability the Greeks called fate or destiny. The Mannon family carries a curse as did the House of Atreus, but its root is in their subconscious, not in the will of the gods.

O'Neill contrasts the harsh, repressed, festering conscience of the Puritan with the freedom of the savage. Though he prefers the latter, neither he nor his characters can escape the former. Neither pagan hedonism nor Aeschylian humanism can save Orin or Lavinia, who can only judge and condemn themselves. A bottomless gloom envelops the characters. They can appeal to nothing outside themselves for help, and as Lavinia sees it, suicide is an evasion and escape. There can hardly be any of that sense of redemption through suffering or emotional

catharsis which has always made tragedies uplifting rather
than depressing.

For much of his career, O'Neill was tempted to write very
long plays or sequences of plays. In 1927, for example, he
produced *Strange Interlude,* the story of Nina Leeds' search
for love, developed in nine acts of double dialogue: actual
conversation plus the characters' stream of inner thoughts.
Toward the end of his life, he was involved in developing an
ambitious cycle of plays which would analyze the paradoxes
of the American psyche by tracing the history of a single
family. Like Bernard Shaw, whose work he somewhat grudg-
ingly admired, O'Neill chafed at the limits of the three-act,
two-and-a-half-hour play. Shaw felt he needed extra time to
develop the complexities of his ideas. O'Neill was more interested in immersing his audience in the emotional experience
he was creating. *Mourning Becomes Electra* is his longest
single work, lasting some six hours of playing time (performed
with a dinner break).

For all his contempt for his father's success in the cheap
melodrama of *The Count of Monte Cristo,* Eugene O'Neill's
theatrical values are not too different. Scene after scene of
Mourning Becomes Electra is a powerful confrontation between impassioned people quarreling, threatening, or exposing
each other's secrets. The cumulative effect, however, is numbing rather than overwhelming. The psychology, no longer
novel, is too diagrammatic, and as the author piles horror upon
horror the characters become more transparent and less interesting. Perhaps because the emphasis is so much on ab-
normal personalities, the broader ethical issues have little significance.

Another serious weakness of *Mourning Becomes Electra* is
its pedestrian dialogue. The clumsy phrases and limited vocab-
ulary of *Desire Under the Elms* will not serve, nor will the
racy slang or profanity of the sailors and derelicts in O'Neill's
other plays. O'Neill frequently deplored his own lack of eloquence, and perhaps never completely accepted the fact that
he was generally most successful when he was least pretentious. In *Mourning Becomes Electra,* where verbal economy
would be welcome, inflated rhetoric and clumsy repetitiousness become doubly unfortunate.

The trilogy has also been severely criticized for borrowing
its rationale and significance from Aeschylus. What tragic

stature the characters achieve depends greatly on our recognizing their classical prototypes. This, however, is not entirely the author's fault. In French drama, for example, the Greek tragedies have frequently been reworked by the greatest dramatists (Racine's *Phèdre* and Anouilh's *Antigone*), and an awareness of sources has added a dimension of complexity and significance. In asking his audience to bring some literary knowledge to the theater, O'Neill ignored the American demand for self-explanatory novelty, and he should not be judged more harshly than his European colleagues.

Despite its limitations, *Mourning Becomes Electra* remains one of the major works of American drama. The brooding darkness of the play, rising more from O'Neill's deeply troubled psyche than from the motives he ascribes to the characters, is almost tangible, and triumphs over narrative details. The optimism that so largely prevails in American drama seems escapist beside O'Neill's plunge into endless guilt and retribution. O'Neill knew he was testing his powers to the utmost and challenging the theater and its audience. The resulting work, though flawed, has a solidly established place in American literature.

Ah, Wilderness!

by

EUGENE O'NEILL (1888–1953)

The Characters

Nat Miller—publisher of the *Evening Globe,* in his late 50s; a loving father and husband, sensible and judicious, rarely solemn and never pompous.

Mrs. Miller—his wife. She tries to be a stern disciplinarian to counteract her husband's easygoing attitude, but she can never remain firm for long.

Arthur—their son, 19; a Yale undergraduate, very conscious of being a sophisticated college man.

Richard—another son, 17; an adolescent in the grip of "Life" as defined by the turn-of-the-century aesthetes, pessimists, and socialists. His fascination with the temptations of flesh and spirit, however, are no match for his wholesome idealism.

Mildred—15 ⎫
Tommy—11 ⎬ the youngest Miller chlidren.

Lily Miller—Nat's sister, 42, a spinster schoolteacher; gentle and kindly, but firmly committed to a high moral ideal.

Sid Davis—Mrs. Miller's brother, 45; high-spirited, always joking, and a heavy drinker.

David McComber—owner of one of the town's biggest stores;
a fierce, tyrannical businessman and father.

Muriel—his daughter, in love with Richard.

Wint Selby—a classmate of Arthur's at Yale.

Belle—a prostitute whose clientele consists mainly of college
men.

The Setting

It is July 4, 1906, in a town very much like New London,
Connecticut. The Miller house is large, cheerful, and comfortable, the home of a moderately well-to-do, conservative
family. On the other hand, the bar at the Pleasant Beach House
is grimy and repellent.

The Story

The Miller children plan to spend the Fourth with friends.
Nat and Sid will be off to the Sachem Club picnic, but
promise to return for dinner and take the ladies to see the
fireworks. Sid promises, as he has obviously done for many
years, that he will not get drunk, and Lily has some hope, as
she has had for many years, that he will keep his promise
and start on his reformation. Before the men leave, however,
Mrs. Miller insists that Nat discipline Richard for reading
lurid books by Oscar Wilde, Swinburne, and Shaw. She is
startled to discover that even her prim sister-in-law is familiar
with, and enjoys parts of, *The Rubáiyát,* though naturally
not the parts about drinking and loose living.

They are interrupted by the arrival of McComber, who
confronts Nat with Richard's love letter to Muriel, bits of
verse with sexual overtones, copied from his favorite poets.
Nat tries to laugh it off as the excesses of a romantic adolescent, but McComber cannot be placated. He demands Richard be disciplined, as Muriel has been, and delivers a letter
to Richard in which the girl announces the end of their friendship.

By dinnertime, Richard has brooded his way into a tragic
and cynical mood. He disdains food and polite conversation.
When Wint arrives to ask Arthur to join him for an evening

with a "couple of swift babies," Richard offers himself as a substitute for his absent brother. He pretends to be an experienced philanderer.

Nat and Sid return from the picnic, both drunk. Nat tells the same stories of his youth that he tells every time he has had too much to drink, and Sid clowns around until he decides he had better go to bed. First, however, he proposes to Lily, as he has been doing for fifteen years, and, as usual, she rejects his offer.

Later that night, at the Pleasant Beach House, Richard struggles to maintain an air of worldliness, but Belle's smoking, drinking, and coarse talk shock him. When she suggests that they go up to a private room so she can earn her rent, Richard offers her money just to stay and talk to him. He is not really disappointed when Belle moves to the table of a traveling salesman. However, when the bartender, learning that Richard is under age, throws him out, the boy is in despair.

His return home is painful for everyone. Mrs. Miller, who has been anxiously waiting up, is alternately furious and protective. Nat tries to be stern, but cannot help sympathizing with his son.

The next day, Mildred delivers a note from Muriel telling Richard that her father forced her to write her letter of condemnation. She will sneak out that night to meet him at the beach. Though he, too, is being punished by being restricted to the house, Richard dares his parents' displeasure to keep the rendezvous. At first the boy feigns a pained bitterness, telling the girl that her cruel letter had sent him into the arms of a tart. When Muriel angrily tries to leave, Richard apologizes profusely, tells her nothing happened, and they are reconciled.

Richard returns home, expecting dire punishments. His father is more intent on discovering whether the boy has actually had any relations with the prostitute. He is delighted by the boy's indignant denials, and after a fumbling attempt to explain why Richard should stay away from such women, Nat is happy to end the conversation.

The crisis has passed.

Critical Opinion

O'Neill said that the idea for *Ah, Wilderness!* (1933) came to him in a dream. Certainly the play, his only comedy, is very much an idyllic dream, O'Neill's version of a youth he never had. It contrasts sharply with *Long Day's Journey into Night*, in which the author faced fully the painful truths of his family. In the earlier play, he chose only a few elements of his own past, combined them with details drawn from the lives of friends and neighbors, and placed them in a familiar story of troubled adolescence.

Richard Miller shares with the young O'Neill a taste for writers who speak of rebellion. Unlike the O'Neills, however, the Millers are a warm, protective family in which radicalism is tempered by love and theatrical posturing is corrected by understanding and healthy laughter. It is significant that in the first production the role of Nat Miller was played by George M. Cohan, whose own fame rested on his projecting a spirit of sunny patriotism and optimism.

O'Neill called his play a comedy of recollection, and its nostaglic tone gives it its character. All the scenes, whether comic or sentimental, are tinged with a longing for a simpler, purer time. Of all O'Neill's plays, *Ah, Wilderness!* has been the most popular with amateur groups, high schools, and community theaters, appealing on a level similar to that of *I Remember Mama* or *Life with Father*. Only when we know O'Neill's other work do we sense that *Ah, Wilderness!* is not so much recollection as wishful fantasy.

The Iceman Cometh

by

EUGENE O'NEILL (1888–1953)

The Characters

Harry Hope—60, owner of a saloon and hotel. A generous man, he sporadically puts on an unconvincing display of bad temper and stinginess. For twenty years, since his wife's funeral, he has not been out of the building. But he dreams of going out for a walk around the ward in order to re-establish his political connections.

Residents and full-time patrons of Hope's saloon—They are all alcoholics in their 50s and 60s, living from day to day on dreams of returning to their abandoned occupations:

Ed Mosher—Hope's brother-in-law, once a circus pitchman.

Pat McGloin—formerly a police lieutenant, one of Hope's cronies.

Willie Oban—in his late 30s; son of a racketeer and himself a graduate of Harvard Law School, always aware of the irony implicit in his life.

Piet Wetjoen ("The General")—a "hero" of the Boer War, claiming a distinguished record but almost certainly lying.

Cecil Lewis ("The Captain")—a British veteran of the Boer War, whose glamorous past is also highly suspect.

James Cameron ("Jimmy Tomorrow")—a newspaperman; his present condition he blames on his wife's unfaithfulness.

Hugo Kalmar—once an Anarchist writer; now he is almost always in an alcoholic stupor, repeating tags of old songs and slogans.

Larry Slade—once an important member of the Syndicalist-Anarchist Party. Unlike the others, he has no dream of returning to his past; rather, he claims to be a grandstand philosopher, coolly observing the others, cynically deriding their delusions, just waiting for death to end his empty existence.

Others who live and/or work at Harry Hope's:

Joe Mott—a Negro handyman, once the operator of a gambling house; generally he spends his time drinking with the others.

Rocky Pioggi—the night bartender, tough and unsentimental.

Pearl and Margie—streetwalkers whom Rocky manages; they are careful not to call him a pimp, and he in turn calls them only tarts. They are good-hearted but stupid.

Chuck Morello—the day bartender, sentimentally dreaming of marrying and settling on a farm.

Cora—Chuck's "tart," sharing his dream of rural bliss.

Don Parritt—18; his mother is a leader of the Anarchist movement and Larry Slade had once been her lover. Parritt is an awkward, very nervous boy, clinging to Larry for protection though he claims to be a man of the world.

Theodore Hickman ("Hickey")—a hardware salesman, about 50. His success as a salesman is apparent in his friendliness, his flow of cheerful chatter and joking, and his air of supreme self-confidence, but his exaggerated good spirits suggest something sinister.

The Setting

Harry Hope's saloon, in the summer of 1912, is a shabby, dirty place. Most of the paying customers are men from the nearby docks and warehouses who want cheap liquor and quick service. The backroom is where Harry spends most of his time among the derelicts who have settled in as his drinking partners.

The Story

Harry Hope and his cronies have spent the night dozing at their tables. It is Harry's birthday, and for years this has been the occasion of a visit from Hickey, who sponsors a week-long binge. They are all fearful of missing his arrival and the first free drink. As the men drift in and out of sleep, they talk of their various plans to get back to work, or they dully repeat the insults and boasts that constitute most of their conversation. By flattering Harry, a few manage to get some drinks.

Larry is disturbed by Parritt, who arrived the night before. The boy's mother has recently been arrested as part of a bomb conspiracy and she will almost certainly be convicted, perhaps executed. Parritt is eager to enlist Larry's sympathy and understanding, hinting that the older man still loves the woman and the Movement. Larry denies both. In Parritt's stories of quarreling with his mother about prostitutes and in the boy's references to a betrayal, Larry senses a truth he does not want to recognize. Determined to remain the unconcerned observer, Larry rejects Parritt's demands for some emotional response and tries not to listen.

Hickey finally arrives, and at first seems to be his usual exuberant self. However, he startles the men in the backroom by announcing that he no longer drinks, having made peace with the pipe dreams that had made him miserable. He does not intend to preach temperance, but he is sure that when they, too, see the light they will also feel free to abandon alcohol. He begins to challenge them to test their rationalizations.

By evening, the backroom is prepared for the birthday party, Hickey providing money for decorations, food, and champagne. Everyone, however, is on edge, for Hickey has spent the day going from one to the other exhorting and encouraging them to go out and test themselves. Even Larry is threatened, for Hickey scorns the grandstand pessimism as a pipe dream. Parritt's confidences threaten Larry from another direction, for Larry can hardly avoid inferring that the boy was the informer.

The party is gloomy. Hickey fails to infect them with his own sense of release. He assures them that it is guilt which is destroying them as it almost destroyed him. They remind him of his usual jokes about finding his wife in bed with the iceman. He tells them she is dead, then brushes aside their sympathy, insisting that she is now at peace, no longer suffering from marriage with a brute.

By the next morning, Hickey's pushing and prodding have taken effect. Most of the men prepare to go out to do the things they have been talking about. Cora and Chuck agree to get married and go over to New Jersey to look at farms. All are bad-tempered and defensive, eager to delay once more, but Hickey's nagging is too much. Larry remains, sure of the results, still rejecting Hickey's hints that suicide is what Larry should test. Parritt keeps disturbing him, now admitting his guilt but justifying himself on the grounds of momentary anger and a desperate need for money, any reason but true disloyalty.

In a short time, Hope is back from his walk, claiming that he was almost run down by a wild motorist. The others also return, all having failed, but none experiencing the release, the exhilaration Hickey had promised. The only result is their inability to get drunk and hide from the knowledge of their failure. They sit stunned and bewildered.

Desperate to help them, Hickey tells his story. He and Evelyn had fallen in love when they were in their teens, but her parents objected because he was a ne'er-do-well. He had gone off to become a successful salesman, then returned to marry her. She remained constant in her love, always forgiving him for his drinking and adulteries, always confident that he could master his weaknesses. His life with her alternated between surrender to his vices (such as his semiannual visits to Harry Hope's) and determined, guilt-ridden efforts to reform. Finally, on the day of Harry's party, recognizing his inability to resist the call to degrade himself and agonized by the thought of once more hurting his wife, Hickey murdered her. Almost reliving the story as he retells it, he repeats what he said immediately afterward: "Well, you know what you can do with your pipe dream now, you damned bitch." Staggered to discover the truth, Hickey says he must have been insane. The others eagerly accept this explanation, for it frees them from his accusations.

Two detectives, called by Hickey, have also heard the story, and now they take him away. Harry and the others insist they will be happy to testify to Hickey's insanity, though obviously he is already becoming part of a story with which they will all console themselves in the future.

As Hickey tells his story, Parritt, half-listening, confesses that he informed on his mother because he hated her. Larry realizes that Hickey was right, that his yearning for death was a lie, a way of protecting himself from the demands for sympathy he saw all around him. Unable to act himself, he tells Parritt that suicide is the only answer. Larry sits tensely near the window until he hears the body fall; then he, too, can join the drinkers rapidly returning to their old ways. Larry, however, has been changed, for he now yearns for death but also accepts his cowardice.

Critical Opinion

In the title of this play, O'Neill combines many of the thematic lines of the play. The iceman is the source of Hickey's jokes in which his own philandering is unconsciously transferred to his wife. The iceman is also death, in the person of Hickey, who not only has murdered Evelyn but whose message is one of self-destruction, for without illusion there can be no life. The author's use of "cometh" gives the title a Biblical sound, suggesting revelation and salvation, which Hickey claims to bring. Thus, the ribald and apocalyptic are ironically blended in the title as well as in the work itself.

Like so many of O'Neill's later plays, *The Iceman Cometh* (1939; produced 1946) is an attempt to deal with the author's own past. Harry Hope's is modeled in part on Jimmy-the-Priest's, a waterfront saloon where O'Neill lived for a while when he returned from sea. Another model was the Hell Hole, a Greenwich Village speakeasy where O'Neill sought refuge in drinking bouts through much of the twenties, even after he was successful. Here he also, at one point, tried to take his own life. In both places, O'Neill came to understand the defensive behavior of the failures he so vividly recreated in his play. In *The Iceman Cometh* as in *Long Day's Journey into Night* he dealt sympathetically with those damaged spirits who can survive only by clinging to illusions.

O'Neill was aware of the parallels between his play and Gorki's *The Lower Depths* (1902). In both, a "savior" presents himself to a group of derelicts, bringing the message of truth, which becomes a burden rather than a release. In each, the messenger is revealed as a fraud, and most of the characters return to their dreams, though at least one is destroyed by the knowledge of his own worthlessness. Like *The Lower Depths*, *The Iceman Cometh* is a masterwork of naturalistic staging, demanding a scrupulous reproduction of its grimy setting and minute attention to the behavior and speech of the characters. The intensity of O'Neill's involvement, the thoroughly American context, and the richness of detail and thematic variation make it much more than an echo of Gorki's play. Where Gorki draws on Russian piety and mysticism, O'Neill discovers profound parallels between American commercialism and philosophy; Gorki's saintlike wanderer becomes O'Neill's salesman of salvation.

Like most of O'Neill's plays, *The Iceman Cometh* has been disparaged as well as praised. Its staggering length and its repetitiousness have been attacked. Critic Eric Bentley says it can be shortened with little loss of effect or meaning. More serious is the question of how persuasively the author has developed his theme. Are these derelicts and their half-crazed visitor representative of the human condition? There are many ironic parallels here to Christ and His disciples (particularly to the Last Supper) as well as pagan, Dionysiac echoes. But the very accuracy of the author's portrayal puts his ugly, self-destructive characters at a distance both from their great counterparts and from the audience. It has also been pointed out that by withholding the truth about Hickey's actions, O'Neill creates a powerful melodramatic effect, but this deprives the earlier acts of the complexity they need. Thus, the overall pessimism of the play is not as fully universalized as O'Neill intended, and the world outside Harry Hope's backroom is relatively untouched by the demonic forces Hickey releases.

Paradoxically, these very objections themselves are a testament to the stature and scope of the play. No other American playwright has attempted so much and achieved so much. O'Neill measured himself against the great novelists as well as against the great dramatists, and like Melville, he pushed at the limits of form and of his own abilities. The results transcend the rough, unbalanced works he produced.

Long Day's Journey into Night

by

EUGENE O'NEILL (1888–1953)

The Characters

James Tyrone—65, an actor famous for a single romantic role he has played for more than three decades. He is compulsively stingy, always fearful of financial and physical disaster, yet resolutely opposed to expressions of pessimism. He is sharp-tongued and bad-tempered, grudging in his respect for others.

Mary Tyrone—54, his wife. A sense of the lovely, innocent, convent-educated girl lingers about her faded, nervous appearance.

Jamie—33, their son. He is cynical and dissipated, though he can be charming and sophisticated. Essentially he is self-destructive.

Edmund—23, another son. Like his brother, he is adept at drinking and whoring, but he is far more sensitive, and seriously concerned about becoming a writer.

The Setting

The Tyrone summer house is in a seacoast town very like New London, Connecticut. The living room, like the rest of the house, is spacious but furnished with an assortment of shabby, nondescript pieces. An air of transience and exaggerated thrift is underlined by the reading lamp attached by a cord to a socket in the overhead light fixture.

It is late August, 1912, after a chill and foggy night. As the play begins, the sun warms and brightens the scene, but by early evening the fog returns, denser than ever.

The Story

The conversation among the Tyrones following breakfast is cheerful, filled with bits of old family jokes, but a hint of strain lies beneath the surface. Though her husband and sons compliment her on her appetite and good health, Mary is plainly nervous. Her hands stray to her hair or to her skirts, and she is conscious that everyone is watching her. References to her sleeplessness the night before are treated with a slightly exaggerated carelessness. When the talk turns to Dr. Hardy's treatment of Edmund's "summer cold," she bursts into condemnation of all doctors, then resumes her air of sensible motherhood. She encourages Edmund to go up to rest.

When Mary bustles out to discuss the day's menu with the cook, Jamie and his father drop the mask of family cheerfulness. Tyrone admits that the doctor suspects that Edmund has tuberculosis and will phone later that day to tell them his final diagnosis. Jamie attacks his father for miserliness, charging that Edmund might now be well if they had not gone to such a cheap doctor. He suggests that his father, remembering that Mary's father had died of tuberculosis, has probably already given up hope for his son and will inveigle the doctor into suggesting some shabby, inexpensive sanatorium. In quarreling, they draw on many years of bitterness, Tyrone condemning Jamie for corrupting his brother, Jamie sneering at his father's career. Their talk soon leads to the sensitive subject which occupies the center of their attention, Mary. Jamie is certain that her sleepless wandering about the house the night before portends a return to her earlier condition. Tyrone angrily rejects Jamie's conclusions, though clearly he has been thinking along similar lines.

Tyrone and Jamie go out to work in the garden. Mary and Edmund joke about them, but Mary soon reverts to a familiar theme, her unhappiness because she has never since her marriage had a home, or friends, or an opportunity to move in polite society. Edmund, hoping to prepare her for the doctor's diagnosis, suggests that his cold may be something more serious, and again his mother reviles all doctors as sadists. Like his brother and father, Edmund is beginning to sense a familiar pattern in his mother's behavior and urges her to be calm, but she furiously objects to being watched and suspected. Determined to show his trust, Edmund goes out to talk to his brother, while Mary tensely struggles to overcome her terror.

Before lunch, the brothers sneak a drink, carefully watering the whiskey so that the bottle will show nothing missing. The news that their mother is napping in the spare room jolts Jamie, who is now certain that she has gone back to taking drugs. When she comes in, his conclusion is confirmed by her calm air of detachment, though she pretends utter lack of understanding when Jamie confronts her. When Tyrone comes in, he also understands. Alone with his wife, he scornfully dismisses his earlier hopes, but she persists in denying any understanding of what he is talking about.

After lunch, Dr. Hardy phones. He asks to see Tyrone and Edmund later that afternoon. The implications are clear. Mary angrily condemns the doctor for the way he has humiliated her, refusing help. Just such a cheap quack, she says, started her on the medicine. Pretending that she needs her glasses, she goes up to her room.

The three men avoid facing Mary's addiction by attacking one another. Tyrone reviles Jamie for his tawdry cynicism, Edmund for his fashionably pessimistic poems. The brothers sneer at their father for his hypocritical religiosity. Edmund goes up to dissuade Mary from taking more of the narcotic. Again Jamie warns his father not to let his poorhouse mentality prevent Edmund from receiving proper treatment.

Mary returns, her drugged state more obvious than ever.

She pleads with her husband to stay with her, but he is too anxious to go to his club. He recommends that she go for a ride in their car. Scornfully, she reminds him that the second-hand limousine and inexperienced chauffeur, like all his investments, embarrass her and make it impossible for her to meet other ladies in the town. As the drug takes effect, she begins to reminisce about Edmund's birth following the many years of traveling, cheap hotels, bad meals, and loneliness, and about the stupid doctor who prescribed a pain killer. Going through her litany of complaints and accusations, she reminds Tyrone of the death of Eugene, their second child, who as a baby died of measles contracted from Jamie.

Before leaving for town, Edmund tries to persuade his mother to stop taking drugs. She pretends not to understand, yet admits that she would like to stop, but cannot.

By dinnertime, Mary has reached a stage of almost dreamlike calm. Yet, when the maid mentions their afternoon trip to the drugstore, Mary automatically denies any knowledge of the subject, then turns the talk to pain in her hands, her lost chance to become a concert pianist, and the rest of the memories of her youth. She is continuing to retreat further and further into the past.

Edmund and Tyrone return, both drunk. Mary rambles on erratically about her early years of marriage. Edmund breaks through her trance with the announcement about his going to a sanatorium, and she tries to shout down his story with repeated attacks on the doctor. Driven to complete despair, Edmund calls her a dope fiend, then rushes out of the house.

Around midnight, Edmund returns, very drunk, as is his father by this time. They continue to drink while waiting to see if Jamie will return by the last trolley. Edmund talks of his near-suicidal feelings. His father quotes lines from Shakespeare, attacking Edmund's taste in literature. The talk turns to Mary and the blame for her condition focuses on Tyrone and his insensitivity. And Jamie was right, for Tyrone has maneuvered the doctor into recommending a cheap state institution. But the young man refuses to go. Guilt-ridden, Tyrone tries to explain his past—the poverty of his childhood, his great promise as an actor, and then his fear of destitution driving him to surrender to the popular but shoddy play in which his career froze. Aware, for the first time, of his father's inner turmoil, Edmund also reveals more of himself.

He describes the exhilaration of life at sea during the years he worked on board ship, and he talks of his hopes of becoming a poet.

Tyrone leaves when he hears his older son returning. Jamie immediately launches his attack on his father, but Edmund is in a more forgiving mood. Jamie then recounts his visit to a brothel. Edmund laughs along, but when Jamie asks, "Where's the hophead?" his brother punches him. Startled into partial sobriety and candor, Jamie warns his brother to beware of him. For all that he loves Edmund, Jamie says he has a great need to destroy this boy who stole his parents' love and who may well succeed as a poet where Jamie has failed. Edmund recognizes the warning as valid.

Mary wanders in, now almost completely out of touch with the present. She clutches her wedding dress, which she found in the attic. She remembers wanting to be a nun, but the Mother Superior recommended that she test herself outside the convent. So she left, confident that she would never lose her faith, but she fell in love with James Tyrone, "and was so happy for a time."

Critical Opinion

Autobiographical novels are a literary staple, but autobiographical plays are a rarity. Certainly few have been as powerful and revealing as *Long Day's Journey into Night*. After many years of struggling with bits and pieces of his past, O'Neill compressed the anguish of his youth and the discovery of his vocation into a single masterwork, one of his finest plays. Substantially completed late in 1940, it was not produced until 1956, three years after the author's death.

O'Neill began work on *Long Day's Journey into Night* just as he was completing *The Iceman Cometh*, his fullest exploration of the theme of necessary self-delusion. In his study of the Tyrone family, he again showed how the weak and insecure could find refuge in alcohol, drugs, and pipe dreams, but he also asserted the strength of young Edmund, who could face the truth about his family and himself and transmute their pain into poetry. The play itself is the fullest affirmation of that strength, for its final effect is neither gloom nor escape, but rather a sense of purification akin to Aristotle's catharsis of pity and terror.

Long Day's Journey into Night is basically simple in form. There is no attempt to experiment with symbols, classical parallels, masks, or inner voices. There is almost nothing one can call a plot, only a series of incidents which prompt the characters to dig or retreat into their pasts, while one, Edmund, can begin to come to terms with the future. Much of the force of the play derives from the sense that artifice has been abandoned in favor of naked truth. A closer look, however, shows that the years of experimentation had served O'Neill well.

The Tyrones wear masks and speak in many voices, and there is not one moment of the ostensibly rambling dialogue that is not rich in overtones. Slowly and with what almost seems like a disregard for theatrical excitement, O'Neill's characters grow to dominate the audience's consciousness and achieve a tragic substance. While we are always aware of the author telling his story, we do not experience the play as an explanation but as a reenactment of an archetypal situation that transcends the author's own life. By focusing on the reality of a personal crisis, O'Neill gives a far truer sense of the mingled hatreds and loves that a family can sustain than he was ever able to do when he drew upon the neat patterning of Freudian or Jungian theory. Finally, by using the remembered speech of his own family—with its repetitions and outdated slang—he achieves a richness and concreteness of expression he was never able to find when he deliberately strove for eloquence.

O'Neill's reputation went into a decline during the late thirties, following the unsuccessful *Days Without End* (1934). The first production, in 1946, of *The Iceman Cometh*, a play out of tune with the immediate postwar world, did little to reawaken interest in an ostensibly dated, overpraised writer. Then, in May of 1956, a powerful revival of *The Iceman Cometh* created a new interest in the playwright, and the opening, six months later, of *Long Day's Journey into Night* at once marked O'Neill as America's foremost dramatist. These two plays demonstrated that the writer's greatest skill, as he had shown from those earliest short plays about life at sea, lay in the presentation of experiences he had known. His own life had always been his best subject.

The Author

In *O'Neill: A Biography*, Arthur and Barbara Gelb have written the most detailed and sympathetic account of the playwright's life and work. The length of their book is justified not only by O'Neill's significance in American and world drama but also by the fascination of his private life and career.

As *Long Day's Journey into Night* indicates, O'Neill's mother generally accompanied her husband on his tours with *The Count of Monte Cristo*, so the boy spent much of his childhood moving between boarding schools or second-class hotels and the family's drab summer cottage in New London. His older brother introduced him to prostitutes and alcohol. Eugene was already a dissipated man-about-town when he dropped out of college in his first semester. During the next few years, he worked with his father's company, went off on a mining expedition to Central America (after secretly marrying a proper young lady, who divorced him when he made no effort to see her and their child on his return), and worked as a seaman. He also spent a short time in a tuberculosis sanatorium. Between jobs he stayed in shabby waterfront hotels and saloons. All this time he was reading widely and trying to write. A year in George Pierce Baker's 47 Workshop at Harvard gave him the confidence and direction he needed.

O'Neill's first production (*Bound East for Cardiff*, 1916) was mounted by the Provincetown Players, a group in rebellion against the emptiness of commercial theater. When the Players moved to a theater in Greenwich Village, O'Neill was their chief playwright. For years many of his plays were first produced by the Players. O'Neill later worked with the Theatre Guild, which had also developed out of a non-Broadway experimental troup. His first full-scale Broadway production was *Beyond the Horizon* (1920), somewhat tentatively presented in a series of special matinees. This tragedy of two brothers who followed the wrong dreams was critically praised and won the Pulitzer Prize for drama in recognition of the young playwright's power and the seriousness he brought to the New York stage. More than any other writer, Eugene O'Neill helped American drama come of age.

Between 1916 and 1933, O'Neill provided the theater with a steady stream of material. The range of his subjects and dramatic styles was wider than that attempted by any other writer, though the basic themes are often less varied than the surfaces suggest. In 1920, for example, he wrote both *Anna Christie*, a stark, realistic study of a prostitute, her barge-captain father, and a hotheaded Irish seaman who falls in love with her; and *The Emperor Jones*, a study of a Negro chain-gang fugitive who has made himself ruler of a Caribbean island and is driven to reliving his own and his race's past, being finally destroyed by the horrors of the jungle and the insistent beat of voodoo drums. In 1921, in *The Hairy Ape*, he drew on his memories of steamship stokers, which he expressed in highly expressionistic and surrealistic terms to trace the tragedy of a man who has no sense of identity in a mechanized society. At the time he was writing *Desire Under the Elms* (produced in 1924), he was also working on *Marco Millions* (produced in 1928), a spectacular, pageant-like play dealing with Marco Polo's visit to China and satirizing the values of the American businessman. O'Neill experimented with the use of masks in *The Great God Brown* and *Lazarus Laughed* (both completed between 1925 and 1926). In the former, contrasting a poet and his businessman friend, O'Neill used masks to illustrate the division between public and private personalities; in the latter, based on the Biblical source, he suggested masks for a Greek-chorus effect. Then, in 1928, in *Strange Interlude*, he returned to the public-private dichotomy, each character using two voices, one to express the stream of consciousness and the other for traditional dialogue.

Consideration of O'Neill's work leads us to a recognition of a few key themes. One critical study is aptly titled *The Haunted Heroes of Eugene O'Neill*. Almost all his protagonists are haunted by a sense of inescapable doom, retribution for some act of *hubris* or grim failure. Like his contemporary William Faulkner, O'Neill saw life shadowed by disillusion and guilt. Though his literary references are often to such European figures as Beaudelaire and Swinburne, O'Neill is a literary descendant of Hawthorne and Melville, who also dealt with tormented souls. Like them, O'Neill identified a dark strain in American life and spent much of his career trying to trace it to its source. At his death, he was still at work on a vast cycle of plays that would illuminate the defeat of the American poetic spirit by greed and insensitivity. Fragments of that cycle, to be called *A Tale of Possessors Self-Dispossessed*, survive in *A Touch of the Poet* (written 1941, produced 1957); *A Moon for the Misbegotten* (written 1943, produced 1957); and *More Stately Mansions*. O'Neill destroyed his copy of the last of these plays shortly before his death, but a massive draft survived, and this has been the basis for both Swedish and American productions, the latter edited and directed by Jose Quintero in 1967. During his last years, O'Neill was also working on a series of one-act plays to be called *By Way of Obit*. He completed only one, *Hughie* (written 1941–1942, first produced in Sweden, 1964).

In 1936 Eugene O'Neill won the Nobel Prize for Literature.

Winterset

by

MAXWELL ANDERSON (1888–1959)

The Characters

Esdras—an old rabbi. Poverty, grief, and brooding over the tragic ironies of existence have left him deeply pessimistic and desperately clinging to life.

Gurth—his son, about 30. Bitter and frightened, he finds in playing his violin some brief relief from his sense of onrushing doom.

Miriamne—Esdras' daughter, about 15. Beautiful and innocent, she is radiant with purity and selfless love.

Mio Romagna—a road boy, about 17. Superbly well-read although he has had little formal education, passionately idealistic despite many years of wandering and hardship, he has dedicated his life to exonerating his father.

Carr—another road boy and Mio's only friend.

Trock Estrella—a notorious criminal. He is the very spirit of destructiveness, of more-than-human evil.

Shadow—Trock's henchman. A cold-blooded killer, he is appalled by Trock's extremism.

Judge Gaunt—an old man. Half-crazed by a guilty conscience, he clings to his aristocratic values and attitudes. Even in his madness he tries to reconcile the competing demands of justice, legality, and expedience.

The Setting

The heavy masonry arch supporting an approach to one of Manhattan's great bridges dwarfs and shadows a cluster of shacks, rock outcroppings, and narrow, crooked alleyways. Pressed against the arch is an old tenement building. In the damp cellar, where pipes and boilers fill most of the space, the Esdras family makes its home. It is a dark, raw December day in the mid-1930s.

The Story

Trock Estrella, just out of prison, confides to Shadow that he has tuberculosis. He expects that he has no more than six months to live. In his fury at approaching death and his hatred of mankind, he swears that nothing and no one will interfere with his remaining time on earth. The chief threat is Garth Esdras. Ten years before, a sensational murder case had resulted in the conviction and execution of Romagna, a professed anarchist whose political affiliations became more of an issue than the crime for which he was tried. Garth is the one witness who could have pointed the finger at Trock as the true murderer, but he was never called to testify. Now a law professor studying the case has published an article pointing to Garth's absence from the witness stand and asking that the case be reopened.

Trock and Shadow burst into the Esdras house. Garth assures them he has no intention of talking. What could be gained at this point? But Trock is not reassured, and leaves a threat of death hovering over the family. Terrified, Miriamne wants to run away, and Garth must tell her the story, explaining that any attempt to run or hide would only intensify Trock's suspicions and anger. His story appalls Miriamne who cannot accept her father's and her brother's assurance that it is better to lie and live.

The professor's investigations have interested others besides Trock. Gaunt, the presiding judge at Romagna's trial, is out of his mind with the fear that he may have blood on his hands, and comes searching beneath the bridge. So does Mio, Romagna's son, who has crisscrossed the country in quest of evidence to prove his father's innocence. Both Gaunt and Mio become involved in a quarrel with a policeman over a street musician's right to play. Garth recognizes Gaunt and gets him into the basement. Mio, when the officer and the crowd have left, is drawn to Miriamne, in whose tender beauty he recognizes an almost angelic purity. She, in turn, immediately falls in love with him, offering to follow him anywhere, despite his dark warnings. Then, pressed to identify himself, he tells her of his father and his quest. Painfully, she urges Mio to go away. They hide as Trock and Shadow appear, the latter urging Trock to forget about killing witnesses. Trock seems to be listening, but when Shadow leaves, Trock signals his two gunmen. They follow Shadow and shoot him.

Miriamne returns to her family. Garth is preparing to lead the judge to the bus. At this point Mio arrives, briskly introduces himself, and demands the truth from Garth and an admission of a prejudiced charge to the jury from Gaunt. Both men defend themselves well, Gaunt building a complex, legalistic justification for his behavior. Mio is shaken. Could it be that his father was guilty? Discovering Miriamne's identity adds to his confusion; his love for her conflicts with his hatred for Garth.

Mio is almost ready to surrender to his doubts when Trock returns, clearly intending to have the judge murdered. A moment later, Shadow staggers in, near death, ready to shoot Trock, but he drops the gun and collapses. Garth and Esdras pull Shadow into the other room, while Mio pockets the revolver. It takes only a few minutes to extract the truth from Trock, and the appearance of the police looking for Gaunt offers a chance to accuse the murderer. However, Shadow cannot be found (Garth and Esdras have managed to move him into a further room), and the policeman, who was angered by Mio during the street quarrel, refuses to listen to his accusations. They take Gaunt away, while Trock clearly hints that Mio will never leave the neighborhood alive.

Outside, Mio and Miriamne cling together in the shelter of the entranceway. He tries to persuade her to return to her family, but her love is now so intense that she would rather

die with him than live alone. Mio decides to try what looks
like an unwatched path, but is fatally wounded by a burst of
machine-gun fire. He staggers back to Miriamne and dies in
her arms. Desperate with grief and anger, she runs toward
the path shouting her defiance, and is shot down in turn.
Esdras, crouched over the two bodies, praises these children
for their courage, nobility, and readiness to die rather than
yield.

Critical Opinion

After writing a succession of impressive historical plays in
verse, especially *Elizabeth the Queen* and *Mary of Scotland,*
Anderson attempted in *Winterset* (1935) a grand poetic tragedy on a contemporary subject. He noted in his preface to
the play that "poetic tragedy had never been successfully
written about its own time and place," yet he felt he had a
subject that could carry the weight of such treatment. Nearly
a decade before, he had written an overheated melodrama
about the Sacco and Vanzetti case, *Gods of the Lightning,*
and now he returned to the case for his theme. He focused
on a son dedicated to clearing his father's name and on the
tortured consciences of the guilty parties. To give the play
grandeur and philosophic scope, Anderson used Shakespearean blank verse and borrowed essential elements of incandescent, star-crossed romance from *Romeo and Juliet,*
troubled questionings from *Hamlet,* and the mingling of grief,
madness, and assertion of human worth from *King Lear.*
(Anderson had no intention of concealing his borrowings. He
has Mio refer to Ben Jonson's defense of mining the classics.)

That the author did not succeed in his grand attempt is
not surprising. Some of the play's flaws are very serious.
Unfortunately, as a poet Anderson has very little voice of
his own. Occasionally an image or line will catch fire, but the
dialogue is best when it is most prosaic. Too often it is florid
and bombastic, too self-consciously imitative and "poetic."
The tragic matters of the plot have many of the echoes, but
little of the substance, of greatness. Instead of adding weight,
the Shakespearean parallels too often become mere pastiche.
Even worse, much of the action, largely because of Anderson's deliberate patterning, is flatly implausible. For example,

Gaunt and the Hobo carry on a conversation that is modeled on the dialogue between Lear and the Fool, but it takes place in a literary universe beyond the boundaries of the Manhattan riverside and is ludicrous in the tenement cellar. Another example: Anderson works so hard to explain Mio's literary knowledge that in effect he only makes it more glaringly unlikely. Only in the scenes between Mio and Miriamne does Anderson create moments of lyric intensity, suggesting that their purity and their love have lifted them and their language out of time and place. The greatest poetic drama, however, has always served to illuminate the real world. Anderson's rarely does this.

Winterset succeeds in those elements which are least Shakespearean. Unlike the Elizabethan playwright, Anderson has at his disposal modern illusionistic staging, which he uses to excellent effect. The bridge foundations, crushing yet soaring, the cavelike tenement basement, the rain, the dark rocks, Garth's violin playing, the lights and shadows—all these are elements of the poetry of the theater, and here Anderson's hand is sure. Rendered with great power are his intense feelings about the injustice of the Sacco and Vanzetti trial, and his fascination with Trock, a figure of pure malevolence. Here more than with Mio, Gaunt, or Esdras, each inflated with significance, Anderson achieves a larger than life-size figure.

In part Anderson proved the great dramatists were right to take "advantage of a setting either far away or long ago." *Elizabeth the Queen,* for instance, is a far neater play, smoothly modeled and polished. *Winterset* is more like a monumental statue that is both unfinished and damaged, yet expressive in its very incompleteness. In the American theater, eloquence and daring appear all too infrequently. In *Winterset* Maxwell Anderson struggled to create a play that would challenge comparison with the classics, something far beyond the reach of the narrow studies of domestic crisis that dominate the contemporary stage. The resulting work, though deeply flawed, comes closer to that ideal than all but a handful of American plays.

The Author

The first play to bear Maxwell Anderson's name was *White Desert* (1923). It was quickly forgotten. The next year, his *What Price Glory?* virtually revolutionized the stage treatment of war. This might suggest that Anderson made a swift conquest of playwriting. Actually, his development as a dramatist was slow and difficult, and at the end of his career, thirty years and almost thirty titles after his first success, he was still exploring, still growing.

Anderson was the son of a Baptist clergyman in a small Pennsylvania town and was educated in Pennsylvania and the Midwest, graduating from the University of North Dakota in 1911. For several years he taught English in California colleges, then shifted to journalism in San Francisco and New York. Collaborating with Laurence Stallings, whose experiences suggested the subject of *What Price Glory?*, converted Anderson into a playwright. However, their subsequent collaborations failed, and after 1925 Anderson worked alone except for two musical plays, *Knickerbocker Holiday* (1930) and *Lost in the Stars* (1949), both with scores by Kurt Weill. Between 1923 and 1955, Anderson had a play on the stage almost every year. Some were well-made realistic works, some verse tragedies, some fantasies, some documentaries, some experiments in structure; many were outstanding successes, many were dismal failures; all were the products of a distinguished talent deeply concerned about the human condition.

Historical figures and events frequently provided Anderson with the kind of subject that most stimulated his imagination. *Elizabeth the Queen* (1930), *Mary of Scotland* (1933), *Valley Forge* (1934), *Joan of Lorraine* (1946), *Anne of the Thousand Days* (1948) (about Anne Boleyn and Henry VIII), and *Barefoot in Athens* (1951) (about Socrates) all deal with people whose personalities, ideas, and actions profoundly affected history and in whose struggles of conscience or conflict of wills the playwright saw modern significance.

Contemporary events especially attracted Anderson. In *Key Largo* (1939) he dealt with the effects of the Spanish Civil War on a young American. In *The Eve of St. Mark* (1942) he dramatized the tragic heroism of young soldiers in World War II. *Winterset* is his most notable attempt to combine the nobility and timelessness of the historical plays with the immediacy of present-day events. A full account of Anderson's contribution to the stage must also include such diverse plays as *Both Your Houses* (1933), a satire on Congressional chicanery; *High Tor* (1937), a blend of realism and dream fantasy on the subject of conformity; and *The Bad Seed* (1955), a melodrama about an evil child.

Maxwell Anderson's dedication to drama is clearly set forth in *The Essence of Tragedy* (1935) and in other essays in which he developed in some detail his principles as a writer. Although he saw himself as essentially a follower of Aristotle, Anderson's theoretical works reveal his chief weakness: a tendency to define dramatic conflict in simplistic moral terms, more Victorian than Aristotelian. In his statements on tragedy, for example, he discusses the moral conflict as a struggle between good and evil, ignoring the moral and psychological complexity that Sophocles, Shakespeare, and Ibsen took for granted. At his best, however, Anderson rose above narrow strictures. He is almost universally acknowledged as one of America's most important dramatists.

You Can't Take It With You

by

GEORGE S. KAUFMAN (1889–1961) and
MOSS HART (1904–1961)

The Characters

Martin Vanderhof (Grandpa)—a vigorous, cheerful man of
75. Beneath his folksy ingenuousness he is a shrewd critic
of the world and a nonconformist.

Penelope Sycamore (Penny)—his daughter, in her early 50s.
A sweet, homey woman, but a bit vague, she could be knit-
ting and rocking with the same naïve concentration she
devotes to painting and playwriting.

Paul Sycamore—her husband. His life is entirely taken up
with the manufacture of fireworks in the cellar.

Essie Carmichael—the Sycamores' older daughter, 28. She
wants to be a ballerina, is remarkably untalented, and
spends all her time in ballet shoes, practicing between ses-
sions of candymaking.

Ed Carmichael—Essie's husband. His pleasures are playing
the xylophone and operating a small hand printing press.

Alice Sycamore—the Sycamores' younger daughter, in her
early 20s. A lovely, intelligent girl, she is the only member
of the family with a regular job.

46

Mr. DePinna—Paul Sycamore's assistant. Eight years before, he arrived at the house to deliver ice, and stayed.

Tony Kirby—the son of Alice's employer. He is a good-looking, romantic young man.

Mr. and Mrs. Kirby—his parents, wealthy and conservative.

Kohlenkov—Essie's ballet teacher, a hot-tempered Russian émigré.

The Setting

The Vanderhofs live in a big, rambling, comfortable house "just around the corner from Columbia University." The spacious living room is where most of the family's activities take place. It has a large dining table at one side, and an assortment of surprising furnishings everywhere: Penny's typewriter and a stack of manuscripts sharing a shaky card table with one or more kittens; Grandpa's snake cases; Ed's xylophone and printing press—in short, a clutter that mirrors the free and easy ways of the family.

The Story

It is a typical afternoon at the Vanderhofs'. Penny is working on her religious play. She will turn to her war play when her inspiration changes direction. Essie is practicing her ballet steps while waiting for the Love Dreams, the candy she makes and sells, to harden. Paul and Mr. DePinna are making fireworks to meet their July 4 orders. Ed plays the xylophone or sets up type for the literature he likes to include in his wife's boxes of candy. He favors short, pithy expressions like Trotsky's "God is the State; the State is God," though he is totally unconcerned about the meaning of such messages.

Grandpa returns from the Columbia commencement exercises, the high point of his year. He is delighted by the solemn inanities the speakers present as profundities, though he is saddened by the graduates who will wake up in forty years wondering about their wasted lives. Alice returns from work and tells the family that she is going out to dinner and to the ballet with Tony Kirby, with whom she is clearly in love.

The next arrival is Mr. Henderson, from the Internal

Revenue Department, come to demand twenty years of back income taxes. Grandpa asks what his money will be used for, and the tax collector is soon reduced to shouting and threatening. His visit is cut short when Paul tests a new firecracker near him. Grandpa is delighted with the hat Mr. Henderson forgets as he rushes out.

Tony arrives and meets the family, plus Kohlenkov, who tells everyone that the Monte Carlo Ballet "stinks" (his favorite epithet.) After the young couple leave, the rest sit down to a dinner consisting mostly of corn flakes and watermelon. Before they begin, Grandpa says grace, addressing God as an equal, expecting Him to take care of their health. The rest they will manage for themselves.

When Alice and Tony return that night, he proposes to her. Alice is afraid that her unorthodox family will be rejected by his parents, but the young man convinces her that the two families will get along.

A week later, the Vanderhofs are even busier than usual. Penny has brought home an actress to read her plays; however, the actress is happier drinking whiskey, and soon goes to sleep on a sofa. Paul is building a ship with an Erector set. Alice reminds them all that on the following evening the Kirbys are coming to dinner, and everyone should be prepared to be on his best behavior. Mr. DePinna brings from the cellar an unfinished portrait of himself as a discus thrower, a painting Penny had been working on before she began her writing career. She gets into her artist's smock, Mr. DePinna dons his Greek costume, and the painting is resumed. Kohlenkov arrives for the ballet lesson, and the living room becomes a maelstrom of activity when the Kirbys arrive one day too soon.

Attempts at conversation are disastrous. Penny's offer of canned salmon or frankfurters as an elegant dinner causes special distress to Mr. Kirby's ulcers. Kohlenkov decides that Kirby should become a wrestler, and promptly pins him to the floor. Penny introduces a word-association game, which, because Mrs. Kirby's answers reveal a profound unhappiness in her marriage, leads to a quarrel. These events are terminated by the appearance of federal agents who have been reading Ed's inflammatory leaflets and have come to arrest this band of revolutionaries. Rounding everybody up, they get Paul and Mr. DePinna out of the cellar. They refuse to listen to the latter's pleas to get his lighted pipe, left on the workbench in the cellar. The inevitable follows: all the fireworks stored below explode.

The following day, after a night in jail, the Vanderhofs try vainly to return to their usual activities. They are deeply disturbed because Alice has broken her engagement, quit her job, and is leaving on an extended vacation. Tony comes to argue with her, but she will not listen. The Vanderhofs' spirits revive somewhat when Kohlenkov arrives with the Grand Duchess Olga Katrina, now a waitress at Childs, who volunteers to make blintzes.

Mr. Kirby appears looking for his son. Grandpa begins talking to him about happiness and lost dreams, and Tony tells his father the truth—that he brought his parents on the wrong night deliberately, so they could see the wonderful Vanderhofs as they are. He has no intention of going back to work and becoming chained to a pointless job as his father has been. In fact, he reminds his father of the older man's quarrel with *his* father about joining the circus, playing the saxophone, and the pursuit of other romantic dreams before "common sense" led to his enslavement. Mr. Kirby softens and agrees to the marriage, even decides to stay to dinner when he discovers that Grandpa has managed to outsmart the tax bureau. The play ends with Grandpa's grace, another of his man-to-man talks with the Lord.

Critical Opinion

Henry David Thoreau had nothing like the Vanderhofs in mind when he said, "If a man does not keep pace with his companions, perhaps it is because he hears a different drummer," and "As long as possible live free and uncommitted." He was thinking of a life of austerity, dominated by the observation of nature, serious reading, and orderly contemplation. Yet, like *Walden*, *You Can't Take it With You* (1939) is one of the strongest expressions in literature of a deeply American unconventionality. Where Thoreau wanted quiet, the Vanderhofs thrive in a zany hubbub; where he asked to escape the demands of the machine and gadgets, the Vanderhofs exist by making the machinery of the modern world serve their human needs. Penny, after all, would not be a playwright without the typewriter, nor could the family survive without the nearby grocery store with its supply of corn flakes and Campbell's soup. But, like Thoreau, the Vanderhofs have shaken off the preoccupation with making money and have found Time. As Grandpa says, since he stopped going to an office thirty-five years before, he has had "time enough for everything—read, talk, visit the zoo now and then, practice my darts, even have time to notice when spring comes around."

The argument of the play rises to the surface with dramatic clarity in the scenes with the Kirbys. Since Grandpa had himself once been a successful businessman, he can challenge Tony's father on his own ground until Mr. Kirby responds only with blustering. The main thrust of the play, however, is less direct. What the audience remembers is a delightful chaos, a strangely idyllic madness. Except at making candy and fireworks, all the Vanderhofs are frightfully untalented and totally disorganized, but their self-assurance, gusto, and uninhibited self-dramatizing enlist our admiration. The audience is quickly attracted to their side. Ultimately, the laughter is directed against the madness and emptiness of "normal" life, "common sense," "business," and "success."

George S. Kaufman always took pains to brush aside any suggestion of profound meaning in his work. Moss Hart also argued that entertainment was his only goal. Both are right only if entertainment is seen as inconsistent with seriousness of purpose. The history of drama, however, proves them wrong. Such great comic writers as Aristophanes and Molière never hesitated for a moment to deal with fundamentally serious ideas in their most knockabout farces. *You Can't Take It With You* will probably outlast many consciously significant and weighty plays because in essence it is actually more serious and more significant than they appear to be. The lightness of its touch, the gaiety of its approach add to its durability as farce and as commentary on the human condition.

The Authors

At this point, one can only guess at the true dimensions of George S. Kaufman's contributions to the American theater. Of the more than two dozen stage works that bear his name, only one, *The Butter-and-Egg Man* (1925), carries his name alone. All the rest are collaborations with writers as dissimilar as Marc Connelly, Edna Ferber, Ring Lardner, and Abe Burrows. In addition, Kaufman was frequently employed as a "play doctor" to salvage an unsatisfactory script. His name does not appear on these plays. He also acted and directed occasionally, and for a long time wrote a weekly column on theater for *The New York Times*. American popular drama, especially comedy, during more than three decades—1921–1955—owed much to Kaufman.

His first collaborator was Marc Connelly, with whom he developed such satires as *Merton of the Movies* (1922). With Edna Ferber he wrote half a dozen plays, including two very different works about the theater—*The Royal Family* (1927), a witty picture of an eccentric family of actors, and *Stage Door* (1936), a tender portrait of young actresses waiting for their big chance—and an ingenious comedy-melodrama about society and social climbing, *Dinner at Eight* (1932). Kaufman's work for the musical theater includes *Of Thee I Sing* (1932), with Morrie Ryskind and the Gershwins, and *Silk Stockings* (1953), with Abe Burrows and Cole Porter.

Moss Hart has written in detail of his collaboration with Kaufman in his autobiography, *Act One* (1959). Their backgrounds and personalities were different, and at first, Hart says, they had difficulty working together. Kaufman was fifteen years older and already an established writer when Hart, who had had only one play produced, quite unsuccessfully, came to him with the proposal that they collaborate on *Once in a Lifetime* (1930), a satire on Hollywood. Hart was a Brooklyn boy who knew the world of crowded apartments, small businesses, and entertaining on the Borscht Circuit, while Kaufman, originally from Pittsburgh, had come to the stage from journalism. He was also, Hart discovered, rather austere, silent, and a bit frightening. However, as they grew to understand each other, they became close friends as well as collaborators. They wrote six plays and two musicals together, most of which were successful.

The most popular of their other works is *The Man Who Came to Dinner* (1939), a farce about an outrageous egotist who breaks his leg outside his host's house and spends his convalescence tyrannizing over his secretary, the nurse, the doctor, and the hapless family whose house he takes over.

Unlike Kaufman, Hart also worked on his own. His *Lady in the Dark* (1941) was more a play with music (by Kurt

Weill) than just another musical comedy. It imaginatively explored the fears and fantasies of a lady executive undergoing psychoanalysis. In 1943, Hart wrote and produced *Winged Victory*, a patriotic spectacle. *Light Up the Sky* (1948) gave a vivid, amusing look behind the scenes during the tryouts of a Broadway play. His greatest success as a director was the production of *My Fair Lady*.

Of Thee I Sing

by

GEORGE S. KAUFMAN (1889–1961) and
MORRIE RYSKIND (1895–   )

Music by GEORGE GERSHWIN (1898–1937)
Lyrics by IRA GERSHWIN (1896–   )

The Characters

John P. Wintergreen—candidate for President; a handsome
bachelor whose face looks good on posters.
Alexander Throttlebottom—candidate for Vice-President; a
bumbling but sweet incompetent.
Mary Turner—an efficient secretary and a baker of superb corn
muffins.
Diana Devereaux—a beauty-contest finalist; very blonde, very
Southern, very determined.
Louis Lippmann } national committeemen; complete
Francis X. Gilhooley { politicians.
Matthew Arnold Fulton—a newspaper publisher and poli-
tician.
The French Ambassador—very French.
Senators, Supreme Court Justices, etc., etc., etc.

The Setting

Convention halls, hotel rooms, Madison Square Garden, the White House, the Senate—all gorgeously exaggerated. The date is 1931, in the midst of the Depression, but the real time of the play, like the scenery, is in the mind of a brilliant, savage political cartoonist.

The Story

The convention is over, and John P. Wintergreen has been nominated for the Presidency. The delegates also had to choose a Vice-President, and settled for—what was his name? Pitts? Barbinelli? Schaefer? No! Throttlebottom. But when he appears at the campaign-planning session no one recognizes him or pays much attention to him. They tell him to keep out of sight.

The main problem is to find a campaign issue. It may be that the public has grown disillusioned, particularly since Rhode Island was sold. What's to be done? Questioning the chambermaid elicits the fact that most people are concerned about love. Of course! They will run a contest to pick the most beautiful girl in America to be Miss White House, and the first prize will be marriage to the President.

On the day of the final judging, Wintergreen is very nervous. How can he marry a stranger? He confides in Fulton's secretary, Mary Turner, that what he wants is a wife who can cook and sew. Mary gives him one of her corn muffins, and love strikes. Wintergreen rejects Diana Devereaux, contest winner, and proposes to Mary. Later, at the great Madison Square Garden rally ending the campaign, she accepts. Wintergreen is swept into office by a landslide.

The inauguration is marred by the arrival of Miss Devereaux, charging breach of promise. The Supreme Court justices consider her charge, but rule that love and corn muffins count for more than contest prizes.

The President and his wife are soon busily involved in running the country. Throttlebottom gets into the White House as a tourist, and is startled to learn from the guide that the

Vice-President presides over the Senate. He rushes out to catch a streetcar for the Capitol.

Miss Devereaux's claims have not gone unheeded. There is considerable unrest in the country which John and Mary cannot quite still. Then comes the worst blow: the French Ambassador announces that Miss Devereaux is the "illegitimate daughter of an illegitimate son of an illegitimate nephew of Napoleon." Her jilting constitutes an insult to France.

The Senate begins impeachment proceedings. Throttlebottom, presiding, is eager to take over as President. The voting begins, but at the key moment, Mary rushes in to announce her pregnancy. Of course, no Senate could impeach an expectant father.

On the evening when Mary is expected to give birth, all of official Washington gathers at the White House. The French Ambassador insists that to ensure peace, the baby must be surrendered to France. The birth of a baby boy is announced, followed almost at once by the birth of a baby girl. Twins make the French Ambassador even more belligerent. However, Wintergreen remembers that "when the President of the United States is unable to fulfill his duties, his obligations are assumed by the Vice-President." So Throttlebottom will marry Diana and the threat of war has passed.

Critical Opinion

Of Thee I Sing (1931) was the first musical to win the Pulitzer Prize for American drama. For the first time a song-and-dance production met the requirements for representing "the educational value and power of the stage." Nothing about this musical is solemn, but in its broadly satirical picture of American politics, it is "educational" and certainly theatrically effective.

Kaufman and Ryskind present politics here as an extension of business, and national politics as totally out of touch with reality. Elections are managed like advertising campaigns and the winning candidate rewards his assistants with lucrative positions. The politicians regard the electorate as boobs who respond to simple slogans. The Southern Senators insist that campaign speeches must refer to the Civil War, though they are not quite sure when it took place. The press serves to manipulate public opinion. Wintergreen and his staff think the Washington Monument is Grant's Tomb, and the President's main relations with foreign diplomats are at poker games. Prohibition is in effect, but the consumption of liquor is staggering. The job of Vice-President is a joke (it is recommended to Throttlebottom that he become a hermit) and, of course, no cabinet officer needs to know anything about the department he administers. The satire is aimed most directly at the complacent, small-town conservatism of Coolidge and Hoover, with obvious references to unemployment, the Hearst newspapers, and fascism abroad.

The "message" of *Of Thee I Sing* is cynical; the approach is flamboyant and farcical. All the resources of musical spectacle are used with relish, but also with a relevance to story and theme that was new for its time. The usual musical-comedy pattern of the 1920s consisted of a slight story of romantic difficulties manipulated to allow for many farcical complications in which the comic couple was often more important than the romantic pair. A full share of songs and dances had to be introduced at regular intervals, often with only the flimsiest of plot justifications. The authors of *Of Thee I Sing* did not reject any of those standard devices, but made them an organic part of the play. John and Mary are the romantic couple, but they are also a delicious parody of Leading Man and Leading Lady. Throttlebottom and Diana Devereaux are the comic pair, and they too spoof theatrical as well as political stereotypes. *Of Thee I Sing* has its full quota of songs and dances, but they are carefully developed in context: the title song, for example, is the campaign song of the love ticket, and another popular number, "Who Cares?," is performed by the President and First Lady at a press conference. (In a witty exchange they comment on their own voices and consider going on the radio for a commercial sponsor. This would help pay the household bills.)

Of Thee I Sing was one of many early creative steps toward the transformation of the traditional musical. Few writers, however, have used the musical as a vehicle for political subjects, and none have equaled Kaufman and Ryskind in their inventiveness, verve, and conviction.

The Authors

For material on George S. Kaufman, see the biographical sketch following the discussion of *You Can't Take It with You.*

Morrie Ryskind and the Gershwins were all born in New York, and all found their way into show business early. Ryskind contributed sketches to revues as early as 1922. Like many other writers, however, he did his most successful work in collaboration with Kaufman. They worked together on two of the Marx Brothers' hits, *The Coconuts* (1925) and *Animal Crackers* (1928); Ryskind also worked on the film adaptations of these scripts. With the Gershwins, they wrote *Of Thee I Sing* (1931) and *Let 'Em Eat Cake* (1933). Ryskind also collaborated with Howard Dietz—*Merry-Go-Round* (1927)— and with Irving Berlin—*Louisiana Purchase* (1940). He has also written light verse and humorous newspaper pieces.

George Gershwin's gift for melody was recognized very early. In 1920, at the age of 22, he was responsible for the entire musical score of that year's edition of the *George White Scandals.* Most of the shows with which he was connected were of the type so popular in the twenties, nothing much more than a skeletal plot on which to hang songs and dances. Almost all have been forgotten. Gershwin's songs, however, have retained their popularity.

Very early in his career, Gershwin began writing works which he hoped would bring the vitality of popular music into the concert hall. *Rhapsody in Blue* (1923) and the Concerto in F (1925) are two of his more ambitious compositions. In *Porgy and Bess* (1935) Gershwin moved far toward creating a distinctively American operatic form. His death at 39 cut short one of the most distinguished careers in modern music.

Ira Gershwin, a few years older than his brother, wrote the lyrics for almost all of George's songs. Since 1937, Ira has worked with other writers, most notably with Moss Hart and Kurt Weill in creating *Lady in the Dark* (1941).

Life with Father

by

HOWARD LINDSAY (1889–   ) and
RUSSEL CROUSE (1893–1966)

The Characters

The Day Family:
Father (Clarence, Sr.)—in his 40s, a successful stockbroker.
 Proud, opinionated, brusque, and hot-tempered; deeply
 devoted to his family, but riding roughshod over the feel-
 ings of others.
Mother (Vinnie)—a few years younger; pretty, warm, equally
 devoted to the family, impractical about handling money
 but very wise about handling her husband.
The Boys: Clarence, Jr. 17 and ready for Yale; *John,* 15;
 Whitney, 13; and *Harlan,* 6. All the children are high-
 spirited but well-behaved.
All the Days have bright-red hair.

Visitors:
Cora—a cousin, about 30; an attractive spinster.
Mary Skinner—a friend of Cora's, about 17; a charming, ro-
 mantic girl.

Margaret—the cook; the only servant Father cannot intimidate.
Annie, Delia, Nora, Maggie—maids; shy young Irish immigrants who work for the Day family for a brief time, sometimes less than a morning.

The Setting

The morning room of the Day house, a bright, informal
room where the family eats breakfast; an informal drawing
room most of the time. The Days live on Madison Avenue and
Forty-eighth Street. It is summer late in the 1880s.

The Story

Breakfast is a delicate time at the Days'. Father can be
bearish if he does not like the food or the service. Yet this is
also the time when such sensitive matters as family finance
must be raised. This morning, the matter is complicated, as it
frequently is, by the presence of a new maid, inexperienced
and unsophisticated. The meal begins promisingly when
Father agrees to let Clarence have one of his old suits, but his
profanity and jocular attitude toward the afterlife shock Annie,
the maid, and she is soon reduced to tears by Father's critical
attitude. When a newspaper item about new taxes draws
an angry diatribe from Father, thunderingly delivered to the
invisible Mayor, Annie rushes out and topples down the stairs
with a tray of dishes. Father goes to work, as usual quite
unaware of the havoc he has created.

Cora arrives to spend a few days, a visit Vinnie has kept
secret from her husband. Another visitor is Mary Skinner, who
tells Clarence she never met a Yale man before. Much to his
bewilderment, Clarence discovers girls can be interesting and
pleasant.

When Father returns from work, he finds the Reverend Dr.
Lloyd at tea. A request for five thousand dollars toward a new
church building sends Father into a rage. He is delighted to
see Cora and Mary until he realizes they are staying in his
house. Once again his temper explodes, and he storms out.

Mary and Clarence begin to share confidences, including
the fact that Mary is a Methodist. The Days are Episcopalians.

When Father returns, Mary questions him to discover whether he might just possibly have been baptized a Methodist. Searching his memory, Father recalls that he has never been baptized at all. His parents were freethinkers who thought their children should choose their own religion. Vinnie is overwhelmed, even fears that they may not be properly married, and insists that Father must be baptized. He curtly dismisses the whole matter as an oversight which it is too late to correct.

The following Sunday brings a host of problems. Clarence finds that while wearing his father's clothes he cannot do anything his father would not do, so he was unable to kneel in church and won't let Mary sit on his lap. She is insulted and says she will never write unless he writes first. In church, Father is so infuriated by Dr. Lloyd's sermon about baptism that he blurts out his opinions. And now the whole congregation knows that he has never been baptized. Going over the monthly bills increases his wrath, for not only is Vinnie extravagant, but he cannot even get her to understand simple arithmetic. Vinnie quiets him in time to say good-bye to Cora and Mary. The latter pointedly ignores Clarence, whose determination to be master crumbles at once. He begins a letter to Mary the moment the door closes behind her.

A few days later, Vinnie is ill. Father's sympathy is limited; he usually swears illness out of his system. Clarence and John intend to peddle Dr. Bartlett's Beneficent Balm. To prove that their own family uses the nostrum, they pour a strong dose into their mother's tea. Later, when Vinnie becomes seriously ill, the doctors are unable to diagnose the problem. Father is so desperate that he promises to do anything to help his wife recover, even get himself baptized.

A month later, Vinnie, fully recovered, awaits the return of Cora and Mary for another brief stay. She has treated herself to a large, expensive china dog, which she places in the center of the table. Once again Clarence's hopes for a new suit are dashed when Dr. Bartlett pays the boys in medicine. Father, in an ungenerous mood, denies Clarence's request for new clothes, orders Vinnie to return the china dog, and refuses to go to another parish to be baptized. Mother interprets Father's vehemence about the dog to mean that he will agree to the baptism if she returns the object. Struck by the price, Clarence asks whether he can use the credit for the dog to buy the suit, which costs exactly the same amount. Vinnie considers this a fine, thrifty decision.

The next morning, Father discovers the stratagem used to get the suit but fails to convince Vinnie that the suit was not free. The arrival of Cora and Mary adds little to his peace of mind. Then, when a complaint of dog poisoning comes in a letter, he learns of the medicine sales and the cause of Vinnie's desperate illness. Father has a moment of joy when he hears that Cora and Mary cannot stay, but his spirits are dashed when the cab arrives to take the family to Audubon for his baptism.

Critical Opinion

Based on the amusing autobiographical sketches of Clarence Day, *Life with Father* has been one of the most fantastically successful plays in the history of the American theater. It holds the record as longest-running play on Broadway (3,216 consecutive performances, 1939–1947). The many traveling companies, the film version, and innumerable stock and amateur productions have also done exceptionally well. Much of this almost universal acclaim is due to the excellent original production, particularly Lindsay's marvelous portrayal of Father, and the lovely performance by Dorothy Stickney (Mrs. Lindsay) as Mother. Both created superb models for all others who have approached these roles. Still, it is surprising that so slight a story should have had so great an impact. Some of its appeal would seem to be in its period, the late nineteenth century, which has a strong nostalgic hold on most Americans. This era is seen as a peaceful, prosperous, expansive time, when people had few problems and it was perpetually summer. In *Life with Father*, even New York City seems to be of reasonable, human size. The Days live at Forty-eighth and Madison and complain that the area is no longer as rural as they would like it to be. To reach Harlem, which is a well-to-do suburb, one needs to hire a cab. The Days buy their ice cream from Mr. Louis Sherry himself, not from an impersonal store, and though Father frightens all the maids into quitting, there is an endless supply of new ones. The personal problems the Days face are similarly small-scale, domestic, manageable. Clarence's first romance will fail unless he can replace Father's puritanical trousers, but his mother's financial vagueness solves the problem. The boys are exploited by the manufacturer of a near-poisonous panacea, but Vinnie recovers nicely and Father will repay the customers. Above all, Father's baptism, or lack of it, is amusing because to the audience of the thirties and forties the problem had little weight but harked back to a simpler, better era.

Life with Father had a special effect on its audiences when it first appeared, only two months after the German invasion of Poland. It continued its phenomenal run into the post-World-War II period.

Another appealing element in *Life with Father* is the mother-knows-best theme. Vinnie may be hopelessly incompetent about money (the man's province), but she has a perfect grasp of one essential, managing Father for his own good. He is, after all, just her biggest boy. Though everyone quakes before his thundering "Damn!," she knows how tender and kind he really is. Just let him get the steam out of his system, and he will be as sweet and cooperative as anyone could want. This leitmotif runs through much popular American comedy, particularly on television. It has rarely been handled so gracefully, so charmingly, so unforgettably as in *Life with Father*.

Lindsay and Crouse write with professional polish. Each scene is deftly honed to a sharp, comic point. There are very few funny lines, but skillful repetition and variation bring the key dramatic points to a delightful climax. The affection Lindsay and Crouse feel for their characters, their times, their customs, their values has been joyously shared by audiences all over America.

The Authors

The American theater between world wars was characterized by the development of an unusual number of successful writing teams. By far the most successful of these collaborations was that of Howard Lindsay and Russel Crouse. They came together almost by accident, but once they had discovered their affinity, they worked not only as writers but as producers until Crouse's death in 1966.

Howard Lindsay began life in Saratoga, New York. While he was a child, his mother left her husband and took her children to live in Atlantic City. There the boy became a board-walk entertainer and a frequent visitor to the theater. Atlantic City was then an important stop for traveling companies as well as the home of active stock companies. In his teens, Lindsay's family lived in Massachusetts, and for a while Howard seemed headed for a future in the ministry. But the attractions of the theater proved too great. He attended the American Academy of Dramatic Arts and went on tour as an actor and stage manager. After World War I he settled in New York as actor, director, and playwright. His writing was moderately successful, and in 1934 he was asked to take P. G. Wodehouse's script for *Anything Goes* (music and lyrics by Cole Porter) and rewrite it in ten days. Lindsay agreed, provided he had a collaborator. The producer suggested Russel Crouse.

Originally from a small town in Ohio, Crouse, like so many playwrights, started out as a newspaperman. He worked in Cincinnati and in Kansas City before entering the Navy in World War I. After his discharge, he decided to stay in New York, where he became a reporter on the *Globe*. In 1930 his first successful play, *Mr. Currier and Mr. Ives*, was produced. In the next three years, he had three other works presented, all well received. However, collaborating with Lindsay on *Anything Goes* proved to be pleasanter and more productive than working alone. So the team was formed.

In addition to *Anything Goes*, Lindsay and Crouse were responsible for the books of such popular musicals as *Red, Hot and Blue* (1936), *Call Me Madam* (1950), *Happy Hunting* (1956), and *The Sound of Music* (1959). The last has many of the qualities of *Life with Father*, including its extraordinary success. The subject is once again drawn from real life, this time the experiences of the Trapp family. Much of the humor lies in the taming of the irascible father.

State of the Union (1945), a comedy about the campaign of a Presidential candidate, was continually rewritten, even while the play was on tour, to keep all references topical.

In 1948 *Life with Mother* appeared, a pale replica of the earlier hit. After 1950, although the Lindsay-Crouse musicals were usually long-running money-makers, their comedies had more modest success. The vigorous wit and ingenuity that distinguished their plays of the thirties and forties gave way to a pleasant but somewhat routine humor.

Porgy

by

DOROTHY HEYWARD (1890–1961) and
DUBOSE HEYWARD (1885–1940)

The Characters

Porgy—a crippled beggar, whose strong arms contrast sharply
with his withered legs. He gets about in a handmade goat
cart. Compared to the other residents of Catfish Row, he is
a serious, contemplative man.

Crown—a tall, powerful stevedore with a vicious temper.

Crown's Bess—his woman, an attractive girl who proudly
flaunts her sensuality.

Sporting Life—bootlegger and narcotics peddler; a slick, big-
city type quick to exploit his customers' ignorance.

Robbins and Serena—a young stevedore and his wife.

Jake and Clara—a fishing-boat captain and his wife.

Peter—a streetseller of honey; a nearly senile man.

Simon Frazier—an unscrupulous lawyer.

Alan Archdale—a white lawyer sympathetic to the Negroes.

Policemen, a detective, the coroner—all white and generally
brutal in their dealings with the Negroes.

A wide variety of other people—residents of Catfish Row,
fishermen, passersby, etc.

The Setting

Catfish Row was once one of the finest mansions in Charleston, South Carolina, but it is now (1925) a crowded Negro tenement. Some traces of its old splendor still remain, window boxes filled with geraniums add flamboyant color, but poverty is the dominant note. The courtyard is the heart of the house, and there is continual activity as the women wash their clothes at the pump or gossip from window to window, and the men gather to talk or gamble. Through the gate one can see the fishing wharves and part of the bay.

It is summer, hot and humid, a time when sudden storms break and tempers are short.

The Story

The men gather in the courtyard for the Saturday-night crap game. Crown arrives in a bad temper, partly drunk. He gulps down more liquor. The women look with disapproval at Bess, but it is clear that Porgy worships her. The game goes badly for Crown, and his drunken frenzy is increased after he inhales some "happy dust" (cocaine). When he loses once more to Robbins, Crown starts a fight, and kills the young stevedore. He must go into hiding. Bess will have to take care of herself until he returns. Sporting Life offers Bess a job in New York, apparently in a brothel, but she brushes him aside. The women of Catfish Row refuse to shelter her, but Porgy takes her in.

At the wake for Robbins, the police try to discover the identity of the murderer, but the Negroes will not cooperate with the white authorities. A detective accuses Peter, and when the old man panics and tells them Crown did it, they cynically take the honeyseller into custody until the guilty man turns up.

Some days later, the whole house is busy with preparations for the annual picnic on Kittiwah Island. Porgy wants Bess to go, but she still feels that the others despise her. Simon Frazier, discovering that Bess is in love with Porgy, sells her a splendidly embossed, gold-sealed divorce. Archdale, the white lawyer, comes looking for Porgy to arrange for the release of Peter. He catches Frazier at his fraudulent divorce business, but both Bess and Porgy agree to keep the paper as a sign of their new relationship. To her delight, Bess is invited to join the others on the picnic, an even more certain sign that she has achieved respectability. Porgy remains behind to carry out the lawyer's orders.

That night, as the exhausted picnickers leave Kittiwah Island, Crown emerges from the palmetto thickets and stops Bess. She tells him that she wants to stay with Porgy. Crown laughs at her, sneering when she says she has stopped using narcotics. Threatening and employing the sadism which has always thrilled her, Crown gets Bess to stay with him.

When Bess returns to Catfish Row two days later, she is delirious with fever. From her broken talk Porgy figures out what has happened, and when she recovers he forgives her. The others have no time to worry about her, for a hurricane is rising just when the fishing boats are farthest from shore.

The storm is dreadful. Bess and Porgy assume that no one could have survived on the island, but their anxiety ends when Crown returns. Together they all watch for the fishing boats. When an overturned hull appears, Crown goes off to help. They see him on the wharf when it collapses.

Once again Crown survives, and sneaks back at night for Bess. Porgy kills him and gets the body out to the shore. Though the police have no reason to suspect the cripple, he seems a likely prospect to be taken to the morgue to identify the body. Sporting Life frightens Porgy with predictions that the body will bleed when the murderer is in the same room. When Porgy tries to get away, he is arrested and taken to jail. Turning his attention to Bess, Sporting Life tells her Porgy will surely be away for at least a year. He succeeds in getting her to take some dope.

A few days later, Porgy returns. He has not only been released, but he has won heavily in crapshooting with prisoners and guards. He is jubilant and can hardly wait to see Bess. The others tell him she has gone to New York with Sporting Life. Without a moment's hesitation, he starts after her in his goat cart.

Critical Opinion

Porgy is a folk play built on rhythms of joy and grief. In almost every scene there is music: a comforting lullaby for Clara's baby; a wailing spiritual for Robbins while the neighbors pray for enough money for his funeral, followed by a hopeful spiritual when the undertaker agrees to grant credit; an exuberant march for the picnickers; a fearful spiritual as the storm rises, then an assertive one to ward off terror; and a dirge for the dead fishermen. The music underlines the sharp changes in mood, as in the crap game that explodes in violence. The people, like the songs, are deeply emotional, though they do not sustain a single mood for long.

The supernatural plays a prominent role in *Porgy*. After Bess leaves for the picnic, a buzzard settles over Porgy's door, a sign of coming disaster. Bess's delirium is viewed with superstitious awe. Crown's survivals become tinged with wonder, as if he were endowed with superhuman power. And Porgy's fears and attempted flight are due to the superstitions surrounding the behavior of a corpse. On a more subtle level, Sporting Life is the Devil, tempting and manipulating. He circles around Bess with his enticing offers and his sinister laugh. He fairly glitters with corruption. Porgy, on the other hand, becomes more and more the figure of a hero doing battle with evil. It is he, not the storm or the police, who manages to kill Crown. His departure at the end adds a note of epic dedication. He may be crippled and his goat cart may be ludicrous, but who is to say he will not ultimately triumph?

Porgy began as a novel, in 1925. After its success as a play, in 1927, it became the basis for the opera *Porgy and Bess*, with music by George Gershwin. Though the essential story remains the same, each version has a distinctive character. The novel gives the fullest details of life on Catfish Row. In the play, with its emphasis on spirituals and visual effects, the story becomes almost secondary to the spectacle. Gershwin's music adds a romantic and more sophisticated dimension. Though it does not mirror the deep and fundamental changes in the status, point of view, and condition of the Negro today, *Porgy*, written over four decades ago, still vitally documents his perennial fears, joys, and sorrows.

The Authors

DuBose Heyward was born in Charleston, South Carolina, the locale of most of his works. His formal education ended when he left school at fourteen and went to work on the Charleston waterfront. By the time he was twenty-one he had established himself in the insurance business, but he was also beginning to write stories and poems. In 1921 he met Dorothy Hartzell Kuhns at the MacDowell Colony. Two years later they were married. She had been a student in the 47 Workshop at Harvard, and it was her interest and skill in drama that helped turn some of DuBose's stories into plays.

Porgy was Heyward's first published novel and his first play. He remained chiefly dedicated to fiction and poetry. He published five more novels before his death in 1940. One of these, *Mamba's Daughters* (1929), was developed as a play (1939), again with husband and wife collaborating. An attempt to explore more fully the relationship between whites and Negroes in Charleston, *Mamba's Daughters* is less sensational than *Porgy*, but also less dramatic. A play by DuBose alone, *Brass Ankle* (1931), was the only other stage work bearing the Heyward name.

Heyward's abilities were limited, but he applied them to portraying honestly and accurately the life he understood, particularly the experiences of the Charleston Negro. His sensitive ear caught with high fidelity the local speech patterns. Heyward rejected the false accents of the stage stereotype. He was one of the first white authors to attempt a sympathetic, unpatronizing approach to the Negro.

The Green Pastures

by

MARC CONNELLY (1890–   )

The Characters

The play includes more than fifty speaking roles, plus an all-Negro choir. Most characters, however, appear in only one or two brief scenes and represent a single idea or moral issue. The following few stand out as important individuals.

God (De Lawd)—an old-fashioned parson. Austere, deeply concerned about his work, he is quick to anger, and more than a little proud.

Gabriel—God's secretary and assistant. Polite and efficient, he is a bit skeptical about some of God's decisions, eager to blow his horn and put an end to mankind.

Noah—a poor country minister. Pious and obedient, he has remained firm in his faith despite the ineffectiveness of his preaching.

Moses—a simple shepherd turned into a leader by God.

Pharaoh—a pompous egotist, in love with magic and trickery.

Hezdrel—a simple Hebrew soldier in the Maccabean army, fiercely dedicated to his faith and his people.

69

The Setting

Production calls for both a revolving stage and a treadmill, since scenes change frequently, most lasting only a few minutes. The backgrounds are naïve heightenings of details from the life of poor country Negroes: the Garden of Eden is full of native Louisiana plants, the angels picnic under live oaks plentifully bedecked with Spanish moss, and Pharaoh's throne room is the meeting hall of a Negro lodge.

The Story

A group of six-year-olds are gathered in a small Negro church in rural Louisiana listening to their first Sunday-school lesson. They are more confused then enlightened by the first five chapters of Genesis, and ask the preacher to explain what God looks like, how the earth began, how the angels live, etc. As he begins to translate the Biblical stories into familiar terms, the scene fades and is replaced by the heavenly host enjoying a wonderful picnic and fish fry. The female angels are busily preparing the fish and the custard, the choir practices marching and singing, and the cherubs play happily.

God arrives to bless the gathering, but He is somewhat disappointed that the custard has too little "firmament" in it. To remedy the shortage, He decides to "r'ar back an' pass a miracle," calling for a "whole mess of firmament." The result is a dense, drenching fog. To drain it off, God creates the earth. All the angels are impressed and agree that the fine farming country should not be wasted. To provide someone to enjoy the fine earth, God creates man.

The fall of man, the murder of Abel, and the marriage of Cain follow quickly, and soon the Lord finds that man's sinfulness displeases Him mightily. Reluctantly, He decides to visit earth and examine His creation. Flagrant adultery, children gambling, and widespread impiety are all He can discover at first, but His spirits revive when he meets Noah, a good, pious man. A twinge of Noah's rheumatism suggests to God the idea of a flood. During a brief discussion, Noah argues that the Ark should have at least two kegs of whiskey as snake-bite remedy. God insists on only one. The Ark is built and ready as the rains and flood begin. When the flood has passed, God returns the earth to man, hopeful that all will now be well.

Centuries pass, and once more God finds that earth is doing badly. He decides on a new strategy, selecting a particularly pious family (the descendants of Abraham) and giving them Canaan, after which He will depend on their hard work and devotion to justify Him. God appears to Moses, and sends him off to Pharaoh to accomplish the release of the Hebrews. With the help of his brother Aaron, Moses succeeds in tricking and frightening Pharaoh into letting the people of Abraham go. But when the Hebrews reach Canaan, Moses is prevented from entering; instead, he mounts to heaven with God, who is once more confident that earth will live up to His expectations.

God's confidence is short-lived. The Hebrews also turn corrupt, collaborating with their Babylonian captors and destroying the Hebrew prophets. Enraged, God renounces mankind, abandoning them to their evil ways.

Despite pleas from the saints and angels, God refuses to reconsider His decision. He is, however, troubled by the silent spirit of Hosea, who seems to be accusing Him. Then, on the eve of a battle for Jerusalem, His attention is captured by the thoughts of a humble soldier, Hezdrel. Drawn by curiosity, He descends to earth again. He is startled to learn from Hezdrel that Hosea had redefined God: no longer is He the God of Wrath, but rather the God of Mercy. How had Hosea learned this lesson? By the only means possible, through suffering. God agrees to help men once more, and returns to heaven to ponder the idea that He, too, must learn mercy through suffering. The play ends as God looks ahead to the passion of Christ.

Critical Opinion

At a time when racial issues loom so large in American life, it is easy to dismiss, indeed condemn, *The Green Pastures* as a white man's condescending, patronizing picture of child-like Negroes, charming and amusing, not to be taken too seriously. Unfortunately, some of that condescension is present in such scenes as the heavenly fish fry, in God's taste for "ten-cent seegars," and in numerous other touches throughout. Connelly's original intention, however, was "an attempt to present certain aspects of a living religion in the terms of its believers." He drew much of his inspiration from the works of a Negro author, Roark Bradford, especially *Ol' Man Adam an' His Chillun*. Though no one would approach this subject in this way today, there should be no misreading either Connelly's sincerity or the actual complexity and sophistication of the play.

The comic fish fry begins the play; it certainly does not dominate it. Although the creation of earth and of man is almost a joke, the play grows more serious as the history of man becomes more serious. The idea of an evolving, learning God provides the true unifying thread, not Connelly's clever ways of translating Biblical stories into the idiom of uneducated Southern Negroes. The role of the Lord is one of the most demanding in the American theater. While embodying the believer's simple, pious feelings for a distant, awesome figure, He is also the troubled minister and father, not beyond making mistakes and not eager to be reminded of His weaknesses. He must always provide the weight of meaning which the farcical elements threaten to destroy. The final moments of the play, when God begins to understand the nature and value of suffering, far transcend the comic postcard scenes at the beginning.

The American theater is not rich in religious drama. Maudlin piety and Biblical pageantry are too often the only forms available. The serious dramatist frequently chooses to deal with this crucial element of human experience in a comic or fantastic way if only to avoid the effect of sententiousness. Thornton Wilder's use, in a number of works, of stagehands to speak excerpts from the Bible and the great philosophers is an excellent example of one way a writer can elude the traps. In his choice of the folk-drama approach, Connelly found a direct, affecting way to present the workings of simple faith and his own mature questionings. The result is a play easily damaged by a weak or insincere performance, but powerful and moving when its elements are kept in subtle balance.

The Author

Few members of the American theater have been as active and as versatile as Marc Connelly. Beginning as a reporter, he entered show business in 1916 as a writer of song lyrics. He has gone on to writing plays, both alone and in collaboration, to directing and producing, to acting, writing scenarios, television scripts, short stories, and teaching (at Yale).

Gentleness, good humor, professional polish mark all of Connelly's work. His first major directing job of another author's work was *"Having Wonderful Time,"* which for all its urban sharpness approaches its subject with an amused delight not out of keeping with the tone of *The Green Pastures.* Connelly made his New York acting debut as the Stage Manager in a revival of *Our Town.* Interestingly enough, that character's tone of sympathetic detachment is so much Connelly's own.

Aside from *The Green Pastures* (1930), Connelly did his most important playwriting as a collaborator with George S. Kaufman on *Dulcy* (1921), *Merton of the Movies* (1922), and *Beggar on Horseback* (1924). Each happily satirizes some aspect of American life. *Beggar on Horseback* is particularly interesting in that, like *The Green Pastures,* it draws upon Connelly's gifts for fantasy. Based on a German comedy by Paul Apel, the play presents a young composer's dreams, or nightmares, of what will happen if he marries the businessman's daughter and is absorbed into the world of mass production and conspicuous consumption. The techniques involve expressionistic, imaginative exploitation of theatrical distortions. But, quite unlike the grim German expressionists, Connelly and Kaufman view the absurdities of this world with a mischievous hilarity.

They Knew What They Wanted

by

SIDNEY HOWARD (1891–1939)

The Characters

Tony—a 60-year-old Italian immigrant, owner of a prosperous vineyard. Jovial and exuberant with friends and employees, he is inwardly insecure about his attractiveness to women.

Amy—in her early 20s, a pretty, warmhearted young woman who is scarred by many years of hard, unrewarding work and fearful of an empty future.

Joe—the foreman, a young, handsome, virile man, critical of the world around him, restless, unwilling to settle down.

The Setting

The living room of Tony's house in the Napa Valley of California is large and airy, furnished with new, garish furniture. In the first two acts, the room is hung with colored bunting, lanterns, and other decorations for an Italian *festa*. The time is the mid-1920s.

The Story

Tony is preparing to drive down to the railroad station to meet Amy who is arriving from San Francisco to marry him. He is very nervous, almost terrified, and keeps drinking wine to fortify himself. Without offering a very clear reason, he hints strongly that Joe should leave before the bride arrives, but Joe is too eager to join in the celebration to listen. Finally, hearing the train whistle, Tony rushes out to his car and drives off. Joe explains to the priest, who has been trying to dissuade Tony, how the engagement came about. The old man, after many years of hard work, finally feeling secure in his prosperity, went off to Frisco to find a wife. He saw Amy waiting on tables in an Italian restaurant and fell in love with her. Too shy to approach her, he got her name and address from the restaurant manager, and with Joe's help courted her by mail.

Joe and his friends are interrupted by the arrival of the rural postal deliveryman who has brought Amy from the station, where no one had come to meet her. She is furious, but quickly calms down as she talks to Joe. The beauty of the scenery and the comfort of the house remind her of the few happy years of her childhood, before alcoholism and bankruptcy destroyed her parents. As she relaxes, she even becomes a bit coquettish, and the truth emerges: Tony had sent Joe's photograph and she naturally assumes that this handsome young man is her fiancé. Before Joe can enlighten her, Tony, who has driven his car off the bridge, is carried into the house with both legs broken. Amy is stunned and infuriated when she learns that this fat old man, with a thick Italian accent, is the bridegroom. Her first impulse is to leave at once. But she has used all her money for a trousseau and the train ticket, and she cannot face the ridicule and drudgery that await her if she returns to San Francisco. Grimly she decides to go through with the wedding.

The neighbors celebrate in the yard while Tony lies encased in pain in plaster casts. Joe tells Tony that he intends to leave, but now Tony needs the young man's help in running the vineyard. Besides, he concludes that the switch in photographs will be forgiven and insists that the foreman stay. For a wedding present, he gives Amy some expensive diamond earrings. This generosity and her growing awareness of Tony's goodness intensify her decision to stay and she insists that she will look after him herself and not hire a nurse.

When the guests have gone and Tony has been carried to the bedroom, Amy and Joe are left alone. He convinces her that he knew nothing of the change in pictures. Then, exhausted by the events of the day and terrified of the future, she lets Joe sense how much she is attracted by him. He makes advances which she tries in vain to repel.

Three months later, Tony is recovering remarkably well and can move about on crutches. Joe is once more ready to leave, this time to work with labor unions. The doctor gets him alone and tells him that Amy is pregnant, something Amy herself does not yet know. He rightly surmises that Joe is the father. When Joe tells Amy, she is disturbed by the pain the news will cause Tony, whom she has come to love. Almost hysterical, she decides to run away with Joe, but when Tony comes in, she blurts out the truth. Despite his crutches, Tony staggers across the room to get a gun, but Joe easily disarms him. Amy explains that she and Joe had sexual relations only once, on the wedding night, when she was confused and desperate. Tony's anger takes a new turn when he realizes that the two young people intend to leave together. He foresees that Joe will desert Amy when times become difficult. Desperate for a wife and a child, he insists that Amy stay; he will say he is the father, despite the certain disbelief this will produce. Both Amy and Joe are relieved. He is now free to go on his way unfettered. She can stay with Tony, whose love and home can provide the security she needs.

Critical Opinion

"Fallen women" have always been popular subjects of drama, but the unwritten law of the popular theater is that the price for infidelity must be paid, usually by death. The soap opera and the tearjerker still honor this law today. In 1924, to reject this idea was daring. That Amy is rewarded with a magnanimous husband and a secure future is a sign of how far the vanguard of American dramatists had gone toward dealing with characters and situations realistically, ignoring the theatrical stereotypes. *They Knew What They Wanted* makes an instructive contrast to Eugene Walter's *The Easiest Way*, which had been treated as sensationally realistic only fifteen years before. In the earlier play, the heroine is redeemed by love, but only temporarily. When, as the result of overwhelming pressure, she falls again, the puritanical lover rejects her. The audience's sympathy is all she can have; her sin has doomed her, and Walter, despite some naturalistic touches, settles for the unwritten law. Sidney Howard, writing in the decade that followed the first World War, is more concerned with truth of character than with such theatrical manipulation and comfortable moralizing.

Each corner of the triangle in *They Knew What They Wanted* could fit a standard model. The December-May romance could lend itself to farce. Tony's obesity and his broken English make him an easy figure to ridicule. According to the formulas, Joe, the handsome libertine, should be either reformed or properly punished. And Amy, if she is not to be destroyed by sin, should at least redeem herself by giving her child its real father. All of these possibilities are explored. The first act is very funny, with Tony desperately drinking to prepare for the great moment. In the last act, Amy and Joe respond at first to the promptings of convention. They prepare to run away more because that is what conventional mores expect them to do. Tony's attempt to shoot his rival is another instance of a conditioned response. However, once all three stop playing these roles, a more honest conclusion becomes possible.

If there is a weakness in the play, it lies in the diagrammatic patterning that makes the title too neat, the whole too consciously a rejection of the stereotype. Howard's play is nonetheless marked by a maturity of viewpoint and workmanship rare in any period.

In 1956 Frank Loesser made a musical version of Howard's play, retitled *The Most Happy Fella*. With few changes in its basic structure, the story remained convincingly realistic and contemporary.

The Author

Well-to-do parents who were enthusiastic about music and literature started Sidney Coe Howard on his literary career. As an undergraduate at the University of California at Berkeley, he tried his hand at playwriting. After receiving his degree, he went on to study drama wih George Pierce Baker at Harvard. World War I interrupted his studies. He first served with the American Ambulance Corps, later with the aviation corps of the U.S. Army. After the Armistice, he returned to writing, including work as a feature writer for *The New Republic*. After his first play, *Swords*, opened in New York in 1921, he devoted almost all his efforts to the theater until his untimely death in 1939.

The range of Howard's subjects is wide, though almost all his plays explore the qualities of American life and the difficulties of marriage. One of his most successful works was a dramatization of Sinclair Lewis' *Dodsworth* (1933), the study of a businessman's marriage disintegrating under the influence of a European tour. In *The Silver Cord* (1927) he examined the destructive power of a possessive mother. *Lucky Sam McCarver* (1926) deals with the rise of a ruthless speakeasy proprietor whose personal life deteriorates as his public success grows. The heroism of the men who experimented with yellow fever is the subject of *Yellow Jack* (1934). In *The Late Christopher Bean* (1933) Howard created a comedy of character, pitting a tough New England woman against greedy art collectors. At the time of his death he was working on a play about Benjamin Franklin.

In all his work Howard revealed himself as a careful technician. Though his plays are perhaps too muted for modern tastes, it is always clear that a serious, critical mind is at work analyzing the stereotypes, brushing aside cant, and exploring the relationships between real, fully conceived characters.

Street Scene

by

ELMER RICE (1892–1967)

The Characters

Tenants of the apartment house:

The Maurrants:
> *Frank*—about 45, a Broadway stagehand. He is sullen, bad-tempered, easily angered, and given to violence, especially when drunk.
>
> *Anna*—his wife. Still attractive, she is a kind, neighborly woman who has tried to make a good home but is defeated by her husband's surliness.
>
> *Rose*—their daughter, about 20, a beautiful, intelligent girl, eager to leave the slums but dedicated to her family. She works in an office.
>
> *Willie*—their son, about 12. A street boy, fighting and shouting, difficult to control, already much like his father.

The Kaplans:
> *Abraham*—in his late 60s, a Russian Jew. He writes for radical periodicals and lectures his neighbors on the evils of capitalism.

Shirley—his daughter, about 35, an unattractive spinster schoolteacher, devoted to her father and brother.

Sam—his son, about 21, a sensitive, poetic young man, preparing to enter law school, and much in love with Rose Maurrant.

The Olsens—the janitor and his wife.

The Joneses—a quiet husband and a gossiping wife. Their son, a swaggerer, drives a taxi; their daughter is a shopgirl with an easygoing morality.

The Buchanans—a young couple. The wife, never seen on stage, has a child during the course of the play.

The Fiorentinos—both husband and wife (she is of German heritage) give music lessons; they are unhappy about their childlessness.

The Hildebrands—Mrs. Hildebrand, deserted by her husband, lives on charity with her two children.

Miss Cushing—a spinster who lives with her ailing mother.

Others:

Steve Sankey—in his early 30s; the collector for the milk company. A married man, with two children, he would like to be thought a lothario, though only a woman as lonely as Mrs. Maurrant could be attracted by him.

Harry Easter—office manager where Rose Maurrant works. He is infatuated with Rose, and prosperous enough to offer to set her up as his mistress in an apartment.

Visitors to the house, and passersby—a vivid cross section of New York's population.

The Setting

The stage is occupied by the exterior of an ugly Manhattan brownstone apartment house built in the 1890s, and parts of its neighboring buildings. The broad stoop leads up to the main entrance, and acts as a gathering place for the residents. To one side is the door to the basement. On one side of the apartment house is a warehouse; on the other is a building being demolished. The area is not quite a slum, but is generally shabby, crowded, noisy, and oppressive.

The action of the play covers an evening and most of the following day, June of 1929.

The Story

The unseasonable late-evening heat brings most of the apartment-house women tenants to their windows or to the front stoop. They discuss the weather and their domestic problems, but the main topic of their conversation is Mrs. Maurrant's love affair with Sankey. When Maurrant comes home, he is in a nasty mood; working on a dress rehearsal in the heat has worn him out, and the next day he must travel to Hartford. He is furious to discover that Rose has not yet come home. He is further irritated when his wife offers vague explanations about overtime work, since Rose will be off the next day because of the death of one of the firm's owners. Shortly after Maurrant goes upstairs, Sankey strolls by. He chats briefly with the ladies, and after he leaves, Mrs. Maurrant goes looking for Willie, in the direction Sankey took.

The gossipers are interrupted by the arrival of Miss Simpson, representing the charity agency that has been helping the Hildebrands. Discovering that Mrs. Hildebrand had used some charity money for the movies, Miss Simpson threatens her client with eviction. Mr. Kaplan scolds Miss Simpson for her un-Christian attitude. The neighbors agree, but can hardly admit any identification with this Bolshevik Jew.

As it grows late, the various tenants go up to their apartments and to bed. Rose arrives home with Harry Easter. He suggests she leave her family and try the stage, with his help. Rose is tempted to escape her father's anger and her shabby life, but she wants love more than comfort. Their discussion is interrupted by a scream from Mrs. Buchanan, who is in labor. Rose rushes off to phone for the doctor. When she returns, she meets Vincent Jones, who talks coarsely to her and tries to manhandle her. Sam Kaplan tries to stop him, but is terrified of the other man's strength. Laughing, Vincent leaves the two alone, and in their common loneliness and dreams of a better life, they talk quietly, unwilling to recognize their love but unable to conceal it.

The next morning, the neighbors discuss Mrs. Buchanan's painful night and the successful birth of a daughter. Mr. Maurrant, surlier than ever and still somewhat drunk from the night before, leaves for his trip. Mrs. Maurrant, aware of the dangers her adultery is leading to, tries to enlist her daughter's sympathy without quite naming her problem. Rose leaves for the funeral without offering any help to her mother.

Sankey comes on his collecting rounds, and Mrs. Maurrant invites him upstairs. Soon afterward, Maurrant, who has decided not to go away, returns, drunk and angry, and rushes upstairs. There are shots, and Maurrant rushes out of the house and down into the cellar. The police discover Sankey dead and Mrs. Maurrant seriously injured.

A few hours later, Rose returns from the hospital where her mother has died. Again Easter tries to persuade her to let him be her protector, but she asserts her need to raise her brother and make her own life worthwhile. Suddenly, the police discover Maurrant in the furnace of the neighboring building. They allow him to speak to his daughter. He tells her he is resigned to his execution, and can only say that the heat, the hints of the gossips, and whiskey had combined to drive him mad.

Sam suggests to Rose that they go off together, but she is unwilling to bind herself to anyone, and recognizes that Sam is too immature to deal with the responsibilities of marriage. Gently she kisses him and bids him good-bye.

Life on the street goes on. The children play; a music student practices in the Fiorentino apartment; the neighbors turn to a new topic for gossip.

Critical Opinion

The title of Elmer Rice's play embodies his chief concern as a playwright: to present the drama of big-city life. The Maurrant story serves as a focus for the play, but it is the mingling of a variety of stories and themes that gives the work its rich texture. The murder becomes a symbol of the explosive passions simmering beneath the surface, of the private life always spilling over into the public street.

In structure and tone, the play is in many ways like a Greek tragedy. The chief actions, whether childbirth or murder, take place offstage and are vividly reported. On stage, with the steps of the apartment house serving as a public platform, the characters meet to chat and quarrel, share their grief, and confide their secrets. On those steps the most important confrontations take place, the most meaningful decisions are made. For example, here Rose easily rejects Harry Easter, who wants to make her his mistress, and here she painfully rejects Sam Kaplan, who would make her his wife. The action, as in a Greek tragedy, covers only a day, and at the opening curtain the Maurrant story is already very near its violent climax. The gossiping women form a chorus, the voice of the society most closely touched by the action.

However, it is not the formal stylization of Greek drama that Rice depends on, but rather the carefully chosen realistic details. His stage directions in themselves provide a picture of street life. Rice has chosen his characters with such careful attention to their varied occupations, national origin, and age that at times the play is in danger of becoming a mechanical cross section of New York's population. But all the characters are vividly and accurately realized. Rice is particularly good at capturing the rhythms and clichés of New York speech, filtered through the various dialects.

Like so many other plays of the twenties, *Street Scene* is implicitly focused on social ills. Mr. Kaplan is the only conscious spokesman of social criticism, but throughout there is a strong sense of life being twisted or destroyed by the city and its materialistic, dehumanizing values. Though the play appeared before the Depression, it was filled with a bleak recognition and foreshadowing of social breakdown. The crowding, the children playing in the streets, the lack of privacy, the niggardly help for the poor—these all are major elements of the play.

The Author

The setting for *Street Scene* (1929) could well have been modeled on Rice's childhood home, for he grew up in a similar locale. His father, a cigar salesman, suffered from epilepsy and was frequently unemployed; the family survived by taking roomers. An only child, Elmer Reizenstein (he changed his name legally to Rice when he became successful) found relief from the family problems in reading at the public library and in occasional visits to the theater with his grandfather. At eighteen, he went to work as a file clerk in a cousin's law office and began attending law school at night.

Though he graduated with honors and passed his bar examinations with ease, Rice was certain that he did not want to spend his life in an office. He gave up his job and decided to become a playwright. Luckily, his first play, *On Trial* (1914), was a great hit and he never regretted his decision.

Rice's experience with the law was invaluable in his first play, which dealt with a murder trial and an unexpected confession. Other works in which Rice drew on his legal background were *For the Defense* (1919), *It's the Law* (1922), and *Counsellor-at-Law* (1931). More important than the actual legal subjects was the knowledge of human motives which his work in the law office gave him.

Rice's best work combines insight into human passion with experiments in form. In *On Trial* he used flashbacks which illuminated the court testimony; he even helped to design the "jackknife" set that permitted rapid changes of scene. *The Adding Machine* (1922) presents Mr. Zero, a repressed bookkeeper who kills his employer when he is replaced by a machine. Even in heaven, Mr. Zero cannot succeed, for there the machines are also taking over. The play is presented in powerfully expressionistic form. For example, Mr. and Mrs. Zero have guests, in a room decorated with numbers, and conversations consist entirely of ritualized clichés. In a lighter spirit, *Dream Girl* (1945) dramatizes the fantasies of a shy bookstore salesgirl. Each of her dreams is presented in an appropriate literary style. In *Street Scene* Rice achieved his finest synthesis of subject and form.

Other successful plays by Rice were *See Naples and Die* (1929); *The Left Bank* (1931); *Two on an Island* (1940); and *Flight to the West* (1940). During the Depression, he was head of the New York Region of the Federal Theatre Project, and helped to develop *The Living Newspaper*, dramatizations of current news. He also directed many of his plays, beginning with *Street Scene* (which might otherwise not have been produced). In *The Living Theatre* (1959), he wrote as a drama historian. *Minority Report* (1963) is his autobiography.

J. B.

by

ARCHIBALD MACLEISH (1892–   )

The Characters

Circus vendors, both old actors resentful of being reduced
to selling balloons and popcorn:

Mr. Zuss—an imposing, dignified figure, with a resonant
voice and a somewhat priestly presence. [Zeus]

Nickles—a gaunt, abrasive man, with a sardonic point of
view. [Old Nick]

J. B.—a prosperous banker in early middle age, an expansive,
self-confident optimist, with a rich enthusiasm for living
and a secure faith in a just God. [Job]

Sarah—his wife, more cautious and doubting than her husband, and subject to despair.

David, Mary, Jonathan, Ruth, and Rebecca—their beautiful,
healthy, glowing children.

The messengers—one brash and loud, the other more subdued, haunted by their experiences; they appear as soldiers,
reporters, and policemen.

The comforters:

Zophar—a priest.

Eliphaz—a psychiatrist.
Bildad—a Marxist.

The Setting

It is night in a corner of an enormous circus tent. Overhead, the canvas disappears into darkness. It is sometimes brightened by strings of bulbs that suggest stars. To one side is a stage or platform, part of a sideshow, with a clutter of costumes and masks. In the center are a table and chairs, which become parts of the scenes in which J. B. appears.

The Story

Mr. Zuss and Nickles hesitantly consider enacting the drama of Job. Zuss will play God, of course, and Nickles, who has planned to play Job, will play Satan. After all, "There's always someone playing Job." From the start they are on opposite sides of the issue. Zuss sees the story as that of a man who comes to understand that God's justice is part of the divine mystery. Nickles sees the story as a challenge to a brutal God and an absurd world. They select masks: Zuss's is white and beautiful, with lidded eyes, impenetrable; Nickles' mask has wide-open eyes and a mouth distorted into a grimace. They get into position, but first a mysterious, unpleasant laugh seems to come from the Satan mask, and then for a moment the lines of God seem to come from the air. The two men accuse each other of trickery, but then proceed.

J. B. and his family are seen at Thanksgiving dinner. Father and children are in a holiday mood, making jokes about the turkey and the other food. Sarah feels they should be thinking more about being thankful to God, whose favor she fears they may lose. Her husband disdains such dark thoughts. He knows himself to be honest and outgoing, a lover of life. His success he owes to God's grace. God, he insists, is dependable; so Sarah's worries about punishment seem unfounded.

Mr. Zuss and Nickles comment on the scene. Zuss recognizes J. B. as a "perfect and an upright man" (the lines of the Book of Job are woven into the text at many points), but

Nickles sees him as a fool. Only when Job is on his dunghill will he be a man, seeing that life is not turkey feasts but agony. Zuss argues that God must teach man about the wonders of His powers and His creation. Nickles' sardonic "Why must he suffer then?" catches Zuss off guard. "To praise," he replies, but Nickles points out that J. B. already praises. No, he says, it is to learn "to wish we'd never lived." Zuss says J. B. will never say that. The test of J. B.'s faith begins.

From two drunken comrades of their soldier son, J. B. and Sarah learn that David is dead, killed in a senseless way after the war was over. From two reporter-photographers eager to capture the look of a mother receiving dreadful news, they learn that Mary and Jonathan have been killed in an automobile accident. From the police, they learn that Rebecca, the youngest, has been raped and murdered. Finally, an enemy bombing flattens J. B.'s bank and buries his last child in the rubble. Though Sarah refuses to say it with him, J. B. reasserts his faith: "The Lord giveth. The Lord taketh away. Blessed be the name of the Lord."

Having failed to bring J. B. to his pessimistic view by destroying his children and his property, Nickles-Satan demands the right to attack the man's own body. Zuss-God agrees, and J. B., covered with sores, huddles in an air-raid shelter. Sarah, disgusted by her husband's condition and haunted by the memory of her children, is bitter and despairing. When J. B. insists that God is just, she rejects him and his faith. "Curse God and die," she shouts, and rushes away.

The comforters assemble. Bildad dismisses J. B.'s sufferings as incidental to the movement of history. At the end there will be justice for all. Eliphaz identifies J. B.'s guilt and pain as manifestations of the subconscious, not real. Zophar preaches repentance for sin, but when J. B. denies sinning, the priest charges him with Original Sin, of which all men are guilty and for which all suffer. J. B. argues that such an idea makes God a party to the crimes He punishes, and Zophar agrees, for otherwise the cruelties and agonies of man would be unbearable.

J. B. dismisses the comforters and once again calls on God for an answer. In the whirlwind comes the voice challenging J. B. with thundering questions, each asserting the power of God and man's inability to understand or judge. Bowed, J. B. whispers, "I abhor myself . . . and repent. . . ."

Nickles is disgusted, for J. B. has failed to express contempt for a brutal God. But Mr. Zuss is also unhappy; he sees J. B.'s last responses as arrogant in their humility, calming an angry God while retaining human separateness. Still, Zuss and Nickles must finish the job, bringing back to J. B. what he has lost. Nickles still hopes the man will reject his wife and once more refuse to accept the burden of human life with all its potential pains and agonies. For the first time, he speaks directly to J. B., tempting him to suicide, but in vain.

Sarah returns. She has also considered suicide, but the sight of a forsythia bush in bloom stopped her. Life and its ability to renew itself save her. She concludes, and J. B. does not disagree, that there is no justice in the universe nor love in God. There is, however, love in man, and an awareness of life. On that they can begin anew.

Critical Opinion

In an early sonnet, "The End of the World," MacLeish developed the image of human life as a giant circus. When suddenly the big top blows away, the audience looks up toward "the cancelled skies" and sees "nothing, nothing, nothing—nothing at all." Both the setting and the theme reappeared years later in *J. B.* (1958) as the author wrestled with the meaning of the Book of Job and its relevance to his own times.

The poet suggests many meanings in the circus setting. Life is a continual, wild show, full of dangers, laughter, oddities, struggle, and repetitions: the same acts, the same rings. The circus also provides escape, shutting out the sky and the stars, yet is timeless. Thus J. B. is one of the millions of Jobs who have ever lived and relived the same agonies and raised the same questions. Only the costumes and references are a little different. And when the top is ripped away, there is nothing there.

The Book of Job has inspired more discussion than most Old Testament books because it raises some of the profoundest questions at the heart of any theology, particularly the issue of undeserved suffering. No other work accepted as part of Holy Writ so baldly and powerfully challenges God's justice. Since the nineteenth-century scholars began exploring the Bible as a work of human thought rather than divine dictation, the Book of Job has become a key problem for scholarly discussion and analysis. For one thing, the frame story of God testing Job in response to Satan's challenge has been recognized as a naïve, folklike "explanation" which is quite out of keeping with the sophisticated language and arguments of the main body of the story. Such simple and inaccurate formulations as "the patience of Job," a phrase picked up from the New Testament, have also been rejected. All of this has brought even more sharply into focus MacLeish's reading of Job as a very modern, existentialist document.

MacLeish has a multiple approach to the problem of Job. Mr. Zuss and Nickles not only read God's and Satan's lines, but their own personalities reflect different interpretations of the Job theme. Though neither man is religious, Mr. Zuss can identify with the majesty of God, mysterious and omnipotent. Nickles is more complex, for he is no traditional devil. Rather than collecting damned souls, he wants men to reject supernatural consolation and recognize the world as essentially illogical and unjust. Though Nickles does not succeed in driving J. B. to despair, his point of view does triumph in a modified way. When Sarah returns, she tells J. B. that there is no justice, only the uncaring world: "Cry for justice and the stars/Will stare until your eyes sting." J. B.'s last comment on the God he has been seeking is, "He does not Love. He/Is." This is to say, as Sarah does, that there is only the world. However, if J. B. and his wife accepted Nickles' complete disgust, they would be damned by turning from life. Instead, Sarah points out that love and justice are human concerns and human wonders. To go on with life they must "blow on the coal of the heart." Perhaps there is something beyond man, but man cannot grasp it or depend on it. Certainly there is undeserved suffering, but through pain man can learn to love. Sticking close to the Biblical source until moments from the end, the author concludes with a modern, humanist, existential view of man making his way alone in an empty universe. Many critics, however, particularly clergymen and theologians, reject the author's solution in human love as a sentimental evasion of the terrifying questions being asked. Most, however, recognize the force and immediacy of his picture of modern suffering as one of the unending repetitions of the eternal pattern.

In the twentieth century, many poets have attempted to create a new form of verse drama. Like T. S. Eliot, MacLeish writes a loose line that is not much more than heightened prose, at only a few points expanding into a more sonorous or lyric mode. This style helps him to overcome the restrictions of the conventions of realistic conversation. The most eloquent passages are those taken verbatim from the King James Bible.

Unlike MacLeish's other plays, which are directed almost entirely to the ear, *J. B.* is vividly theatrical. The setting, masks, and lighting combine with the virtuoso roles to create a powerful, resonant production. It is MacLeish's most fully realized stage work.

The Author

Archibald MacLeish's life has reflected the dramatic changes that American literature and society have experienced in this century.

He was born in Glencoe, Illinois, in 1892. He received a bachelor's degree from Yale, fought in World War I, went on to receive a law degree from Harvard, and for a number of years was a teacher and practicing attorney. His first book of poems, *Tower of Ivory*, published in 1917, consisted of competent but traditional pieces. There was little to distinguish MacLeish from many other bright young men moving smoothly into secure places in a flourishing country.

By 1923, however, like so many young writers, MacLeish had become deeply unhappy in America, where the current prudery and gross materialism posed a deadly threat to the artist. He moved to Paris, where he became one of the large group of stimulating and productive expatriates who dramatically altered the outlines of modern literature. His reading in the French symbolist poets and his contact with experimental poets like Ezra Pound and T. S. Eliot helped MacLeish to develop a free, flexible style and a tone of controlled antiromanticism. His published collections of 1924 and 1926 include some of his best lyrics. In 1926 he published a verse play, *Nobodaddy*, about Adam, Eve, and their two sons. The theme, as the author summed it up, could well apply to *J. B.*: "self-consciousness in an indifferent universe."

In 1928 MacLeish returned to America with a new assurance in and awareness of himself as a writer and an American. He worked for the new *Fortune* magazine, and wrote many poems about New York and American history, often with satiric overtones. He also wrote verse plays which reflected his growing concern about contemporary life. *Panic* (1935) is about mob hysteria. *The Fall of the City* (1937) is a prophetic picture of how fear and skillful propaganda can undermine a society. In *Air Raid* (1938), the horrors of the modern world are explored. The last two of these plays were given highly effective radio productions and brought MacLeish wide recognition. In 1939 he was appointed Librarian of Congress, a position he held for a number of years. He has held other government posts, including an appointment to UNESCO and Assistant Secretary of State (1944–1948). In recent years, he has been active as a lecturer and teacher at Harvard. Thus, in his life as in his work, MacLeish has moved from acceptance of traditional values to total rejection of his country and of conventional art, then to a sharply critical reinvolvement in American life, and finally to membership in what might be called the Establishment. He has, however, not surrendered his critical detachment or concern. Many of the ideas that he and other writers of his generation helped to develop have played a major role in creating the intellectual climate of our time.

In MacLeish's most recent play, *Herakles* (1967), the Greek legend is reenacted in a modern setting. As in *J. B.*, the author is searching for the eternal and universal in contemporary events.

Biography

by

S. N. BEHRMAN (1893–   )

The Characters

Marion Froude—a painter, in her late 30s. Radiantly attractive, intelligent, and warmhearted, she has both the strengths and the weaknesses that come with sympathetic awareness and comic detachment.

Richard Kurt—a magazine editor, 25, very proud of his probity and furious about injustice and corruption.

Leander Nolan—a Senatorial candidate from Tennessee, in his early 40s; a pompous, ambitious man, with traces of the gentle, shy person he once was.

Orin Kinnicott—ruler of a publishing empire, a famous health fanatic, about 55. Dictatorial, without a shred of humor, he is never aware of how other people feel.

Slade Kinnicott—his daughter, in her early 20s. Superficially brash, she yearns for romance and fights off her father's dominance.

Melchior Feydak—a Viennese composer, a quietly perceptive friend of Marion's.

The Setting

Marion Froude's studio apartment in New York City is a comfortably spacious, old-fashioned place. The cluttered furnishings, mostly imitation Renaissance and shabby, are the congenial legacy from former tenants, for this is for Marion only temporary quarters as have been all her studios and apartments. The effect is pleasantly unconventional, mellow, a little anachronistic, and relaxed. The time is 1932.

The Story

A respect for appointments is not one of Marion Froude's virtues, and now, half an hour after the time set for their interview, Richard Kurt is raging at Marion's tardiness. He is joined by Melchior Feydak, just arrived in America. Richard mistakes Feydak for his late brother Victor, a far more successful composer. Melchior wryly explains that others continue to make the same mistake and he is now off to Hollywood with a fat contract based on this error. When Marion arrives, she asks Kurt to leave so she can talk to her old friend. With bad grace, he agrees to waste another half hour waiting for her. Marion, who had loved Victor Feydak deeply, encourages Melchior to treat the mistaken identity as his brother's finest gift.

Melchior leaves when an impressive-looking gentleman arrives, apparently to commission his portrait. The new visitor greets Marion as an old friend, and he identifies himself as "Bunny" Nolan, a hometown boy and, as he proudly remembers, her first lover. They reminisce, and he explains his financial success and his present campaign for the Senate, backed by the Kinnicott papers. He is also engaged to Kinnicott's daughter. Ostensibly he has come to have his portrait done, but actually he wants to test his memory of his early sweetheart, who has gone on to achieve a disturbing, tantalizing notoriety as mistress to as well as painter of world celebrities. Marion does not deny her reputation, only denies that her promiscuity has been as extreme as gossip has reported. She asks Leander to believe that there are moral standards other than his very conventional ones.

Kurt returns, more bad-tempered than before. He can barely be civil to Nolan, and chafes visibly until Marion sees her visitor to the door. Then, violently and abruptly, he attacks her friends, her way of life, her attitudes, and her condescending tone to him. Finally, he explains his business. He offers Marion a substantial fee for writing her autobiography for the magazine he edits. He makes clear that the people she has met, painted, and loved should be the main theme of her book. At first reluctant, Marion is challenged and intrigued by the idea of reviewing her life, and finally agrees to write her life story.

Some weeks later, Kurt's magazine announces the forthcoming publication of Marion Froude's memoirs, hinting broadly at sensational revelations. Nolan is frightened, assuming that Marion's story will destroy his chances for election. She is at first amused by his fears. Whatever the advertisements may say, she has no intention of writing a scandalous exposé, and is insulted that Nolan should suspect that. Besides, she cannot seriously believe that her story can be so damaging, and brushes aside his complaints. When Kurt arrives, Nolan suggests that Kinnicott could certainly get the editor a better job. Richard threatens to publish the book himself if his publisher is intimidated. Nolan leaves when he fails to convince either Kurt or Marion to drop the project.

Marion tries to explain Nolan to Kurt, and suggests that he, too, will be more cautious when he reaches forty. This understanding, compassionate attitude infuriates the young man, and he lashes out at her, accusing her of being a casual, irresponsible, parasitic force for preserving injustice. All her attempts to present a case for intelligent detachment are unsuccessful. But her charms and generosity do reach him, and he begins to confide in her. His dream is to be a "critic-at-large of things-as-they-are," able to "laugh the powers that be out of existence in a great winnowing gale of laughter." Touched by the undercurrent of painful self-awareness that lies behind his arrogance, Marion asks him about his life and his family. He tells her of the senseless death of his father, killed by a stray bullet during a strike. Having revealed his grief, Richard tries to resume his tough, unsentimental manner, but Marion's love is too strong, and he surrenders to her.

Two weeks later, with the date of publication rapidly approaching, Nolan brings his father-in-law-to-be to see Marion. As usual, she is not at home, and Kinnicott fumes. They are joined by Slade, who has come to meet her fiancé's old sweetheart; she is hoping this meeting can somehow make her engagement to stuffy Leander more meaningful. Kurt also comes to visit Marion and soon begins to quarrel with everyone.

When Marion arrives, she greets them all as if this were a purely social gathering. While playing the innocent, she reveals that she understands the laws of libel and that she has no letters or other evidence to prove her affair with Nolan. Left alone with Kinnicott, Marion charms him by listening respectfully to his advice on metabolism, but avoids promising him anything. Kurt, however, jumps to the conclusion that she has succumbed to Kinnicott's threats or bribery, and storms out.

Alone, Marion looks through the completed manuscript, then wistfully burns it in the stove. Nolan returns to say he has broken with Slade and wants to marry Marion. Flattered but amused, she refuses, gently explaining that their values are too different. He understands her when he realizes that she has been having an affair with Kurt, and rushes out when the younger man arrives. Marion explains to the editor that in her book the romance with Leander was too idyllically disguised to be identified. Besides, she has destroyed the manuscript since she refuses to be a source of distress to anyone. To Kurt this is one more sign of her tolerance, a quality he sees as preventing her from attacking the cruel and powerful. Yes, she says, what he hates is her essential nature, and if they stayed together she would try to change him, destroy what is his essential being, his anger. She tearfully sends him away.

Luckily, a telegram from Feydak rescues Marion from despair. He has arranged for her to do a group of portraits in Hollywood. She calls to her maid to begin packing, for new places and new adventures.

Critical Opinion

In his "Essay on Comedy," George Meredith describes the Comic Spirit as "luminous and watchful," with a smile and a laugh that are "finely tempered, showing sunlight of the mind, mental richness rather than noisy enormity."

> Its common aspect is one of unsolicitous observation. . . . Men's future upon earth does not attract it; their honesty and shapeliness in the present does; and whenever they wax out of proportion, overblown, affected, pretentious, bombastical, pedantic, fantastically delicate; whenever it sees them self-deceived or hoodwinked, given to riot in idolatries, planning short-sightedly, plotting dementedly . . . ; whenever they offend sound reason, fair justice; are false in humility or mined with conceit, individually, or in the bulk; the Spirit overhead will look humanly malign, and cast an oblique light on them, followed by volleys of silvery laughter.

While Meredith was defining an idea, his description fits certain characters, frequently women, who stand at the center of the finest high comedy. In American drama, there is no finer embodiment of this Comic Spirit than Marion Froude. What makes Meredith's noble claims for the Comic Spirit particularly relevant to *Biography* (1932) is that the play is in effect about the place of such detachment in a society which demands involvement and commitment.

Marion's dilemma is that she can deal with people as individuals, recognizing at once their need for warmth or assurance or simple friendship. These she is prepared, even eager, to provide, but she is also asked to endorse a position or denounce an enemy. This she cannot do. Thus she is likely to be condemned, at least misunderstood, by almost everyone. To Leander she is morally corrupt because she is promiscuous, though he would be ready to forgive her if she accepted his glamorization of first love and remorse. To Richard she is a parasite fattening on the evil her tolerance prevents her from attacking. To Kinnicott she is the product of poor nutrition and can easily be reformed by a change of diet. To Slade she is some kind of *femme fatale*. Marion understands them all, laughs at the ludicrous, loves the injured, but cannot surrender her nature. She must remain above the battle.

The challenge to Behrman in *Biography* is to keep the tone light, the struggle like an elegant game, at the same time pointing to a less amusing struggle on the sidelines, just offstage as it were. Leander is a country boy turned into a Babbitt-like businessman, but it is 1932 and he is running for the Senate, backed by a publisher who is politically conservative, perhaps reactionary. And since it is 1932, Richard's angers and hatreds are not merely youthful rebelliousness; they are a call for revolutionary action, a demand for something even more than the New Deal. Can one reasonably be above such a battle? The play is a plea for noninvolvement as a respectable choice. For Marion, Behrman says, this must be true; what she has to offer is that sunny intelligence which is at the heart of civilization. Yet Richard puts the other answer strongly, and Nolan and Kinnicott, though they may be charmed by Marion, demonstrate the accuracy of Richard's indictment. The playwright's sympathies are divided. Between the two poles, the play stretches taut and resonant.

Although *Biography* is somewhat dated in its specific references, it remains one of the finest examples of high comedy in the American theater. The dialogue is elegant and witty, a model for the way sensible, truly sophisticated people should talk. There are few jokes or epigrams, but the dialogue flows smoothly, each idea clear and pointed. The plot has a similar fluidity and clarity. The play as a whole beautifully embodies its own idea of civilized poise and grace.

The Author

Writers of high comedy rarely have the elegant, aristocratic backgrounds that their characters take for granted. Noel Coward's family was suburban middle class, always on the edge of bankruptcy. Bernard Shaw's parents had gone far over that edge. W. Somerset Maugham, who achieved fame first as an author of witty plays, had a youth full of hardship and financial problems. Samuel Nathaniel Behrman is a member of the same company. From his autobiographical sketches collected in *The Worcester Account* (1954), a picture emerges of a sensitive boy growing up at the turn of the century in a world of poor, struggling Jewish immigrants. The dreamlike glitter of the comedy of manners owes a great deal to the authors' awareness of the distance between the civilized drawing room on stage and the world outside the stage door. With Behrman, that distance is itself a crucial element in many of his best works.

Behrman defined his major concern most directly in the

pointedly titled play *No Time for Comedy* (1939). The protagonist is a writer of clever comedies who is led by the Spanish Civil War to question the pertinence of his work. He decides to write a serious, impassioned, propagandistic play. His wife, an actress for whom he has written his finest comedies, finally convinces him that he is wrong to deny his gift of laughter, which, she argues, people need even more than ever in times of crisis. Ironically, following this affirmation, Behrman's own work underwent a change. Since 1940, his plays have been mostly light and transparent, lacking the underpinnings of serious questioning that gave such strength and individuality to his work in the late twenties and early thirties.

In addition to *Biography*, Behrman's most distinguished and characteristic work includes *The Second Man* (1927), his first success, a study of a sophisticate whose shiny facade conceals a pained self-awareness; *Rain from Heaven* (1934), an anti-Nazi play surprisingly prophetic for its time; and *End of Summer* (1936), a symposium on the proper use of wealth. He has written sketches and short stories, and two excellent biographies: *Duveen* (1952), a portrait of the famous art dealer, and *Portrait of Max* (1960), the account of his friendship with Max Beerbohm. Like his best comedies, these profiles are distinguished by a lucid style and a warm, unsentimental humor.

Among Behrman's popular successes are a number of adaptations: the brilliant *Amphytrion 38* (1937), drawn from Giraudoux's French play of the same title, and *Jacobowsky and the Colonel* (1944), based on a play by Franz Werfel.

What Price Glory?

by

LAURENCE STALLINGS (1894–1968) and
MAXWELL ANDERSON (1888–1959)

The Characters

Captain Flagg—commander of L Company, U.S. Marines. A
professional soldier, virile, tough, hard-driving, he can
also be gentle and compassionate.

Sergeant Quirt—company top sergeant. Also a professional soldier, he is hard-boiled and blustering, less subtle than
Captain Flagg, but in most respects they are two of a kind.

Charmaine—a French village girl, daughter of the local inn-
keeper and, at least since the Americans arrived, a tart.

Members of L Company—a mixture of experienced soldiers,
full of self-glorifying tales and ribald comments, and raw
recruits.

The Setting

The battlefront in France, early in 1918, is an area where
everything and everybody show the effects of nearly four
years of war. Act I is set in a room in a French farmhouse

temporarily serving as company headquarters. In the second act, headquarters have been moved into a deep wine cellar in a farmhouse on the edge of a village still partly in German hands. The final act is in the barroom of Pete de la Cognac's inn. Acts I and III take place behind the lines, and contrast sharply with the crowded, dirty, oppressive cellar.

The Story

Quartered in a small village, L Company waits for orders. The men assigned to company headquarters loaf about, swapping stories about their past military and amorous adventures. They enjoy predicting the course of the captain's romance with Charmaine, the village beauty.

Their gossip is interrupted by the arrival of Quirt, replacement for their top sergeant. He briskly takes command, bullying and snapping. When Flagg appears, he is delighted to see Quirt. They have worked together in the past and respect each other as topnotch military men. They have also competed bitterly over women, the record about evenly divided between them. Quirt's arrival gives Flagg a moment's pause, but he is so eager for his eight-day leave in Paris that he rushes off as soon as he can. Within minutes of Flagg's departure, Charmaine is in Quirt's arms.

A week later, the captain returns in a state of furious intoxication. The leave has been a disaster; he has spent almost all of it in the stockade for refusing an order to give up his swagger stick. He never got to Paris and was not even able to spend his money. Immediately he is faced with a complaint from Cognac Pete that someone has corrupted his daughter. When Pete accuses Quirt, Flagg gleefully commands the sergeant to marry the girl. All of Quirt's efforts to avoid the ceremony fail until he discovers that orders have come for immediate troop movement. Flagg had hoped to conceal the news until after the wedding, but now the sergeant can abandon his "fiancée" and report for duty.

The company is ordered to take a well-defended village. There will be a special leave for anyone who captures an enemy officer. Day after day, the Marines battle, but the Germans still control the railroad station and dominate the area. American losses are heavy, and those who survive are exhausted. When one of the officers is seriously wounded, his closest friend breaks down, hysterically shouting, "What price glory now?" Flagg and Quirt manage to calm the nervous, rally the despondent, and carry on their feud about Charmaine.

Quirt returns from patrol wounded in the leg, gloating at this excuse to go behind the lines and try his luck with the girl again. Flagg is infuriated by the sergeant's "luck," and exasperated by the arrival of two new, totally inexperienced lieutenants. Some of his men, however, have already captured an Alsatian lieutenant, and the battle is soon over. The price of victory is the loss of more men, including shy, naïve Private Lewisohn, who dies in Flagg's arms.

When Quirt reaches the hospital, he absconds and heads for Cognac Pete's. Flagg arrives almost immediately afterward. Quarreling and drinking in a murderous mood, they settle on a game of blackjack, the winner to get the revolver, the loser a head start. Quirt loses, but upsets the table and escapes in the dark. Flagg settles down with Charmaine, but new orders arrive for the company to return to action at once. Cursing, but recognizing his near-religious dedication to the "profession of arms," he bids farewell to Charmaine and goes off to assemble his men.

Quirt appears from his hiding place upstairs. He is delighted to have outwitted the captain, but he, too, must answer the call of battle. He kisses Charmaine good-bye and rushes out shouting, "Hey, Flagg, wait for baby!"

Critical Opinion

Produced six years after the end of World War I, *What Price Glory?* (1924) was one of the first works to deal with the war without glamorizing it. Though preceded by a few novels like John Dos Passos' *Three Soldiers* (1921) and E. E. Cummings' *The Enormous Room* (1922), Stallings' and Anderson's play appeared five years before the peak outpouring of World War I literature: *All Quiet on the Western Front, A Farewell to Arms,* and *Journey's End* all appeared in 1929. In contrast to the sentimental pictures of war that all but monopolized both fiction and drama of the time, *What Price Glory?* was a shattering revelation. The importance of the play lies in its bringing to the stage a picture of war that mixed the comic and tragic in a newly realistic manner.

The authors concentrate their attention entirely on the Americans. The enemy is there to be fought, not condemned or caricatured. The real enemy is, in fact, the bureaucracy behind the lines, ordering troops to risk their lives tacking up posters, jailing officers for carrying swagger sticks, or blithely sending hastily trained officers to the front. Praise is reserved for the tough, professional Quirt and Flagg, roistering philanderers but heroes in battle.

In their choice of heroes, however, the authors still reflect an older tradition. They hardly recognize the new kind of soldier, the drafted or volunteer civilian dominant in World War I and usually the hero of later writers. Flagg and Quirt are descendants of a long line of melodrama Marines, and their delight in violence, both in war and in personal competition, somewhat neutralizes the bitterness implicit in the play's title. Only in the secondary characters, especially Private Lewisohn, does the play begin to explore the agony, the waste, the tragic absurdity of modern war. This limitation is surprising in view of Stallings' own experience as a Marine in France. The explanation lies in the changed perspective with which the post-World War II reader looks at the play. In 1924 the cynicism and anguish, though largely limited to only one-third of the play, the second act, were overwhelming. To many in the audience, just hearing profanity in the theater was an intensely shocking experience, and the authors felt it necessary to defend, somewhat apologetically, their use of realistic dialogue. A more completely naturalistic view, one which would be taken for granted today, was more than the authors could have expected their audience to accept.

A similar adjustment of viewpoint must be made in looking at the comic elements in the play. To the contemporary eye, the struggle over Charmaine seems contrived. Like so many successful theatrical inventions, this triangle has been drained of vitality through countless film and stage treatments. Seen in context, however, the "romance" effectively frames the agonizing scenes of wounding and death.

What Price Glory? is a landmark in the history of the American theater. It is one of the earliest plays to deal realistically with a major subject, and reveals how both the drama and the society it reflects were beginning to come to terms with a profound national memory.

The Authors

For commentary on Maxwell Anderson, see the discussion following *Winterset*.

Much of Laurence Stallings' most successful work has been associated with World War I. In this he reflects not only the enormous effect that confict had on his whole generation, but also his own painful history. In his novel *Plumes* (1924), the hero's experiences are nearly identical with the author's: an idyllic romance at college is followed by dreadful war experiences, culminating in the loss of his leg at Belleau wood. The passionate antiwar feeling that shaped the most forceful sections of *What Price Glory?* also contributed to the power of Stallings' best-known movie script, *The Big Parade* (1925), his dramatization of Hemingway's *A Farewell to Arms* (1930), and his best-selling book of photographs and commentary, *The First World War* (1933).

After the success of *What Price Glory?*, Stallings collaborated with Anderson on two more plays. *First Flight* (1925) is about the young Andrew Jackson; *The Buccaneer* (1925) deals with Sir Henry Morgan. Neither was well-received, and the two men went their separate ways thereafter. In the years since, Stallings has written film scenarios, dramatizations, operas, and fiction, but nothing very significant.

The Front Page

by

BEN HECHT (1894–1964) and
CHARLES MACARTHUR (1895–1956)

The Characters

Hildy Johnson—reporter for the Chicago *Herald-Examiner*. Tough, quarrelsome, and ebullient, he is a crusader despite his surface cynicism.

Walter Burns—city editor of the *Herald-Examiner*. Quick-witted, ingenious, he is relentless in his drive to keep his newspaper at the top.

Peggy Grant—Hildy's fiancée. Only 20 years old, she has an iron will and fixed ideas about middle-class propriety.

Earl Williams—a confused, shy man who vaguely professes anarchism.

Mollie Malloy—a warmhearted streetwalker with a strong loyalty to anyone who treats her decently.

Sheriff Hartman—an inept, cowardly official who considers himself a clever realist.

The Mayor—pompous and sharp-witted, the epitome of the corrupt politician.

The Setting

The action is limited to the press room of the Criminal Courts Building, Chicago, during three hours on a Friday night in spring, 1928. The room is shabby, lighted by unshaded light bulbs, and furnished with a few old chairs and tables. There is a large number of battered telephones, each connected to a city newspaper. The only distinctive item in the room is a huge rolltop desk belonging to the reporter from the Chicago *Tribune*.

The Story

The press room might better be called the poker room; as usual, most of the reporters are deeply involved in a game while one of them has been delegated to phone all the police stations and hospitals to see if there is any news they can feed to their city desks. On this evening, they are waiting for late developments regarding the execution of Earl Williams, sentenced to be hanged in the morning for shooting a policeman. There is no question of his guilt, but the reporters are aware that the sheriff and mayor have blown up the case into a triumph over the Red Menace and intend to use the execution to enhance their vote-pulling powers in the coming elections.

The cardplayers are interrupted by the arrival of Hildy Johnson, usually the worst scapegrace of them all. They are startled by his elegant attire, complete with gloves and a cane, and even more by his announcement that he is leaving the newspaper to go to New York, where he will get married and work for an advertising agency. Untouched by their envy-inspired wisecracks, he goes off to say his farewells to others in the building. The reporters try to resume their game but are interrupted by the entrance of Mollie Malloy, who tearfully scolds them for their hardhearted treatment of Williams. Despite their jeers, she explains how she had met Williams wandering in the street, and had listened to him pouring out his despair all through one night. In her own surprised way, she is in love with him.

Mollie leaves when the sheriff enters. He tries to bully the reporters into stopping their persistent belittling of his actions and statements, but he is unable to respond to their taunts and is reduced to buying their goodwill by distributing extra tickets to the hanging. Hildy returns, ready to leave for the railroad station, and phones his city editor to announce his resignation. Just as he finishes, delighted with catching his boss off guard, there is a volley of shots and the news that Williams has escaped. Without a moment's hesitation, Hildy reverts to his job as a reporter.

The press room is awash with rumors, and each reporter goes off to follow some lead. Hildy bribes a guard to get the true story: Dr. Eglehofer, a psychiatrist interviewing Williams at the request of a strong citizens' group, had asked Williams to reenact the crime; the condemned man requested a gun, which the dim-witted sheriff handed him; Williams shot the psychiatrist, and in the confusion managed to get away. To get this story, Hildy has used the pay advance he needed to get to New York.

Now he tries to get Burns to send the money over so that he can leave. While he waits for Burns, Hildy must face both Peggy's and Mrs. Grant's wrath about the delays. He takes them out to find a cab, solemnly promising to join them at the station in plenty of time to catch the train for New York.

With all the reporters out of the room, the sheriff and the mayor start to discuss their plans, but they are interrupted by the arrival of the governor's messenger bearing a reprieve for Williams. The reprieve, coupled with Williams' escape, is bound to ruin their image. The mayor sends the messenger off with a promise of a lucrative city job if he will pretend that he was delayed in delivering the reprieve. The sheriff notifies all his men to shoot Williams as soon as he is found.

Hildy returns to the phone and the frustrating task of convincing his boss to send over money, but Burns obviously prefers to have Hildy on the job. Mollie comes in to ask Hildy's help, and while they are alone in the room they are joined by Williams, who has come down the rain pipe from the roof. Hildy hides the fugitive in the rolltop desk and asks Burns to come over to the press room. The temptation of getting a scoop and using it to expose the corrupt city officials is more than Hildy can resist.

The other reporters get suspicious of Hildy's and Mollie's

closeness and suggest to the police that Mollie may know something about Williams. But rather than tell them, she jumps from the window; she is seriously injured, but will survive. Mrs. Grant, who had stormed in a few moments earlier to summon Hildy once more, had overheard something of Hildy's conversation with Mollie, and now is stunned by the girl's suicide attempt. Burns arrives at this crucial moment and orders one of his henchmen to take Mrs. Grant away for a while, then calls his office for some men to come for the desk and the man hiding in it. But neither plan works. Diamond Louie, given the job of hiding Mrs. Grant, has an automobile accident (colliding with a police car), and regains consciousness to discover that the woman has disappeared. No men arrive to move the desk, despite all of Burns's frantic telephoning.

Hildy and Burns become more and more ingenious in keeping people away from the desk, but the return of Mrs. Grant leads to the discovery of Williams. Hildy and Burns are about to be arrested for harboring a criminal when the governor's messenger arrives again, staggeringly drunk, with the announcement that he will not be bribed. The reprieve is delivered along with the story of the sheriff's and mayor's behavior. Followed by the reporters, the two officials try in vain to leave the room with some dignity.

Peggy bursts in furiously. Hildy apologizes and resigns again, announcing his determination to change his ways. Burns suavely encourages him to follow the dictates of his heart, and magnanimously gives the couple his famous watch as a wedding present. As soon as Hildy and Peggy leave, Burns phones his assistant and instructs him to call the police at the train's first Indiana stop and tell them to arrest Hildy for stealing a valuable watch.

Critical Opinion

The authors of *The Front Page* (1928) say they started out to show their disdain for newspapers and reporters and ended up writing a valentine. All is not sweetness, of course. The reporters as a whole are an unsavory lot. In the opening minutes of the play particularly, they come off badly: gambling, inventing news stories, sarcastically tormenting Mollie. Their archetype is Walter Burns, a man who will do anything for a good story, even take on the role of muckraker, but certainly not because he has any feelings about truth or honesty or civic virtue. Hecht and MacArthur draw these characters with emphasis on their weaknesses, but they cannot help admiring the masculine camaraderie and how obviously superior the newspapermen are to the politicians and the police.

Though the tough, hat-on-the-back-of-the-head, semigangster reporter was rejected by professional newspapermen as preposterous from the moment the play first appeared, the audience instantly welcomed him into the American pantheon. He emerged from *The Front Page* as an urban equivalent of the independent, self-possessed Westerner.

The attractiveness of Hildy lies in the way he combines sentiment and cynicism, the reformer competing with the newspaperman hot on the trail of a story. Like the Western hero, he is fully masculine, master of his fate, a free spirit. Even though he seems to have succumbed to Peggy, a pure schoolmarm type (backed up by a mama, a double hazard the cowboy rarely faces), we cannot really believe he will ever be domesticated. Not only Burns's trick to get him back, but his own nature will prevent his accepting a life of routine work. Of course, he is on the side of justice even if some inner code is to him more important than conventional morality. He embodies Walter Burns's dynamism without his brutal insensitivity, and the reporters' freedom without their aimlessness.

Aside from Hildy, the play is an exciting, slick melodrama well leavened with elements of farce and simple satire. Coincidence plays a major role, and the characters are neatly labeled types, whether goodhearted tart or bossy mother-in-law, corrupt politician or dumb cop. The success of its production depends on carefully exaggerated acting and well-timed, ingenious direction. The original production was staged by George S. Kaufman, who as writer and director was one of the creators of a distinctive American theater style: fast-moving, fast-talking, superficially realistic but at heart all make-believe. A successful Broadway revival in 1969 demonstrated the continuing vitality of this skillful piece of entertainment.

The Authors

Ben Hecht and Charles MacArthur met as reporters in Chicago, and later spent a good many years collaborating on plays and motion-picture scripts. For a time they even had their own movie company.

Charles MacArthur was born in Scranton, Pennsylvania, into a settled American family. He worked successfully as a reporter both in Chicago and in New York, and as a magazine writer. However, except for his collaborations with Hecht, he wrote nothing of importance.

Ben Hecht has left a far more distinctive mark on American letters. Born in New York of Russian immigrant parents, as a child he moved with his family to Chicago. At first a prodigy on the violin, he later became an acrobat with a small circus and, at sixteen, ran away from home. He soon was involved in the art-theater movement and in journalism. He became an integral part of the "Chicago renaissance" of the post-World War I period. He published stories, novels, poems, and, for a while, his own newspaper, the Chicago *Literary Times*.

After the success of *The Front Page*, Hecht and MacArthur turned their talents to the theater and motion pictures, though Hecht never stopped writing on his own. *Twentieth Century* (1933) was another Hecht-MacArthur stage success. *The Scoundrel* was the best of the films their own company made. After the early 1940s, however, their collaborations tapered off. Neither ever succeeded in writing plays alone.

Hecht's nontheatrical work includes a long list of works all infused with a strong individuality, outspoken, flamboyant, and a bit sentimental. *Erik Dorn* (1921), his first novel, is still considered his best, and a major work of the Chicago school of realism. More recently, *A Child of the Century* (1954), his autobiography, was widely hailed as a vital picture of American life.

The Male Animal

by

JAMES THURBER (1894–1961) and
ELLIOTT NUGENT (1899–   )

The Characters

Tommy Turner—associate professor of English at Midwestern
University, in his mid-30s. A quiet, somewhat absentminded
man, with a dry sense of humor, he impresses people as
not very dynamic.

Ellen Turner—his wife, about 30, a sweet romantic who
imagines herself to be a counterbalance to her husband's
impracticality.

Patricia Stanley—her sister, 19, a student at the university, a
bright, quick-witted, and spirited girl.

Wally Myers—star player on the university football team;
healthy, muscular, and unsophisticated.

Michael Barnes—editor of the student magazine; a brilliant
student and a political idealist.

Joe Ferguson—the star halfback of the team ten years before,
now a successful businessman; hearty and boisterous, still
enamored of football and living in memories of his great
college days.

Ed Keller—one of the university's trustees; a superpatriot, intolerant of any values other than his own. He considers the intellectual life of the school less important than athletics.

Dean Damon—head of the English Department. Decades of submitting to direction by his intellectual inferiors have left him with a wry awareness of failure.

The Setting

The Turner living room is dominated by books. The furnishings show good taste but a limited budget. It is home-coming weekend at Midwestern, the most important time of the year.

The Story

It is Friday evening, and Ellen is preparing for a small party before the big rally. The guest of honor will be Joe Ferguson, once her beau, who is returning to campus after an absence of ten years. Dean Damon arrives with some chilling news. In the issue of *The Literary Magazine* to appear the next day, Michael Barnes has written a hot-tempered editorial calling the trustees fascists for dismissing two professors "ignorantly called Reds," and praising Professor Turner for the courage to read in class a letter by Vanzetti. Tommy explains that he mentioned that he intended to read the letter someday, and scolds Michael for not consulting him. He is interested in the letter as a piece of prose, not as a political statement. Ellen and Damon encourage Tommy to issue a denial.

Joe Ferguson arrives with flowers and gifts. He has remembered Ellen's birthday, though her own husband forgot. Joe is full of talk about the coming game. Though he jokes and laughs, he does let slip the fact that his wife is divorcing him. Soon after the Kellers arrive, talk turns to the editorial. The trustee is furious, insisting that only Americanism be taught. Tommy is ready to quarrel, but an attack of nausea sends him rushing upstairs. When he comes back down, he discovers Joe and Ellen dreamily dancing to one of the songs they loved as undergraduates. Tommy refuses to go with them to the rally.

The next day, with the editorial now public knowledge,

everyone awaits Tommy's denial, but he is nowhere to be found. Patricia, who has been courted by both Michael and Wally, decides she prefers football players any time; they don't get into trouble. Tommy returns, explaining that he has decided that he must read the letter. He has also concluded that Ellen really loves Joe, and he will politely step out of the way. Ellen is furious, and Joe is bewildered, but Tommy is so determined to be a calm, sophisticated gentleman that he gives no one a chance to argue with him. Before matters can come to a head, Ellen and Joe leave for the game.

Tommy stays with Michael, and together they get very drunk. The liquor washes away all of Tommy's "reasonableness," and he berates himself for failing to fight for his mate as any male animal should. When the others return, Tommy challenges Joe to a fight. They go out to the garden, where Joe knocks Tommy down. In falling, he hits his head and is carried in unconscious.

On Monday morning, still in pain, Tommy prepares to meet his class and read the letter. He still assumes that Ellen is leaving with Joe, interpreting her denials as pity.

Keller arrives to announce that the trustees have suspended Michael and intend to fire Turner unless he issues an immediate denial. Instead, Tommy insists on reading the Vanzetti letter to everyone there; this now includes Damon and Patricia. The letter is a short piece, in broken English, in which the condemned man sees the irony of the situation in which he has been made a hero to his ideals virtually by accident. There is no reference to any political beliefs. Keller is puzzled, since the letter is obviously harmless, but when he remembers who the author was, he is once more determined that even a hint of dissent must be stifled. Damon is driven to espouse the right of free inquiry and free discussion of ideas. Michael appears with a student petition including signatures of some of the biggest football heroes, but Keller is unmoved. Patricia, who has been tremendously touched by the letter and Tommy's quiet heroism, goes off with Michael.

Tommy goes to dress. Ellen tells Joe that she is now more in love with her husband than ever. Tommy overhears this, and he and his wife are reconciled.

Critical Opinion

Much has changed in college life since 1940. The emphasis on sports has diminished, the absentminded professor is no longer such an obviously ludicrous figure, and contemporary attacks on academic freedom involve more complex, inflammable issues than the reading of a letter written by an anarchist. Tommy Turner's story was probably a bit oversimplified even for 1940. Yet the play is not as dated as conditions at Berkeley, Columbia University, and the Sorbonne might suggest. The essential problems have not been resolved; they have only grown uglier. *The Male Animal* is still relevant because the core of the problem is unaltered. Significantly, when the play was revived in 1952, when McCarthyism was at its peak, it had a longer run than it did in its first production.

Simply stated, the issue in *The Male Animal* is academic freedom, the teacher's and student's right to examine ideas which to the simplistic mind seem subversive. To make matters worse, the Vanzetti letter does not even contain any subversive ideas. The trustees' judgment is based solely on what they considered an infamous name. By their obstinate illogic, they succeed in repeating the very point Vanzetti makes: they create a hero out of an otherwise unimportant man. What is only implied in the play but has loomed much larger since is the question of the trustees' role in deciding academic policy, ignoring student and faculty participation. In the background is also the press, reporters always hovering about ready to exaggerate and distort in the name of news.

The political theme is, of course, only half the play. The other half is a light comedy of errors. Tommy thinks his wife is still pining for her football hero, while she quickly recovers from a momentary surrender to nostalgia. She thinks he is stubborn and impractical, but is surprised to find him a hero. Joe is briefly enticed by the idea of marrying Ellen, but as the complications mount he decides to try a reconciliation with his wife. Patricia rejects Michael in favor of her predictable, if dumb, halfback, only to come rushing back when her head clears. Most hilariously of all, Tommy, in an alcoholic haze, decides that he must act like a male animal—his models include the tiger, the wolf, the sea lion, and even the penguin, all of whom respond to the "first law of human nature," defense of the home.

Whether as light comedy or as satire, *The Male Animal* is distinguished for the adroitness of its language and the clever bits of stage business. *The Male Animal*'s wit and point have relevance for today's audiences.

The Authors

James Thurber and Elliott Nugent were classmates at Ohio State University. Their memories of some of their professors helped to shape *The Male Animal*. Nugent's father was an actor and playwright, his mother was an actress, and their son seems not to have wavered much about his future. He made his Broadway debut in 1921 and soon after began collaborating on plays with his father. Gentle, somewhat bemused, or inept were most of the characters he created. Tommy Turner in *The Male Animal* was the epitome of the type. Nugent played the role in both of its New York runs. He has also been active as a producer and director. His autobiography, *Events Leading up to the Comedy* (1965), includes the story of his friendship and collaboration with Thurber.

The idea for *The Male Animal* originated with Nugent, who asked Thurber to help him with it. By 1940 James Thurber was already recognized as one of America's finest humorists. After some years as a newspaperman, he found himself almost accidentally hired as managing editor for *The New Yorker* in 1929. He quit that job after six months, but continued to write for the magazine the rest of his life. With E. B. White, Thurber helped to set the tone of sardonic sophistication that distinguishes the magazine. It was White, also, who picked up Thurber's doodlings of sad dogs and lumpy, faintly sinister women, and decided that they had to be published. Most of Thurber's books consist of essays, stories, and drawings which originally appeared in *The New Yorker*. His book *The Years with Ross* (1959) provides the best history of the magazine and of its eccentric founder.

The Thurber Carnival (1960), a collection of sketches drawn from his work, was Thurber's only other contribution to the stage. Some of his fables and children's stories have been the source of dance works and musical productions. His best-known story, "The Secret Life of Walter Mitty," was turned into a highly successful film.

The Animal Kingdom

by

PHILIP BARRY (1896–1949)

The Characters

Tom Collier—a publisher of avant-garde works, in his early 30s. Open, honest, naïvely assuming that anyone he likes must share his values, he fails to understand how unconventional his ideas and behavior are.

Cecelia Henry—a lovely, well-bred, bright young woman. Apparently warm and understanding, she is actually an opportunist who uses any wiles to achieve social status and power.

Daisy Sage—an illustrator for elegant fashion magazines. Vibrant, independent, hard-working, she asks to be treated as an equal; she refuses to use femininity as a weapon.

Rufus Collier—Tom's father, a banker. Used to having or buying his own way, he is frustrated by his son's blithe disregard of material gain.

Richard Regan—Tom's butler, a former prizefighter, a tough, outspoken man on a first-name basis with his employer.

Owen Arthur—a close friend of Tom's, in love with Cecelia.

Joe Fisk—a writer
Franc Schmidt—a violinist } friends of Daisy.

Grace Macomber—a well-to-do, social-climbing, insensitive neighbor.

The Setting

Tom Collier lives in a converted farmhouse in an unfashionable section of Connecticut. It is a cheerful bachelor residence, furnished with a random collection of comfortable pieces. After his marriage, the house undergoes a change, quickly showing the hand of a woman of Good Taste; the result has less character and less warmth.

Daisy Sage's apartment is very different. Its Victorian style reflects individuality; and since her living room is also her workshop, sketches, portfolios, easels, and magazines are scattered about. The combination of femininity and professionalism is characteristic of Daisy.

The Story

Three people are nervously waiting for Tom, already two hours late. One is his father, who has never before been invited to his son's house. He is worried that Tom's important news will be an announcement of his marriage to Daisy Sage, with whom Tom has had an unconcealed affair. Cecelia calmly corrects him. Tom is going to marry *her*. Owen Arthur is deeply disappointed, since he is also in love with Cecelia. The poise with which Cecelia listens to the gossip about Daisy suggests that she is as open-minded as Tom and his friends.

Tom finally arrives, quite undisturbed by everyone's scolding. He is relieved that C., as he calls her, has already announced their engagement and calls for a celebration. At this point, a telegram from Daisy announcing her return from France interrupts the party. Tom tells C. that Daisy is his closest friend and he must welcome her home. He innocently assumes that Cecelia can accept his relationship with Daisy as the purely intellectual relationship he believes it to be.

Soon after Tom arrives at her apartment, Daisy tells him that she wants to get married and have a child. He is staggered. She admits that the physical aspects of love are not very important to her, but in other ways her love for Tom is more intense than ever. Reluctantly, he tells her that he is getting married, but he feels sure that as civilized people Cecelia and Daisy can be friends. Daisy insists that they must separate completely, but Tom cannot, will not, accept her view.

Eight months later, Cecelia has begun to remake both her husband and her home. She has persuaded Tom to publish a book, a popular success which he considers rubbish. He tries to believe she is right in saying that the profits from this work will help subsidize other ventures. She has also fired Regan, whose free-and-easy ways offend her. She has not, however, convinced Tom to accept an invitation from his father. On this evening she must somehow prevent their driving into New York for Franc Schmidt's concert debut; Cecelia would much rather save her energy for Grace Macomber's fashionable Sunday breakfast. C. changes into a filmy honeymoon negligee and comes down to say she is too headachy and cold to risk the drive. Tom avidly responds to her sensual lure.

A few months later, Daisy's first show of paintings opens. Though it has been more than a year since they last met, Tom is easily tricked by Joe and Franc into coming to Daisy's apartment and telling her what he thinks of her work. At first ill at ease, particularly when they taunt him with the poor quality of his books, Tom is soon back in stride, criticizing Daisy's show. He begins making appointments for lunches, as if everything were normal. When he leaves, Daisy at once begins packing for a long trip, determined not to get involved again.

Six months later, and it is the morning after Tom's birthday party. Cecelia is so self-assured that she has invited Daisy, Joe, and Franc for the weekend. She senses that Tom's drunken behavior at his party, so amusing for people like Grace, has alienated his friends. Secondly, unworried about Tom's feelings, she is using her appeal to Owen to push through a sale of Tom's company for the exorbitant price Tom had suggested as a way of discouraging the sale. When Owen hesitates to use his influence on the publishers he represents, she promises him that his yearning for her need no longer be unrequited. She now knows that Tom's father has sent a check and an invitation to the young couple to spend the winter with him in his splendid town house. She is not even bothered by the return of Regan. Her method, as we see when Tom speaks to her of the night before, is to withhold herself sexually until he agrees to her demands.

Daisy is appalled by Tom's behavior and by the slick, trivial magazine he is preparing to publish. He pretends to be happy, and drinks more and more heavily. She hastily leaves for New York.

Later that night, Cecelia, once more in a negligee, joins Tom for an intimate, candle-lit supper when he returns from completing the business deal. The setting reminds him of an expensive brothel. He shows Cecelia his father's check, which is much larger than she had expected. In her delight, she ignores all Tom's ironies and hesitations. She also evades Tom's suggestion that they have a child. Believing she has finally won him over, she goes to her bedroom, promising never to lock him out again.

Regan comes in to announce that he is quitting again, permanently. Tom borrows his fountain pen, endorses the check to Cecelia, and leaves with the butler, saying he will drive them both to the city. He tells the bewildered Regan that he is returning to his "wife."

Critical Opinion

The search for the ideal marriage is the most frequent theme in Philip Barry's plays. In some, the handling is light, nearly farcical. In his more serious plays, the treatment is more solemn, with an overlay of unconvincing mysticism. In *The Animal Kingdom* (1932) Barry achieves a complex, mature balance between witty badinage and serious questioning.

In a simple formula, Cecelia would be sexual and Daisy intellectual or spiritual love. Cecelia is Circe, who turns men into beasts, Owen as well as Tom, though her own interest is in power. Her name is ironic in its suggestion of heavenly purity, but it is accurately pretentious. Daisy, on the other hand, like her name, is honest, strong, open, though by no means simple. However, a contrast between the sensual and the spiritual is less than Barry intends. It is a question of balance and true affinity. Tom's rejection of Cecelia is not an argument for celibacy, but for health. It is Daisy who wants a child, while

Cecelia wants no claims on her and no damage to her attractiveness. For her, the flesh is only a weapon in a war for money, for social status, for mastery. With Daisy, his "true wife," Tom achieves a meeting of mind and body in which each person gives without loss, without surrender. The contrast between the two women is strongly reminiscent of Ibsen's *Hedda Gabler*, but without that play's tragic denouement. In Barry's comedy, the hero turns from sterile passion to life-giving love.

Barry's study of marriage probes deeply into American values, particularly attacking the emptiness of fashionable, conservative society. Cecelia and her friend Grace are sharply contrasted with Daisy and her circle, the former concerned only with possessions and appearances, the latter with true self-expression and artistic fulfillment. Tom's career as a publisher mirrors the contrasting views: when he is under his wife's control, he publishes what is superficially clever and easily digested; when he is with Daisy he recognizes that honesty, even if it does not sell, is his true metier. Here, however, the play falters. The differences between the two worlds are not always clear or important. The books that Tom publishes, the paintings that Daisy exhibits, the novels that Joe writes are all discussed in the abstract. Nor do the discussions about aesthetics and cultural values ever go beyond glittering generalities. At times the conflict seems only a preference for one set of superficialities over another. Even Tom's rejection of his father's money and his father's mentality seems personal pique, since the older man says too little to establish a solid position. Eager to press his comedy into the service of major social criticism, Barry does little more than outline what that criticism might be.

Combining a serious play of ideas with a light comedy of manners is a goal which few have achieved. *The Animal Kingdom* has less weight than Barry hoped for, but its elegance, charm, and wit make it one of the few really provocative American comedies.

The Author

Despite his skill at creating elegant comedies in which intelligently satirical, witty dialogue is spoken by charming, unstereotyped characters, Philip Barry throughout his career aimed at writing more substantial drama. He never quite succeeded. In many of his plays, including many of the comedies, he attempted to explore theological and psychological questions with results that are all too frequently cloudy and pretentious. Raised as a Roman Catholic in a well-to-do family, educated at Yale and Harvard, he developed standards which led him to consider his comedies frivolous potboilers.

The most nearly successful of his serious plays are *Hotel Universe* (1930) and *Here Come the Clowns* (1938). They reveal Barry's persistent concerns and his essential weaknesses as a dramatist. In the former, a group of wealthy, important people are gathered on the terrace of a Riviera villa. Their host is a physicist who has found a way to reverse time, and each guest is given an opportunity to relive the crucial, traumatic moment of his life, freeing himself from the guilt and confusions that have held him in bondage. In the latter play, set in a vaudeville theater symbolically named the Globe, a troubled stagehand looks for God to explain the evils and sufferings of the world. At first he succumbs to the pessimistic answers of a satanic magician, but at his death, the hero recognizes man's freedom and responsibility. In both plays, unfortunately, the initial dramatic force is dissipated by lengthy, self-consciously mystical philosophizing that befogs the basically simple ideas.

In addition to *The Animal Kingdom*, Barry's best comedies are *Paris Bound* (1927,) *Holiday* (1929), and *The Philadelphia Story* (1939). All deal with marriage as transcending human weakness and conventional morality. In *Paris Bound*, a husband's adultery threatens a happy marriage until the wife realizes that she can also be attracted sexually by someone other than her husband, yet without any loss of love for him or any desire to end the marriage. In *Holiday*, the hero is a wealthy young man who decides to retire and spend his life "living" rather than working. His fiancée is too much interested in wealth and status to accept his Thoreauvian ideas, but he soon finds a more suitable partner. And in *The Philadelphia Story*, the heroine prepares to marry a stodgy, fatherly young man, but instead remarries her first husband, whose relaxed, unconventional ways she comes to understand once she recognizes similar impulses in herself. Though he was reluctant to admit it, in all these jaunty comedies the playwright deals with more fully developed characters and more provocative ideas than those in the serious plays to which he devoted so much more time and thought.

Idiot's Delight

by

ROBERT E. SHERWOOD (1896–1955)

The Characters

Harry Van—leader of a second-rate dancing troupe called "Les Blondes." Wisecracking and gum-chewing, Harry seems at first just a small-time vaudevillian, but he is levelheaded, perceptive, and romantic.

Irene—a beautiful Russian woman of indeterminate age. Svelte and sophisticated, and a deliberate, fanciful liar, she maintains an air of tantalizing but impenetrable mystery.

Achille Weber—a world-famous munitions manufacturer. Though he is quiet and cool, his great power is suggested by the ease with which he controls others.

Donald Navadel—a young, pompous, naïve American employed as the hotel social director.

Mr. and Mrs. Cherry—young English honeymooners.

Dr. Waldersee—a German scientist. His concern for medical progress is in conflict with his contempt for human foolishness and destructiveness; beneath both lies a profound chauvinism.

Captain Locicero—the officer in charge of the frontier guard. An intelligent, unpolitical man, a civilized drinking companion, he performs his duties without question or commitment.

Quillery—a short-tempered French radical.

Dumptsy—a gentle, aging bellboy born in the region when it was Austrian. Now he is an Italian citizen separated from his family by the new borders.

The Setting

The Hotel Monte Gabriele, in the Italian Alps near the Swiss and Austrian borders, derives much of its income from the pilots at the nearby army airfield. The management has invested heavily in enlarging the hotel and hiring a social director in the hope of attracting wealthy winter-sports enthusiasts, but the season has been disastrous. This is clearly evident in the new, shiny, but sparsely occupied cocktail lounge.

It is a winter day "in any imminent year."

The Story

Italy stands on the edge of war, and the Swiss frontier is closed. Even Dr. Waldersee, a citizen of Italy's Nazi partner, must receive permission from Rome to cross into Switzerland with his laboratory rats. Harry Van and "Les Blondes," en route to Geneva, are also delayed, as is Quillery, returning from a Labor Congress in Zagreb. The Cherrys, on the other hand, had chosen this hotel for their honeymoon, but they are already thinking of crossing the border, too. Irritated, amused, frightened, or resigned, they all settle down until the orders from Rome arrive.

The next unexpected guests are more distinguished. Achille Weber is recognized as a major munitions manufacturer who has just completed semisecret negotiations with the government. With him is Irene, beautiful, superbly dressed, gracious, aristocratic in manner, a striking but distant figure. Harry is less impressed than bewildered; he senses in her something specious and vaguely familiar. For all his importance, even M. Weber must wait for permission to cross the frontier.

Later that day, with the radio mute and the rumors dark,

tension grows. Quillery is vehement, condemning Weber and the arms industry for fomenting war. Then he turns his anger on Dr. Waldersee and the Germans. The doctor claims to be only a scientist, completely unpolitical. Weber confides in Irene that the Italian planes from the nearby base have gone to bomb Paris. They must leave before French planes arrive to bomb in reprisal. Irene's response, subtly hinting that he trades in death, irritates Weber. When she returns to the attack somewhat later, he coldly suggests that their affair is approaching its end. He cannot bear soft people and considers criticism of his work sentimental hypocrisy.

To pass the time, Harry and his troupe perform for the small audience. Toward the end of their act, the fliers come in, tired but full of high spirits. The girls happily join them in drinking champagne, but Quillery interrupts the festivities to announce that Paris is in ruins; he shouts that the pilots are assassins. He is hustled out, and they later learn he has been shot.

That night, Irene and Harry are alone. She is telling him the dramatic story of her escape from Russia at the time of the Revolution. He is fascinated but skeptical; he has earlier overheard her tell a different version. He asks her if she has ever been in Omaha. Years before, while he acted as assistant to Zuleika, the Mind Reader, he had fallen in love with a red-haired Russian dancer, part of another act on the vaudeville bill, and they had spent one rapturous night together. Amused, Irene assures him that she has always been blonde and has never heard of the Governor Bryan Hotel in Omaha.

The following day, the good news arrives that the border is open. Dr. Waldersee, infected by the war hysteria, announces that he is returning to Germany, dismissing the attractions of medical discovery that await him in Geneva. Irene's passport, however, issued by the League of Nations to stateless persons, cannot be honored unless M. Weber vouches for her. Choosing his words carefully, he assures the captain that Madame is quite capable of taking care of herself, thus dooming her. She takes the blow calmly, though she knows the Italian government will soon arrange to silence her. As Harry leaves, she half-jokingly tells him the room number at the Governor Bryan Hotel. Since he does not remember the number and Irene will say nothing else, he storms out, assuming that she is lying again. But after he gets the girls safely aboard the train, he returns, drawn back to Irene although he still cannot be sure she is the girl he loved. Soon they hear the French planes coming to bomb the airfield. Their defiant singing of "Onward, Christian Soldiers" is lost in the din of exploding bombs, machine-gun fire, breaking glass, and crashing timbers.

Critical Opinion

When Weber denies personal responsibility for war, since he is only "the humble instrument of His divine will," Irene ironically agrees: "Yes—that's quite true. We don't do half enough justice to Him. Poor, lonely old soul. Sitting up in heaven, with nothing to do, but play solitaire. Poor, dear God. Playing Idiot's Delight. The game that never means anything, and never ends." Sherwood's play demonstrates both the truth and falseness of her analysis.

The revelations in the early thirties of the role of the munitions makers in World War I account for the sharp focus on Weber. To Quillery, the Communist, Weber embodies all evil and explains everything wrong with society. He makes a strong case, but Harry Van, the voice of common sense, cannot be satisfied with the answer: "Weber—and a million like him—they can't take credit for *all* of this! Who is it that did this dirty trick on a lot of decent people? And why do you let them get away with it? . . . It's God-damned bad management—that's what it is!" All around him the evidence is compelling that munitions makers and greedy capitalists are at most a symptom, not a cause. Don Cherry, the artist and pacifist, is caught in what he himself identifies as bestial frenzy. Dr. Waldersee, the dedicated scientist, is caught though his loyalty is to medicine and the saving of lives. The captain follows his orders and shrugs. Even poor Dumptsy is back in uniform at the end, the victim of a brutal trick of history. An aimless violence, an uncontrollable destructiveness is abroad, and no League of Nations or Soviet Internationale can stop it.

On such a bleak philosophical foundation, Sherwood's *Idiot's Delight* builds in melodrama and high comedy to a bitter but not tragic end. Both Harry and Irene are worldly-wise observers of the deteriorating world around them. His experience as pitchman and entertainer has given Harry a profound awareness of human gullibility. Irene, too, has learned to live without illusions. So, with a lightly Olympian air, they expose the pompous, the ludicrous, the sinister, and the maudlin, in the tradition of the witty couple of high comedy. Yet, in the time of a crisis unknown to Congreve's or Sheridan's heroes and heroines, they reach out to each other, discovering that their feelings of self-sufficiency have been their worst illusions. Together they can defy the bombs with courage and intelligence, asserting that life is more than a game of Idiot's Delight that never ends and never means anything.

Though Sherwood brings his play very near the edge of despair, he can still, in 1936, find amusement in watching the dancing on the lip of the volcano. Though the play ends with war, the tone is one of warning, not of surrender. Stupid American isolationism, as in Navadel, is still comic. The humanity of the Italian captain still balances the hysterical patriotism of Dr. Waldersee. The horror of the rapidly approaching cataclysm in itself seems an excellent reason for avoiding it. Despite his foresight, Sherwood could hardly believe that the conflict was utterly inevitable. He said in an interview at the time that he was sure that memories of World War I would work to prevent the occurrence of an even greater holocaust. Thus, the play remains a comedy, though at times a dark one. A few years later, the undercurrent of optimism had run out. In *There Shall Be No Night* (1940), dealing with the Russo-Finnish War, Sherwood approached his subject with anguish and only a faint hope that human nobility could survive the war.

Idiot's Delight is less dated than might be expected. Since the end of World War II, the sense of inexplicable evil and imminent destruction has become a central premise of contemporary thought; the absurdists and the writers of black comedy start from this position. Sherwood's play, even his somewhat old-fashioned hopefulness, still speaks to the modern consciousness. And as a well-constructed comedy-melodrama, it remains entertaining as well as provocative.

The Author

Robert Emmet Sherwood was born in New Rochelle, New York, but spent most of his childhood and youth in Manhattan. His father was an investment broker, his mother a painter and illustrator. Both loved the threater. They very early introduced their children to the delights of playgoing.

In 1914, after graduating from Milton Academy, Sherwood entered Harvard, where he made his mark as editor of *The Lampoon* and as a member of the Hasty Pudding Club. In 1917 the club presented his first play, *Barnum Was Right,* and Sherwood was expected to provide another play in his senior year. However, when America entered World War I, Sherwood decided to enlist. Rejected by the American Army because he was too tall, Sherwood enlisted in the Canadian Black Watch Regiment.

After the war, Sherwood joined the staff of *Vanity Fair* as movie critic, a job new to journalism and one in which Sherwood distinguished himself. His aim, however, was still to become a playwright, and he gave up movie reviewing soon after *The Road to Rome* opened with both critical and popular success.

The Road to Rome (1927) was the first Broadway production by a writer who would, during the next quarter century, distinguish himself not only as a dramatist, but also as a speech writer for President Franklin Roosevelt and as an active government official during World War II. To historians, Sherwood's *Roosevelt and Hopkins* (1948), growing out of his work with the Office of War Information, is invaluable. In the history of the movies he also made his mark as one of the writers of *The Best Years of Our Lives* (1946), a penetrating account of veterans' difficulties in adjusting to the postwar world. Almost all of Sherwood's important work is, indeed, in some way an attempt to understand and combat war and violence. Such concern reflects at least in part his painful experiences in World War I.

In Sherwood's first play, Hannibal is dissuaded from entering Rome by a lovely and witty woman. The subject is treated satirically somewhat in the manner of Shaw's *Caesar and Cleopatra,* with considerable emphasis on official pomposity and the hollow claims of military glory. In contrast, *The Petrified Forest* (1935) shows civilized understanding as helpless in the face of crude violence. A group of people in a diner at the edge of the desert are terrorized by a brutal criminal. The sensitive young writer and the idealistic girl are the most vulnerable. It is Sherwood's most despairing work. In *Abe Lincoln in Illinois* (1938) and *There Shall Be No Night*

(1940), as in *Idiot's Delight,* the author's bitter and angry awareness of the dark forces is strong, but he finds hope and consolation in the nobility and fortitude of individuals.

Quite different in subject is *Reunion in Vienna* (1931), Sherwood's most polished comedy. An exiled Hapsburg returns secretly to Vienna for a meeting of his followers and insists that to rid his psyche of damaging memories, he must spend a night with his former mistress. Her husband, a psychoanalyst, can hardly refuse the call of therapy. The next morning, though it is never made certain whether the duke has succeeded in persuading the young woman, all go happily on their separate ways. *Reunion in Vienna* is one of the few American comedies in which the game of sex is played with the worldly air one associates with writers such as Molnar or Schnitzler. Having written it, however, Sherwood returned to his more serious concerns and, except for collaborating with Irving Berlin on *Miss Liberty* (1949), he never again wrote a play intended as light entertainment.

As an American writer, Robert Sherwood is an unusual combination of qualities: on the one hand, an intellectual, scholarly, deeply serious about world politics and gripped by a view of the world's tragic madness; on the other hand, a remarkably skilled craftsman with a flair for vivid theatrical situations, striking characterizations, and all the wisecracking of slick farce. Combined in varying proportions, these abilities produced some of the most sharply individualistic and memorable plays of the last three decades.

Our Town

by

THORNTON WILDER (1897–   )

The Characters

The Stage Manager—a friendly, chatty man, with a dry sense
of humor and the air of a small-town homespun philosopher.
He is the narrator and also takes part in key scenes, once
as the druggist, and again as a minister.

The Webbs: Mr. Webb is editor of the *Sentinel; Mrs. Webb*
is a sensible mother and housewife; their daughter, *Emily*
(born 1885), is the brightest girl in the high school; they
have a young son, *Wally.*

The Gibbses: Dr. Gibbs is the town physician; *Mrs. Gibbs,*
like Mrs. Webb, is a hard-working, uncomplaining woman;
George (same age as Emily) is a fine young man, not very
good at his studies, but a good baseball player; and there
is a younger child, *Rebecca.*

Townspeople:

Simon Stimson—organist and choir director; an alcoholic.

Mrs. Soames—a gossipy, good-hearted neighbor.

Joe Crowell, Jr.—the newsboy.

Howie Newsome—the milkman.

The Setting

There is neither curtain nor scenery; the stage is bare except for such pieces of simple furniture as are brought on when needed for the action. George and Emily suggest they are at their bedroom windows by standing on ladders. A board laid on two chairs can serve as a soda-fountain counter or as Mrs. Gibbs's ironing board. A few trellises can indicate gardens. All arrangements of setting are made in full view of the audience, the actors helping to move furniture.

All movement involves some element of pantomime: the newsboy tosses invisible papers; the children carry invisible books; and the milkman scolds his invisible horse.

The Story

The Stage Manager introduces the play and the characters. He describes the setting, Grover's Corners, New Hampshire. The first act deals with a fairly typical day in town, May 7, 1901. It is early morning and Doc Gibbs, returning from delivering twins, chats with the newsboy and the milkman. His wife wakes the children and gets them ready for school. Next door, at the Webbs's, the pattern is much the same. With the children on their way, the two women chat briefly, until the Stage Manager interrupts. He introduces Professor Willard, who gives some background on the geological and anthropological history of the town. The population is 2,640. When the professor has finished, Mr. Webb speaks a bit about the town's commonplace character. Questions from the audience about the behavior and values of the townspeople elicit the information that there is little drunkenness but also little formal culture.

The Stage Manager then calls up an afternoon scene, with the children home from school. Emily agrees to help George with his algebra and tries to get her mother to tell her she is pretty. Again the Stage Manager interrupts, this time to talk a bit about the future of some of the minor characters. Joe Crowell, Jr., for example, will go on to MIT, but will be killed in World War I. The Stage Manager explains that a copy of this play will be placed in the cornerstone of a new bank, so that people in the future will know what everyday life was like.

The scene shifts to evening. The two adolescents are at their windows moon-gazing. George's father scolds him for not chopping wood. Coming home from choir practice, the ladies gossip about Simon Stimson. Rebecca joins her brother at his window and tells him a friend of hers received a letter addressed: Jane Crofut; the Crofut Farm; Grover's Corners; Sutton County; New Hampshire; United States of America; Continent of North America; Western Hemisphere; the Earth; the Solar System; the Universe; the Mind of God.

At the start of the second act, the Stage Manager tells the audience that it is now July 7, 1904. The first act was called "The Daily Life"; this one is "Love and Marriage"; the audience can probably guess what the last will be. It is the morning of George and Emily's wedding day. Both households are in a turmoil.

The Stage Manager stops the action so that we can see the scene, about a year before, when George and Emily discovered they were in love. Coming home from school, George offers to carry Emily's books and asks why she is so angry. She accuses him of being conceited. He thanks her for her candor and invites her to have a soda. Emily is not so much angry as upset because George is planning to spend three years at agricultural college. He is eager to have a reason to accept his uncle's offer of a farm as soon as possible, and agrees that he hardly wants to go away for so long now that he and Emily have discovered their feelings for each other.

At the wedding, both George and Emily have moments of panic, but all goes smoothly. The minister sees the wedding as one of the millions bound to follow the usual pattern: children, work, age, illness, and death.

The third act takes place nine years later, summer of 1913. On one side of the stage are three rows of chairs, a section of the town's cemetery. Among those sitting quietly, patiently in the chairs are Mrs. Gibbs, Mrs. Soames, Wally Webb, and Simon Stimson. The Stage Manager explains how each died. The dead, he says, wait patiently for their hold on earth to loosen and for the eternal part of each to come clear.

Emily Webb's funeral procession appears. She has died in childbirth. The others gently welcome her. She realizes that she can go back and relive her life. The others warn her not to try, but she cannot understand why it will be painful. She decides to try a relatively unimportant day, and a happy one, her twelfth birthday.

The day begins much as any other does, and Emily is struck by the youth of her mother and the beauty of nature and of everyday things. But what begins as wonder turns to grief with her awareness of the future. She realizes that everything is passing too quickly and that no one has time to notice, to experience fully. In minutes the attempt to relive the past becomes overwhelmingly painful. Back at the cemetery, she agrees that the living do not understand much. She, too, will now rest and wait.

The Stage Manager wishes the audience good night.

Critical Opinion

When *Our Town* was made into a film, most of Wilder's nonrealistic approach was omitted. The result was a sweet, gentle story of a small town in which two young people grow up, get married, have a family, and approach death. (In the film, Emily recovers, the ingredients of Act III becoming a dream she experiences in her illness.) This is the plot of the story, but it is not what the play is about. What the camera missed, with its ability to impart solid believability to anything it sees, was the interplay between illusion and reality, Wilder's way of endowing his story with universality, while at the same time ironically commenting on it.

Our Town (1938) is designed to illustrate its own theses: (1) that life runs out so quickly and we take so much for granted that we hardly notice the world about us, and (2) that if we did notice it, we would find the everyday details of life beautiful, fascinating, and symbolic of all human life. We are presented with a bare stage on which each bit of furniture strikes us with renewed wonder and each action has significance, as if rescued from the void. The simplest gestures, like tossing newspapers, become almost ritualistic in pantomime. Yet everything is so completely transient; nothing lasts for long.

In *Our Town* Wilder creates a deliberately ordinary town and story. Grover's Corners is without drama in the usual sense of the word. There is no crime. Even Simon Stimson's domestic problems and alcoholism are treated as part of ordinary life. But the playwright makes high drama of it. He plays the magician in evoking different places and times. He creates a tension between the story we have heard so many times before and the simple but immensely sophisticated way in which the story is told. He extracts the essence of each situation by looking at it somewhat obliquely. Most of all, he insists that the audience use its imagination.

Almost all of these effects depend on the pivotal role of the Stage Manager. As narrator, he keeps the plot straight, filling in the gaps, tying up loose ends. As a kind of lecturer, he manipulates the stage, calling scenes into being, ending them when they have made his point, commenting on their meaning. As a philosopher and artist, he underlines the ideas, particularly the idea of omniscience, since much of the force of the play depends on our awareness of seeing the story in the past. And because he has this omniscience, he becomes something like that God in whose mind all of existence is contained. He is a spokesman for the author but also a completely realized character, a relaxed, unemotional Yankee.

In no other work has Wilder so beautifully synthesized the two aspects of his talent, the sophisticated artist and the humanist praising the simple joys and inherent decency of men.

The Skin of Our Teeth

by

THORNTON WILDER (1897–)

The Characters

Mr. Antrobus—inventor of the wheel and of the alphabet, Man as discoverer and inventor; a good family man but also much concerned about mankind in general, an idealist full of forward-looking plans, but apt to sink into despair when human wickedness seems too great.

Mrs. Antrobus—a fiercely protective mother, ready to put up with her husband's antics so long as the children are taken care of.

Henry—their son, originally named Cain; a rebellious, violent boy, quick to anger.

Gladys—their daughter; a sweet, pretty girl who idolizes her father.

Sabina—the maid; a brassy, pleasure-loving girl, with little sense of responsibility. She is supposedly played by an actress named Miss Somerset, who frequently speaks in her own person; a sentimental woman, not very bright.

Fortune Teller—a swarthy Gypsy whose predictions of doom are usually accurate.

Doctor, Professor, Judge Moses, Homer, the *Muse sisters—*
refugees.
Mr. Fitzpatrick, Mr. Tremayne, Hester, Ivy, and *Fred Bailey*
—backstage workers.

The Setting

Acts I and III take place in the Antrobus home, a conventional suburban house, in Excelsior, New Jersey. Act II is set on the Atlantic City boardwalk, bright with striped canopies.

The walls of the Antrobus house have a tendency to act rather strangely, sometimes leaning precariously over the actors, sometimes flying up out of sight.

The Story

Act I

After some slides and news announcements, one concerning the wall of ice said to be moving south through New England, the curtain rises on the Antrobus living room. Sabina is dusting and worrying whether the master will make it home on this incredibly cold August day. As Miss Somerset, she interrupts to complain to the audience that the sense of the play eludes her. It has something to do with the troubles of the human race, and is not at all as entertaining as are the simple melodramas she would rather be appearing in. When the play resumes, Mrs. Antrobus scolds her for letting the fire go out, and Sabina gives two weeks' notice. A telegraph boy arrives with a message that Mr. Antrobus will be late; he has been busy working on the alphabet, has discovered the number 100, and invented the wheel. The boy also has heard rumors about the moving ice.

The children and the pets, a dinosaur and a mammoth, join the women before the fire, which the telegraph boy has relighted. Mrs. Antrobus warns the children to be well-behaved when their father returns; Henry is to keep his hair well down over the mark on his forehead and Gladys is to act like a lady. Mr. Antrobus arrives, bellowing with joy, laden with packages. But his enthusiasm evaporates when he asks his wife to let some refugees share their house. Reluctant to deprive her family, she refuses, but Antrobus argues that these people include the finest representatives of mankind, a doctor, a judge, a fine poet, and some talented ladies. Mrs. Antrobus agrees, though she insists the animals will have to go. The refugees crowd into the living room and discuss whether all of man's work will be destroyed by the ice.

Suddenly, there is a scream. Henry has thrown a stone and probably killed the boy next door, just as he had killed his brother Abel. Mr. Antrobus is ready to give up mankind's struggle for civilization. Mrs. Antrobus pushes Gladys forward to tell about her successful day at school, Henry starts reciting the multiplication table, and the refugees sing. Faith is restored and everyone cooperates in building the fire. Sabina calls on the audience to sacrifice their theater seats to save the human race, and ushers rush forward with broken chairs.

Act II

The Ancient and Honorable Order of Mammals, Subdivision Humans, is having its annual convention at Atlantic City. Delegations from the other Orders are also present. Mr. Antrobus has been elected president for the year, and delivers a welcoming address. His watchword is "Enjoy yourselves." The other conventioneers need no encouragement. The bingo parlors and bars do an excellent business.

Miss Lily-Sabina Fairweather (the Sabina of the first act) has won the title Miss Atlantic City and sets about seducing Mr. Antrobus. The Fortune Teller acts as her adviser when she is not shouting grim warnings to the people who pass her door. When Mrs. Antrobus goes off in search of raincoats, since severe weather warnings have appeared, Lily begins to entice Mr. Antrobus into her tent.

Abruptly, Miss Somerset stops the scene, announcing that the actors will move to the end of the scene, where Mr. Antrobus agrees to divorce his wife. She explains that the scene so closely parallels what happened to a friend in the audience that she could not play it. The others finally agree to let her have her way.

Mrs. Antrobus returns and is distressed to discover Gladys in shocking red stockings. Her husband's attempts to explain his new decision are interrupted by radio technicians waiting for his address to the world and by signs of the approaching storm. Gladys tells her parents that Henry threw a rock at one of the rolling-chair men and may have killed him. The Fortune Teller urges the Antrobuses to board a boat, taking the animal delegates with them. At first, Henry cannot be found, but his mother frantically calls him by his original name and he runs in and joins them. Sabina begs to accompany them, and Mrs. Antrobus agrees, contemptuously relegating the girl to the kitchen, where she always seems to end up.

ACT III

A war has ended. Sabina, who has been a camp follower, returns to the house, where Mrs. Antrobus, Gladys, and Gladys' baby have been hiding in the cellar.

The action is stopped while the stage manager explains that a group of actors who were to appear in the final scene have all become ill with food poisoning. Various backstage personnel are recruited to handle the material. They will represent the hours of the night, each reciting a passage by a famous philosopher. Ivy explains that the great ideas of man are always around us, ready to inspire us if we will only stop to heed them. They rehearse briefly.

The play is resumed. Sabina tells Mrs. Antrobus to get Mr. Antrobus' books ready and on no account to allow Henry into the house; Henry is the enemy. But Henry does return, sullen, insulting, and terribly hungry, insisting he does not intend to stay. His mother gives him some food, and he goes to sleep.

The women start pulling the house back into shape. (The walls are awry, and Sabina straightens them by pulling on a rope dangling from the ceiling.) The maid is pessimistic, wondering what good it does always to start over again when destruction lies ahead. Mrs. Antrobus scolds her for such lack of faith.

Mr. Antrobus returns, and immediately he and Henry quarrel, the younger man despising the regulations his father wishes to impose on the world. Abruptly, Miss Somerset interrupts, reminding them of how serious the scene became the night before, when both had literally fought. The actor playing Henry says that his resentments against his own family rise up and take over, while the actor playing Mr. Antrobus admits that his devotion to work has turned him cold and unresponsive.

Left alone, Mr. and Mrs. Antrobus discuss the war and the hope for the future. He is happy that his books have survived, once more to spark hope in mankind. Sabina asks permission to go to the movies. With the war over, normalcy begins to return.

Actors, representing the hours, pass as they quote Aristotle, Plato, Spinoza, and the Bible, all on the beginnings of life and society and the search for truth and goodness. The lights go out briefly, and when they go on again, Sabina is dusting, repeating the lines from the beginning of the play. She bids the audience good night, because the play will go on for ages and ages.

The end has not been written, but the Antrobuses "are full of plans" and are "as confident as the first day they began."

Critical Opinion

The Antrobuses are Mankind (from the Greek *anthropos*, "human being"), and *The Skin of Our Teeth* is the story of how Man is constantly threatened with extinction and always survives, though often after a very close brush with death. Wilder playfully mixes past with present, for the patterns of human life are unchanging; reality with illusion, for the actors as human beings share the problems of the fictitious characters; and farce with near-tragedy, for such is the near-absurd nature of life. At the end, he finds some hope for man's continued survival.

In Act I, the ice sheet, a natural disaster, threatens the human race. Some creatures are doomed to extinction, but men are more adaptable, and with faith and cooperation they can survive. Throughout this act, the stress is on man the maker, and if anything saves him it is his mastery of nature through his will to survive. In Act II, the doom is God-sent, a moral chastisement. Though Wilder never refers to God, the parallels to the story of Noah and the Ark make the point for him. What saves the family this time is the very fact that it is a family. Lily-Sabina's temptation fades before Mr. Antrobus' concern for his children. But by saving Henry-Cain, Mr. Antrobus sets up the conditions for the most serious threat of all, mankind's own evil, his will to destroy. War, the subject of Act III, is the fullest manifestation of that danger. (The play was written in the darkest days of World War II.) Henry-Cain, who has been a source of worry throughout, is at first disowned by his father, but in the key scene between the men as actors, a deeper source of trouble is laid bare. The human psyche does not deal separately with simple good and evil but rather with the two inextricably entwined, and the actor playing Mr. Antrobus recognizes his own responsibility for the anger and envy he may stimulate in others. Here Wilder finds part of his answer in man's ability to face the sources of danger within and control them. With this and with the wisdom of the past, the Antrobuses can build a better world.

Though Wilder's theme is serious, *The Skin of Our Teeth* is anything but solemn. Wilder keeps so many glittering ideas in the air that it is difficult to attend to one at a time. His multilevel approach employs surprising parallels and paradoxes, interruptions, incongruities, and anachronisms. As a simple example, take Miss Somerset's difficulties with her role. First, the actress, like the character she plays, prefers not to think; the conventional, neat categories and responses are enough for her; she wishes she could be acting in a nice tearjerker like *Peg o' My Heart.* So each time she comments on her role, she reminds us that this is a play designed to shatter accepted ideas about plays and life, and, through new and refreshing juxtapositions, lead us to new insights and relationships. Secondly, when she does grasp an idea, such as the notion of refugees, she does so by seeing the modern equivalent, thus justifying the playwright's suggestion that human experience is timeless. Finally, while complaining of the play's difficulties, she helps to make it entertaining in ways which satisfy her notion of theater.

Wilder says that he got part of his idea for *The Skin of Our Teeth* at a performance of *Hellzapoppin,* a popular entertainment that relied heavily on continuous wild surprise and crazy confusions. Other influences Wilder is clearly drawing on are James Joyce for the overlapping time levels and the play of language, and Bertolt Brecht for the alienation technique. The actor's comments on the character he is playing keep the audience from staying with the play only on a literal level. The humanistic theme and optimistic tone are, however, fully Wilder's. Though its structure has none of the spare dramatic economies of *Our Town*, *The Skin of Our Teeth* shares with the earlier play a sense of delight in the simple, everyday life of man and a bittersweet appreciation of his limited accomplishments and infinite foolishness.

The Author

Grover's Corners, the quiet setting of *Our Town*, is Thornton Wilder's ideal of a home town, but he did not discover his affinity for New England until late in his twenties. He was born in Madison, Wisconsin, where his father was a newspaper editor. Before he was ten, the family moved to Hong Kong, where his father served as consul general, but Mrs. Wilder soon returned with the children to California so they could have an American education. Thornton Wilder studied at Oberlin College and at Yale, where he began writing fiction and plays. He spent a year in Rome, taught French, did graduate work at Princeton, writing all the while. In 1926 he spent the summer at the MacDowell Colony in New Hampshire.

In his writing, Wilder has alternated between fiction and drama. His best-known novels are *The Bridge of San Luis Rey* (1927), *The Woman of Andros* (1930), *Heaven's My Destination* (1935), *The Ides of March* (1948), and *The Eighth Day* (1967). The novels reflect Wilder's scholarship and his interest in history and philosophy.

As a playwright, Wilder has always been fascinated with the limits of illusion. One of his earliest one-act plays is *The Long Christmas Dinner* (published in 1931), in which ninety years of a family's history are compressed into the comings and goings of people around a dinner table. Two other early plays prefigure the techniques and, to some extent, the subject matter of *Our Town*. *The Happy Journey to Camden and Trenton* (1931) relies on four chairs to represent an automobile and on skillful pantomime to indicate the activities of a family making an uneventful visit to relatives. In *Pullman Car Hiawatha* (1931) a stage manager helps to explain how some simple chairs are arranged to represent compartments on the train. At times the action stops while information is provided about the little towns the train passes through. At the end, there is a sequence involving the planets, very much like the ending of *The Skin of Our Teeth*.

Wilder has also adapted plays by other playwrights. His first work on Broadway was *Lucrece* (1932), based on André Obey's *Le Viol de Lucrece*. In 1938 he presented *The Merchant of Yonkers*, adapted from Johann Nestroy's *Einen Jux will er sich machen* (1842). This farce about how a successful businessman is tricked into marriage was not very successful. Rewritten and retitled *The Matchmaker* (1954), it was a hit. Ten years later it reappeared again, as the fabulously successful musical *Hello, Dolly*.

In recent years, Wilder has presented only one new full-length play, *The Alcestiad*, produced at the Edinburgh Festival as *A Life in the Sun* (1955). In 1962, the Circle in the Square presented three one-act plays by Wilder, which were announced as the first of a cycle dealing with the chief virtues and vices.

Thornton Wilder has written only a few plays. Their importance, however, is considerable. With little fanfare or notoriety, his productions have done more to expand the uses of the stage than has many a widely heralded and soon forgotten "breakthrough." Wilder is also one of the few modern writers who have maintained a sense of humane values and some muted optimism about man's future, neither surrendering to the oracles of despair nor turning his back on the truths they have expressed.

Boy Meets Girl

by

BELLA and SAMUEL SPEWACK
(both 1899–   )

The Characters

Robert Law—a Hollywood screenwriter. He dreams of returning to Vermont, but the fun, challenge, and money
keep him in California.

J. Carlyle Benson—Law's collaborator. He has been in the
movie business since boyhood, and will not disparage
screenwriting, especially since his exorbitant salary is all
that keeps his wife from leaving him. Benson and Law are
ingenious practical jokers and wisecrackers.

C. Elliot Friday (usually called C. F.)—a producer. Conscious of being a college graduate, he has pretentions to
sophistication, but is crass and vulgar.

Susie—a commissary waitress, young, blonde, pretty, and not
very bright.

Rodney Bevan—a young Englishman trying to prove himself
as an actor; good-looking and ambitious, but utterly out of
step with the hectic Hollywood world.

Larry Toms—a Western star with a dwindling following. Like

143

the character he usually plays, he is slow-spoken and un-sophisticated.

Rosetti—Larry's agent, a fast-talking, completely amoral operator.

Green and *Slade*—songwriters in the studio's music department.

B. K.—the head of the studio, a tyrant, never seen, only heard thundering over the Dictaphone.

The Setting

Most of the action takes place in C. F.'s office, an example of middle-level executive opulence, a mixture of periods and styles, all expensive. One scene is set in the corridor of one of Hollywood's most exclusive hospitals.

The Story

Law and Benson are desperately trying to manufacture a script for Larry Toms's next movie. The formula must be "Boy meets girl. Boy loses girl. Boy gets girl," but they are unable to dream up a new variation. Instead, they enjoy themselves by confusing Toms with preposterous plot suggestions and trading insults with Rosetti. C. F. insists that something new and original must be developed, but the conversation is frequently interrupted by phone calls from "casting" about midgets or from Benson's wife about extravagant purchases; by the arrival of a manicurist; and finally, by the appearance of Rodney from the costume department to check on Guards uniforms for *Young England*. C. F. rejects the fur hat, but Rodney insists it is the only authentic part of the costume. Being corrected by a seven-dollar-a-day extra puts C. F. into a fury, and Rodney is fired. Green and Slade appear and insist on singing a new, stupendously banal song for *Young England*. Through it all, Law and Benson clown about, cleverly twitting and confusing everyone.

Susie arrives with lunch. She puts the tray down, and faints. She is pregnant. When she tells them she has no husband, the writers praise her frankness and moral iconoclasm, but she is too much the literalist to understand. Over C. F.'s objections, they reserve a room for her at the best hospital, at studio expense. Then they are inspired to use the baby in the new movie, creating a plot around an abandoned infant and the tough he-man who finds it. All but Susie rush up to B. K.'s office to get his reaction. Rodney returns to argue about the uniform. He and Susie are immediately drawn together. He explains that he must be in at least one picture so that he can claim to have given up films voluntarily. He is very hungry, and Susie encourages him to eat the untouched lunches before he goes.

Law and Benson return and get Susie to sign a contract for the unborn child, already named Happy. No sooner has she done so than she begins to have labor pains.

Seven months later, Happy is a star, surrounded by nurses and servants. Toms is furious about becoming a mere appendage to Happy, and Susie is delighted about going back to finish high school. Rosetti discovers that Law's and Benson's power of attorney has run out, and he tells Larry to marry Susie, thus assuring his career and profiting from the baby's earnings. Half persuaded, Larry invites Susie to the De Mille opening. Though not attracted to him, she finds Benson and Law so involved in their work that they seem to have lost interest in her. She has also been unsuccessfully trying to find Rodney, whose name she does not know, and so accepts Larry's invitation.

When Rosetti tells the writers that he has just completed an agreement on a new joint contract for Larry and Happy, Law and Benson are stunned. They must have full control of the baby if they are to retain their jobs. When Rodney arrives, finally traced by C. F.'s secretary at Susie's request, the writers, not realizing why he is there (nor does he), offer him a job for the evening. He is to rush up to Susie at the premiere and declare he is Happy's father. They explain that it is all a scene from a movie.

The hoax works all too well. The studio is in an uproar. Susie arrives, not so much disturbed by the scandal as by the fact that Happy has been rushed to the hospital with measles. Rodney escapes from the room in which he has been locked, and C. F. guesses the trick. Law and Benson are fired, and Larry rushes in to announce that he, too, has the measles.

At the hospital, two weeks later, Law visits Susie to tell her he is returning to Vermont and serious writing. Benson is there also, totally depressed. Rosetti gloats over his new victories, for he has been dickering with Gaumont-British to buy the studio and has sold C. F. on the idea of a contest to replace Happy. Benson suggests as a practical joke that they call an old friend in Paris, using Larry Toms's hospital phone. Suddenly inspired, Law asks the friend to send a telegram over the name of Gaumont-British offering to buy the studio, with the provision that Happy, Benson, and Law be part of the package.

The telegram has its effect. Benson and Law receive lavish new contracts, while Larry is to be farmed out on loan, at a pittance, to a minor company. Rodney fights his way into the office and proposes to Susie. She explains that she had had a husband, a bigamist later murdered by his other wife, and is hesitant about remarrying. The arrival of Major Thompson, representative of Gaumont-British, clears the air. He reveals that the telegram is not authentic, though no one grasps Benson's and Law's part in the affair. He also recognizes Rodney as a nobleman's son. Susie and the young Englishman go off, while C. F. is left utterly stunned by the whole sequence of events. Benson triumphantly shouts: "Cinderella—Prince Charming—Boy meets girl. . . . Boy loses girl. . . . Boy gets girl! Where's your damned realism now?"

Critical Opinion

Hollywood has had an irresistible attraction for writers of farce almost since the earliest nickelodeon days Nowhere else has the contrast between business and art, between the film as a moneymaking product and the film as a work of the imagination, been so vividly presented. The Spewacks cleverly exploit this contrast. Throughout the play, C. F. is involved with the production of *Young England*, a history of England being presented in extravagant style, obviously a prestige production. Yet everyone involved is ignorant and insensitive, particularly the "intellectual" producer. C. F. judges the costumes by standards that have nothing to do with authenticity. The song writers keep trying to satisfy his desire for a splendid trumpet flourish, only to discover at the end that he really wants trombones. When the length of the film is at issue, great swaths of history are excised. The audience, it is argued, will never know the difference. The problems with *Young England,* which is still not finished at the end of the play, counterpoint the story of Benson and Law. The films they concoct are frankly commercial but probably more intelligent; at least they recognize and revel in the artificiality and exploit the pretensions and confusions.

Artificiality and confusion are the essence of farce, and the Spewacks are ingenious at inventing new turns and variations. The story is full of outrageous implausibilities and coincidences, but as long as the mad logic of the play is retained there is never any need to apply realistic criteria. For example, the way the threads are neatly tied together at the end is preposterous. Would any studio make such decisions on the basis of a single telegram? Has no one ever bothered to ask Susie about the father of her child? But it would not be as funny if matters were handled reasonably. The illogic is a large part of the fun. It is appropriate that the Spewacks have two screenwriters at the center of the action, for they continually remind us that the comedy is all witty invention. We share with the Spewacks their delight in writing the play just as we share with Benson and Law their delight in inventing plots or practical jokes.

Much of the fun in *Boy Meets Girl* also comes from the frank exploitation of stereotypes. Susie is the dumb blonde. Rodney is the dumb Englishman. C. F. is the pompous producer. Larry Toms is the dumb Westerner. At every point, from the title to the closing line, the plot is identified as one enormous parody of a stereotype. There are some elements of satire in the play, but mostly it is a reveling in some of the oldest of all comic materials: the tangle of mistaken identities, misunderstandings, and wild improbabilities.

The Authors

Bella Cohen was born in 1899, in Budapest, Hungary; Samuel Spewack was born in 1899, in Bachmut, Russia. Both of their families came to the United States when the children were small, and Bella and Sam both grew up in New York. They met when both were working on newspapers, Bella as a columnist for the New York *Daily Call,* Sam as a reporter for the New York *World.* In 1922, when Sam was assigned as a correspondent to Berlin and Moscow, they married and in their four years abroad began writing together. Although both have written on their own, their collaborative efforts have been the most successful.

Their first few comedies—*The War Song* (1928), *Poppa* (1928), *Clear All Wires* (1932), and *Spring Song* (1934)— were only briefly successful, but they revealed the Spewacks' skill and wit. In Hollywood, Bella and Sam produced a number of screenplays while gathering the material for *Boy Meets Girl* (1935). They followed this with their first musical, *Leave It to Me* (1938), about a bumbling American ambassador to Moscow.

The music and lyrics for *Leave It to Me* were by Cole Porter. The three worked together beautifully. Porter's tongue-in-cheek witty lyrics combined perfectly with the Spewacks' sharp-edged satire. The trio got together again ten years later and created *Kiss Me Kate* (1948). The story involves an acting company preparing a musical production of *The Taming of the Shrew*, with the two stars repeating offstage a tumultuous courtship very much like that of Petruchio and Kate. The mingling of Shakespeare's play with backstage farce, of the poetic with the slangy, of romance and satire, produced one of the finest works of the American musical theater.

The only other successful play the Spewacks have written is *My Three Angels* (1953), based on Albert Husson's *La Cuisine des Anges,* about three escaped convicts who solve a number of domestic problems in the house they invade. In recent years, Sam Spewack has been writing a good deal on his own. *Two Blind Mice* (1949) is a light comedy about Washington bureaucracy. *Under the Sycamore Tree* (1952), produced in London with Alec Guinness as star, is a satirical allegory with insects as characters.

"Having Wonderful Time"

by

ARTHUR KOBER (1900–   )

The Characters

Teddy Stern—an idealistic young woman who wants adventure but is trapped in an office job. She wants romance but is afraid of being hurt.

Chick Kessler—an unemployed lawyer, bitter about working as a waiter, usually on the defensive, and apt to explode whenever he feels insulted.

Pinkie Aaronson—a small-time Don Juan who presents himself as well-traveled, sophisticated.

Mr. and Mrs. G.—a middle-aged couple who delight in malicious gossip.

Fay Fromkin—Teddy's best friend, fun-loving and compliant.

Abe Tobias—the camp owner. Concerned only with profits, he fawns on the campers and is brutal to the employees.

Other campers, waiters, entertainers, and visitors. Like the chief characters, all are Jewish and from the New York City area.

149

The Setting

Camp Kare-Free is an adult vacation camp in the Berkshires. Though the scenery is lovely, the camp buildings are cheap and crudely constructed, the individual cabins crowded and ugly. The time is August, 1936, in the depths of the Great Depression.

The Story

For three years, Teddy has been saving her money in order to marry stodgy but dependable Sam Rappaport. When he asks her to wait and keep saving for another year, she breaks the engagement and decides to have a fling. She arrives for two glorious weeks at glamorous Camp Kare-Free. The brochures, however, are more than a little deceptive, and she is distressed to discover that she will be sharing a small, ugly cabin with three other girls. The hot-water tap does not work; the cabin provides only minimal privacy. Teddy is offended by Chick Kessler, one of the camp waiters, who approached her on the bus. In her nervous mood, she considers Chick fresh and rude. Only Fay's assurances prevent Teddy from going back to New York.

The waiters at Camp Kare-Free are young men who pay to be at camp, but hope to make some money through tips. But the work is hard, many of the campers are demanding, even insulting, and the tips are minuscule. Chick refuses to be subservient and often quarrels with his co-workers and with the guests. Mr. Tobias fines him or gives him extra jobs, such as washing the windows. Chick is utterly exhausted because he has been working at so many extra jobs, yet he is expected to be a partner to the single women campers in the social hall. Though still irritated with him, Teddy agrees to dance. Afterward, as they talk on the porch, they begin to sense the similarities in their views and values. Both are eager for something finer than the giggly foolishness they see around them.

A week later, Teddy and Chick are in love, and, like all the other romantic couples, they have found Eagle Rock the proper setting for their rendezvous. They sadly compare their home situations, her three years wasted waiting for Sam Rappaport, his years spent studying law with still no job in view. The future looks bleak, and marriage is out of the question. Chick suggests, carefully and gently, that perhaps they could at least make love. Teddy is outraged and they separate angrily.

That night, following the long-awaited Japanese Fiesta, some of the campers assemble in Teddy's cabin to continue the party. Teddy has had nothing to eat for hours, since she could not face seeing Chick in the dining room, but refuses his offers of food and sympathy. Instead, she determines to be a gay party girl and quickly downs some potent highballs. When Chick tries to stop her, they quarrel again and she flounces out with Pinkie Aaronson. Chick follows them to Pinkie's cabin, bursts in and denounces them. When he is gone, Teddy, who has been drinking scotch in an attempt to demonstrate her poise and worldliness, decides to return to her own cabin. But while Pinkie searches for a flashlight, Teddy collapses into a deep alcoholic sleep.

The next morning, despite Fay's ingenious efforts to conceal the fact, Chick discovers that Teddy has spent the night in Pinkie's cabin. To complicate matters, Sam Rappaport, who has arrived to ask Teddy to reconsider their broken engagement, is waiting for her in the dining room. Mr. G. spreads the word at breakfast that he saw Teddy leave Pinkie's cabin early in the morning. When Teddy arrives, Sam rejects her, saying he deals only with "merchandise in A-1 condition." They are interrupted by Chick rushing in with his suitcase, ready to leave. Teddy tries to explain that nothing has happened between her and Pinkie, but Chick refuses to listen. Finally, furious, ignoring the goggling onlookers, she tells him that despite his rudeness and his nasty suspicions she wants to marry him and will support him if necessary. Overwhelmed, Chick humbly agrees. Mr. Tobias is ecstatic and promises them the two-week free vacation that goes to honeymooners who meet at Camp Kare-Free.

Critical Opinion

The boy-meets-girl plot of *"Having Wonderful Time"* is simple and predictable. The misunderstandings which keep it moving are equally familiar. Kober has used these traditional elements skillfully, but the story itself is of small consequence. What keeps the play alive is the vividness and precision with which the playwright has captured the mores of a moment in American history. The present response to the play arises from knowing how much the world has changed since 1937 and how much human behavior has not.

Camp Kare-Free is at once ludicrous and pathetic. The campers are mostly young people, full of gay spirits, yet desperate. For all of them the two weeks in the Berkshires represent an escape either from the dulling routine of work or from the near-hopeless search for work. They are not terribly disillusioned by the shabbiness of the camp, for at home they have lived in sleazy, cramped apartments. So, with the help of alcohol and sex, they simulate a gay abandon.

Kober certainly intended these shadows to frame his picture. The characters all take the Depression as a fact of life, perhaps as *the* fact of life; though the men complain bitterly, they can see no way out. Teddy's decision to support an unemployed husband has a ring of self-sacrifice that underlines the desperation. These are not, after all, the well-educated, well-heeled rebels of the 1920s. Sexual freedom and women's rights are new, not altogether pleasant ideas. Home, family, and a good provider are still the woman's goals, but conditions seem designed to frustrate her.

The historical background of the play must not be overstressed. To the friendly but sardonic eye of the playwright, the main point about these campers is that they are funny. Their urban Jewish dialects and vocabularies are perfectly captured, from Mr. and Mrs. G.'s immigrant English to Fay Fromkin's Bronxese, from Henrietta Brill's socialist clichés to Pinkie Aaronson's smart-guy witticisms. And their urban Jewish mores are in sharp contrast with "camping." Dressing up for dinner and a dance is far more important than exploring nature, and the high point of vacation pleasure is the Japanese Fiesta, a glorious hodgepodge of misunderstood exotica. The camp recreation director, the typical Borscht Circuit entertainer of legend, creates the Fiesta hopefully for fun and games, and with their Chinese pigtails, Mexican hats, and Seventh Avenue kimonos, the campers are one in revealing their marvelous ignorance of the world outside New York.

Camp Kare-Free has now been replaced by glossy resorts where the secretary is promised romance with the swim or après-ski. The waiters are not likely to be unemployed lawyers, and every young woman expects to keep her job at least a few years after marriage. But the young people still arrive with hopes and trepidations, the managers are still delighted to announce engagements, and everyone works very hard to have a wonderful time.

The Author

Born in a small town in Austria-Hungary and brought to New York as a child by immigrant parents, Arthur Kober knows best the world of Jewish New Yorkers he so gently mocks in *"Having Wonderful Time."* His best work has grown out of his fascination with middle-class Jewish life. Even the slightest of his stories is made vivid by his delight in his characters' speech rhythms, their pronunciations, the direct translations of their Yiddish grammatical structures into English. Kober's most characteristic work is the sketch, the lightly patterned short story about adventures in the offices, stores, and apartments of Manhattan and the Bronx. His two excellent collections are *My Dear Bella* (1941) and *Ooh! What You Said* (1958). Most of these loosely shaped, satirical pictures originally appeared in *The New Yorker*. *"Having Wonderful Time"* is based on some of Kober's early stories.

Aside from his successful study of Camp Kare-Free, Kober has done very little writing for the stage. He collaborated with Joshua Logan and Harold Rome in converting his play into a musical, *Wish You Were Here* (1952). With George Oppenheimer, he wrote a light comedy, *A Mighty Man Is He* (1960). Far more of his time has been spent as a screenwriter. More recently, he has written for television, contributing episodes to a number of comic series.

I Remember Mama

by

JOHN VAN DRUTEN (1901–1957)

The Characters

The Hansons, a Norwegian-American family:

Papa (Lars)—a carpenter, a hard-working, unassuming, kindly man.

Mama (Marta)—a warmhearted woman who always senses the needs of others, and who makes innumerable sacrifices for her family without hesitation or complaint.

Nels—the only son, a sturdy, kindhearted boy.

Katrin—"the dramatic one," her father calls her; she wants to be a writer.

Christine—a sensible, matter-of-fact girl.

Dagmar—the youngest, a lover of animals.

The aunts, Mama's sisters: Sigrid, who is bossy; *Jenny,* who whines; and *Trina,* the shy spinster.

Uncle Chris—Mama's uncle, "a black Norwegian," with dark hair, swarthy skin, and a loud, overbearing manner. He has a severe limp.

Mr. Hyde—an unemployed English actor, the Hansons' lodger.

Mr. Thorkelson—a timid little man, Trina's fiancé.

154

The Setting

The play takes place in and around San Francisco beginning in 1910. Katrin is the narrator. In retrospect, she exaggerates the action somewhat. Since there are numerous locales, the scenery must be simple and flexible, not completely solid or realistic.

The Story

As Katrin describes her family, we see a typical scene. Mama and Papa divide Papa's weekly earnings to cover rent, grocery bills, and other important needs. With a little left over, they will not have to go to the Bank. Nels asks whether he can go on to high school. If they take the money from the Little Bank (the box for emergency funds), Papa gives up smoking, Mama once more postpones getting a new winter coat, and Nels does some part-time work, they can manage without withdrawing money from the Bank downtown.

Trina comes to tell Mama she wants to marry Mr. Thorkelson, the undertaker, but is afraid the other sisters will laugh. Mama handles the situation neatly by threatening to tell some embarrassing stories about Sigrid and Jenny. Uncle Chris, however, must be consulted about a dowry, and they are all terrified of him and shocked by his living with a "housekeeper." After the aunts leave, the Hansons settle down to hear Mr. Hyde read. He has not paid his rent, but they are too delighted with his reading to ask him for money.

A few weeks later, Uncle Chris descends on the family for one of his surprise visits. He discovers that Dagmar needs to go to the hospital for a mastoid operation, and he sets about making plans and ordering the doctor about. The doctor agrees to let Chris drive Dagmar in his car, but he insists he will drop the case if the officious old man does not stay away from the operating room. In the waiting room, Mr. Thorkelson timidly approaches the tyrannical Chris and asks about the dowry. Uncle Chris bullies the young man into agreeing that accepting a dowry would show he is not in love.

The operation is successful, but Mama is told that clinic

rules forbid all patients to have visitors during the first twenty-four hours after admission. Desperate, Mama disguises herself as a scrubwoman and gets in to satisfy herself that her little girl is all right. Uncle Chris is barred from the hospital, and in a moment of candor he admits to Mama that he drinks and acts rude because he envies those who have families and homes.

Dagmar recovers beautifully, and her pet cat, Uncle Elizabeth, badly mauled in a fight, is cured by the dose of chloroform meant to put him away. Mr. Hyde announces he must leave, but presents Mama with a check for a hundred and ten dollars and his books. The check seems a godsend until Jenny bustles in with the news that Hyde has no bank account and has passed a number of bad checks all over town. Mama, thankful for the evenings of reading and aware of what Mr. Hyde has sacrificed in leaving his books, says he did not cheat them.

Katrin's grammar-school graduation approaches. She presses her parents for a fancy dresser set as a gift, scorning the heirloom brooch her mother intends for her. On the night of the class play and graduation, Christine, furious about her sister's selfishness, tells her that Mama sold the brooch to get the dresser set. Stunned and contrite, Katrin manages to return the set and regain the brooch. When she returns it to her mother, Papa recognizes the emotional strain Katrin's sacrifice represents, and pours his daughter a cup of coffee, the family symbol of maturity.

Some weeks later, a telegram arrives with news that Uncle Chris is dying. The other sisters resent being called upon to go some four hours by train to his farm and to socialize with "that woman," but their greed gets the better of them. When they arrive, Mama is the only one Chris will speak to. He tells her to take care of Jessie, his woman, whom he could never marry because she had a husband. He apologizes for leaving no money for Nels's medical-school costs. After he dies, Mama finds his journal and discovers that his money has all gone into paying the hospital bills for children with leg trouble.

As she grows older, Katrin keeps dreaming of becoming an author, but all she gets are rejection slips for her melodramatic, derivative stories. She decides to give up writing. Mama, however, manages to see a famous author, with whom she trades recipes in exchange for opinions about her daughter's stories.

Miss Moorhead, the author, advises the girl to stick to subjects she knows. Katrin decides to write about Mama and the hospital.

When a check for five hundred dollars arrives in payment for her story, Katrin is delighted with the opportunity to buy Mama a coat, help pay bills, and make a deposit in the Bank. Shamefaced, Mama admits there is no bank account, that she has never even been in a bank. The parents had agreed on this fiction to give the children security, so that they would always feel there was a reserve of money if it should ever be needed. They settle down to hear Katrin read her story.

Critical Opinion

I Remember Mama is based on Kathryn Forbes's autobiographical sketches, *Mama's Bank Account*. In each the mythical Bank downtown, to be approached only in the direst emergency, is a leitmotiv. However, in adapting the material to the stage, Van Druten put a new emphasis on the development of Katrin as a writer. She is both narrator and participant. By ending the play with Katrin reading the story that has just been enacted, the author neatly rounds out his chronicle.

The chronicle form presents the author with a number of advantages and problems. Unlike the carefully structured, conflict-focused play which is the prevalent modern form, the chronicle allows for rapid shifts of time and place, and the narrator spares the author the difficulties of introducing characters and justifying their entrances and exits. The narrator can also explain the meaning of scenes by directly addressing the audience, a possibility excluded in the realistic play. A particularly good example of the flexibility of the chronicle form comes late in the second act of *I Remember Mama*. In a short scene, Trina's husband tells her how delighted he is with their marriage and their healthy baby. He has decided they should give a party, and since he is determined to give his wife everything he can, he solemnly announces that they will hire a *waitress*, the epitome of luxury. The scene is quite irrelevant to the story of the Hansons, but it is charming and nicely ties up the subsidiary story of Trina and the difficult time she had getting married. Only because the play is so loosely structured can this interlude be introduced.

On the other hand, the loose structure can also lead to shapelessness or repetition. In *I Remember Mama,* the usual scene involves a situation with a mother-knows-best solution, but Van Druten avoids the dangers of monotony and banality in a number of ways. For one, there is a widely varied group of characters, vividly delineated, from fierce Uncle Chris to whining Aunt Jenny, each with his own story. Then there is the evocation of a past period and a typically American experience—the immigrant making his way in a new world. Finally, there is Mama herself, a familiar figure of good sense and self-sacrifice, but neither a martyr nor a paragon. She is not above a little blackmail to protect her youngest sister or a trick to get into the hospital, and she can also laugh at her stratagems. Though she rarely feels self-pity, there is the moment when she weeps over her dead child in Norway, a brief, piercing look behind the facade of competence and assurance. She is complex enough not to be the long-suffering, selfless mother of soap opera, and is a whole person who extends beyond the limits of a role. The audience, too, remembers Mama.

I Remember Mama was turned into a popular television series that helped to shape the pattern of the familiar "family" program.

The Author

Son of a Dutch father and an English mother, John Van Druten began life as a British subject. His first interest was in law. After completing his studies at London University, he went on to become a solicitor and a lecturer on English legal history at the University College of Wales. At the same time, another side of his character revealed itself in the stories and sketches he was writing for *Punch* and other periodicals. *Young Woodley,* the story of a sensitive boy at an exclusive English public school, was refused a performance license by the Lord Chamberlain. It was first produced in New York in 1925, and started the author on a career as a playwright. Van Druten began spending more and more time in this country. He became an American citizen in 1944.

Van Druten wrote about twenty-five plays. With few exceptions, they are firmly constructed comedies or dramas dealing with a small group of articulate characters, sometimes lightly touching on a social theme. Among the best are *Old Acquaintance* (1940), about two competitive women; *The Voice of the Turtle* (1943), a bittersweet romance between a soldier on leave and a young actress; and *Bell, Book and Candle* (1950), a tongue-in-cheek treatment of modern witchcraft. *I Remember Mama* (1944) is one of Van Druten's least typical works.

The title of his play *I Am a Camera,* based on *The Berlin Stories* by Christopher Isherwood, derives from the central character, a young Englishman living in Berlin and reporting on the life around him. As the play unfolds, his position as detached observer becomes untenable as the shadow of Nazism falls across the society of expatriate Englishmen and native Berliners of which he is a part. Van Druten's play was filmed with little change. *The Berlin Stories* have also served as sources for the popular musical *Cabaret* (1967).

In both his autobiography, *The Way to the Present* (1952), and a text, *Playwright at Work* (1953), Van Druten discusses his work, stressing that he sees himself primarily as an entertainer. Both books contain excellent material on the mechanics of dramatic construction.

Of Mice and Men

by

JOHN STEINBECK (1902–1968)

The Characters

George Milton—a migratory farmworker. He is short but tough, intelligent, and compassionate.

Lennie Small—his companion, a big, powerful but feeble-minded man, fascinated by soft, furry creatures; essentially a child.

Slim—the foreman, a quiet, understanding man.

Curley—the boss's son, a small man, bad-tempered and pugnacious, always fearful of being insulted or cuckolded.

Curley's wife—a dance-hall girl, disgusted with her suspicious, unpleasant husband and excited at being the only woman on the ranch. She is a rather naïve, lonely woman.

Candy—an old, nearly senile laborer. Since he lost a hand, he has been kept on to clean and do odd jobs; he lives in terror of being fired.

Crooks—the hunchback Negro stablehand.

Whit and Carlson—laborers.

The Boss—the superintendent of the ranch.

The Setting

All the action takes place on or near a ranch in Southern California. It is late summer, hot and dry. The bunkhouse and barn are rough, graceless, weathered buildings. Only Crooks's room has some faint resemblance to a home.

The Story

On their way to a new job, George and Lennie stop to spend the night on a riverbank. George discovers that Lennie is concealing a dead mouse in his pocket and stroking it. George throws it away. The childlike Lennie is unhappy at the loss of his toy, but obediently settles down to listen to George's coaching on how he should behave the next day. Lennie carefully repeats his instructions: he is not to say anything when they are interviewed; he is to avoid trouble; and if he does something bad, he is to return to this spot and hide in the bushes. When George sends him to find firewood, Lennie retrieves the mouse, only to have George throw it away again in a fury. Contrite and frightened, Lennie promises to be good and begs George to tell about their future. Mechanically but sincerely, George describes the little farm they will have as soon as they save some money. Away from bosses and orders, they will live off the fat of the land, and if he continues to be good, Lennie will be permitted to tend the rabbits.

The next morning when they arrive at the ranch, George is nearly drawn into a quarrel with Curley, who seems eager to fight with anyone he thinks he can beat. Candy warns the newcomers about Curley's wife, who will flirt with any man. Shortly after the other workers come in for dinner, Curley's wife arrives, ostensibly looking for her husband. She wears heavy perfume, much makeup, and bright-colored clothes. Lennie is attracted to her. George warns him to stay away from her.

Slim is happy to have two experienced workers on his team. He quickly grasps Lennie's limitations and George's desire to protect the child-man. George explains that Lennie had almost been lynched at their last job. He had touched a girl's skirt, and when she tried to pull away, all he could do was hold on harder. The girl claimed he had tried to rape her, and only by running away had they saved themselves. Now Lennie is ecstatic, for Slim has let him have a puppy. George warns him not to bring it into the bunkhouse or handle it too roughly. When Candy comes in with his old, blind sheepdog, the other men complain of the smell of the dog, and Carlson persists in demanding that the dog be killed, until Candy tearfully agrees to let the younger man take the old dog out and shoot it.

Believing they are alone, George once more begins telling Lennie about the plan for a farm. Candy is hypnotized and offers all his savings if he can join them. George, who has no luck at saving, is euphoric. Of course they can do it! They are interrupted by Curley's wife, who overhears herself referred to as a tart and furiously defends herself, telling them she is lonely and bored. She gets away just before her husband enters, in a worse mood than ever. When Lennie laughs at him, Curley challenges him. George, carried away by the fever of battle, tells Lennie to "get him." Effortlessly, the big man crushes Curley's hand. When it is over, Lennie is only worried that George may not permit him to tend the rabbits.

Later that night, when most of the men are in town, Lennie goes to Crooks's room, looking for company. Usually treated badly by the others, Crooks enjoys frightening Lennie with thoughts of George's getting hurt or deserting. They are joined by Candy, who is almost in a trance thinking about the farm. George returns from town early, disgusted that he has been wasting money in a brothel. But again their quiet talk is interrupted by Curley's wife. She has figured out that Lennie crushed her husband's hand. She flirts with him until George threatens to strike her.

The next morning, Curley's wife prepares to run away. She comes to the barn to hide her valise, and finds Lennie there hiding his dead puppy. Once again, he had petted the animal too hard, and when it tried to bite, Lennie pinched its head. The girl is too preoccupied with her own concerns to understand Lennie's worries, but in her loneliness she is drawn toward him. In a tentative move toward seduction, she suggests that he stroke her soft hair. He is enraptured. When she starts to move away, he will not let go. She becomes angry, then frightened. His response is a stronger grip. When she cries out, he shakes her violently, and breaks her neck.

Horrified, Lennie remembers about the hiding place near the river. Curley, determined to kill the murderer, rounds up some men for a search. George knows there is little chance of saving his friend. He goes to the riverbank. There he succeeds in sending the posse off in another direction. He finds Lennie and tells him to sit looking across the river while George once again repeats the story of the wonderful farm and the rabbits. While Lennie sits entranced, George moves behind him and shoots him through the head.

Critical Opinion

> The best-laid schemes o' mice an' men
> > Gang aft agley,
> An' lea'e us nought but grief an' pain,
> > For promised joy!
> > > —Robert Burns, "To a Mouse"

The title of Steinbeck's play is subject to two interpretations. First it is about plans demolished, of dreams destroyed. It is not only George, Lennie, and Candy who dream about some wonderful place to settle down and escape the ugliness, the self-destructiveness of their migratory life. Crooks and Slim have the same dream in different forms, but both agree that while most of the migrants talk about settling down, none do. The work is so hard that it is impossible to resist the Saturday night at the brothel, the liquor and the soft chairs offering almost as great an attraction as the girls. In their separate ways, Curley and his wife also have their longings. George and Lennie, however, have more than a dream. They have a specific plan, and with Candy's help they might have made it work but for the passions and brutality in men. A major irony of the play lies in the clash between the good-hearted Lennie, with no intelligence to control his terrible strength, and the vicious Curley, whose intelligence seems directed at destruction. Curley's desire for power triumphs over Lennie's hope for peace and security.

The title *Of Mice and Men* also suggests the basic pattern of the play, the death of mice and men arising not only out of anger but out of an excess of some kind of love. Lennie cannot help stroking anything soft, preferably animals, but his adoration usually destroys them. George loves Lennie in a different way, as if he were a stupid kid brother, a frightful burden but one he cannot drop. Without entirely understanding why, he angrily yet unquestioningly accepts Lennie as his responsibility. For George, Lennie is also a direction and a goal. The child-man is a visible reminder to George of the farm, of the future. He is also, in a deeper sense, a brother, for everyone remarks on how few of the migrants travel together or have close relationships with anyone. Yet this love, too, leads to death.

Steinbeck based his play (1937) on his novella of the same title, published the same year, making little change in the process of dramatizing the story. The play is, indeed, tauter and more concentrated than the story. Everything contributes directly to the sense of isolation and the defeat of love. The setting is bleak, dry, and sterile, and the characters are all diminished by the forces working on them. Candy loves his dog but cannot keep it against the objections of the other workers. He sees in the execution of the old, useless creature the callous way in which he, too, will be discarded. Crooks is so used to mistreatment that it is only with difficulty that he can relax with Lennie and Candy. Curley's wife is actually a pathetic creature hungry for affection. Only Slim and George are briefly undefeated, Slim because he seems to be cool and self-sufficient, and George because his feeling for Lennie gives him a connection with another life. Ultimately, however, Slim's coolness is evident as a defense against pain, and George must destroy what is closest to him.

Serious dramas about crude, inarticulate people are rarely successful. They are too frequently either sentimentally patronizing or implausible. *Of Mice and Men* is one of the few exceptions.

The Author

John Steinbeck was born and raised in Salinas, California, and much of his work draws on his knowledge of life on the farms and ranches of the West. He worked as a reporter, chemist, and bricklayer until his first novel, *Cup of Gold* (1929), was published. During the following years, his reputation grew with the appearance of such works as *Tortilla Flat* (1935), *In Dubious Battle* (1936), and *The Red Pony*

(1937). *Of Mice and Men* (1937) and *The Grapes of Wrath* (1939) brought him great popular as well as critical success.

Steinbeck is admired most for his novels. The Nobel Prize for Literature he received in 1962 rests primarily on his powerful study of Dust Bowl farmers migrating to California, *The Grapes of Wrath*. He was, however, attracted to the theater a number of times. In 1942 he made a play of his novel *The Moon is Down*, a stirring melodrama about the Nazi occupation of Norway. *Burning Bright* (1950) also appeared as a novel, but it seems to have been conceived as a play from the start. In each of the three acts, the same characters appear. However, each act is set in a different century and in a different place, and the characters' occupations also change. The intention is to emphasize the timelessness and universality of the theme, man's desire to achieve immortality through his children.

In his plays, as in his novels and reportage, Steinbeck did best with unsophisticated characters in a rural setting, locked in a struggle between elemental forces and ideas. He combined a sense of the natural struggle for survival with indignation at man's frequent inhumanity to man.

Tobacco Road

by

JACK KIRKLAND (1902–   )

from the novel by ERSKINE CALDWELL
(1903–   )

The Characters

Jeeter Lester—an old cotton farmer, slovenly, lazy, hypocritically pious. If he has any virtue, it is an attachment to the land his family has worked for generations.

Ada—his wife, a tired, sickly old woman.

Grandma Lester—his mother, a feeble crone who never speaks but creeps about collecting bits of firewood.

His youngest children, last of seventeen, still at home:

  Ellie May—about 18. She is disfigured by a harelip; otherwise she would have married long ago.

  Dude—about 16, good-looking but stupid and mean.

  Pearl—about 13 or 14, a strikingly beautiful girl with golden hair.

Lov Bensey—Pearl's husband, a railroad worker.

Sister Bessie Rice—a woman preacher, about 40, recently widowed and lusting for a man.

The Setting

Jeeter Lester's sharecropper's shack is a squalid ruin. The porch sags, the yard is nothing but dust, even the trees are undernourished. The Tobacco Road is a reminder of a prosperous past, but the land will not even support the cotton that replaced tobacco as the main crop.

The Story

Since Jeeter's old automobile is beyond repair, he can no longer earn what little money he used to make hauling wood to Augusta. Complete starvation faces the Lesters, but they are all so listless that it hardly matters. Jeeter daydreams about planting a crop of cotton, but he knows no one is any more likely to lend him money for seed and fertilizer this year than at any other time during the past five or more. With Ada, he talks about getting help from the older children; but they have all gone away and have never kept in touch. Ada's only wish is for a stylish dress to be buried in. Dude viciously predicts his parents' deaths, describing the rats eating their bodies.

Lov comes to visit, carrying a sack of turnips. He complains that Pearl won't talk to him or sleep with him. He demands that her parents order her to behave like a wife. Ellie May is drawn to the virile young man, and rubs against him until he begins pawing her. Thus distracted, Lov releases his hold on the turnip sack, and Jeeter steals it and runs off into the fields. Disgusted, Lov shambles off.

Bessie is the next visitor. She prays enthusiastically with the family. Her real purpose in coming is to size up Dude as a new husband. She promises to return in the morning with her decision. Meanwhile, a neighbor rushes in with the news that Captain Tim, owner of the land, has returned. Jeeter is confident that the landlord will lend him money for a crop.

The next morning, Bessie returns with the announcement that the Lord has approved her choice of Dude as a husband and a new preacher. The boy is not much interested until he learns Bessie has eight hundred dollars in insurance money she intends to spend on a new automobile. At the thought of a car, particularly a horn to toot, he is impatient to be on his way.

Lov returns with somber news. Pearl has run away. He is inconsolable and sadly goes on to work. Jeeter discovers Pearl hiding in the bushes, but Ada protects the girl. She informs Jeeter that he is not Pearl's father, anyway. When Lov returns, Ada beats him off with a stick. Jeeter suggests that Lov take Ellie May with him instead, but he wants Pearl.

Dude and Bessie drive up in their brand-new car. The boy has already damaged a fender. The preacher has bought a license, and she performs her own wedding ceremony. Consummation of the marriage is interrupted by the visit of Captain Tim and a man from the bank. Instead of helping Jeeter, Tim explains that he has lost his property. Jeeter can stay if he pays a hundred dollars a year in rent. The old man sends Dude and Bessie off to get the money from one of the successful children, Tom, in Augusta.

The next day, Jeeter and Ada miss old Grandma Lester. They assume she must have died during the night, but their interest does not extend to looking for the body. Once more Lov comes to bargain for Pearl. He even offers two dollars a week if they give the girl back, but Ada drives him off. Jeeter feels so confident about getting money from Tom that he is not upset by Lov's departure.

The tooting of a horn tells them Dude and Bessie have returned. A broken headlight and a damaged wheel are the newest changes in the car. Tom, of course, has sent no money, only curses. Jeeter decides to take up Lov's offer. He grabs Pearl and starts to lead her back to her husband. Dude starts the car and, destructively clumsy as usual, backs it up over his mother. She creeps back to the yard, and, as her last living act, tricks Jeeter into coming close enough so she can bite his hand. In pain, he lets go of Pearl, who escapes.

Only slightly disappointed, Jeeter asks Dude and Lov to dig Ada's grave in the fields. He tells Ellie May to go down to Lov's house and prepare to be his wife. Then he settles down on the porch to doze.

Critical Opinion

When *Tobacco Road* opened in New York on December 4, 1933, most reviewers took it to be a serious play, and found it exaggerated, grotesque, and distasteful. The audience found it exaggerated, grotesque, and hilarious. The cast responded to the audience and emphasized the laugh-producing lines and situations, and it was as a gamy comedy that the play achieved one of the biggest successes in American theater history: a run of seven and a half years on Broadway, production by innumerable traveling companies, and many revivals.

Jack Kirkland is listed as the author of the play, but he followed Erskine Caldwell's novel so closely that the two men must be considered coauthors. Their intentions were serious. *Tobacco Road* started out to be a mixture of social protest and regionalism typical of the period. The opening stage directions indicate the authors' point of view:

> The back country, Georgia . . . is a famished, desolate land . . . so intensively and stupidly cultivated as to exhaust the soil. Poverty, want, squalor, degeneracy, pitiful helplessness and grotesque, tragic lusts have stamped a lost, outpaced people with the mark of inevitable end. . . . Grim humor pervades all, stalking side by side with tragedy on the last short mile which leads to complete, eventual elimination.

At the end of the play, left alone, Jeeter "takes a pinch of earth between his fingers and rubs it into dust. . . . Seconds of somber silence pass. A rotten shingle falls from the sagging porch, and the curtain falls slowly."

In the play itself, however, there is little indication that these people are anything but dirty, shiftless, bestial, oafish creatures, hardly human. The open sexuality, the illogical planning, the lack of feeling for one another, the ineptness—in short, the primitive mentality—appear to the audience to be nothing but a titillating series of crude and obscene jokes not too unlike cartoons of hillbilly life. Perhaps the authors assume too much knowledge on the part of their audience, but more likely they share some of the same ribaldry. In any event, they make it virtually impossible to identify with any of the characters or to believe that these people feel any pain or emotion. For example, the casual way in which Jeeter and Ada decide that Grandma's absence means she must be dead can be attributed to the numbing effect of hunger, ignorance, and a dumb, animal-like resignation. In context, however, Grandma's death becomes another ludicrous incident like Dude's disasters with the car, Jeeter's well-rationalized thefts, and Ellie May's hard-breathing, wriggling approach to Lov.

The very term "Tobacco Road" has become synonymous with raucous stories of crude, stupid people whose lives consist of sleeping, eating, and fornicating. Caldwell has continued to exploit the same subject matter in his many novels, in most of which thigh-smacking laughs outweigh any cries of protest against poverty. While more recent studies have given ample factual support to Caldwell's pictures of Georgia crackers, no serious writer today could approach the subject with his relish for freakish comedy. As a result, *Tobacco Road* is usually dismissed by most students of American drama as an aberration of popular taste comparable to such crowd-pleasers as *Abie's Irish Rose*. At its best, *Tobacco Road* is a striking drama marred by an unclear point of view and a surrender to the easy smirk.

The Authors

Jack Kirkland was born and grew up in St. Louis, far from the Georgia back country that provided the material for his only important play. He attended Columbia University and for a number of years worked for the New York *Daily News*. His writing talents took him first to Hollywood. He has continued to alternate film scripts with his stage work. His first play was *Frankie and Johnnie*, produced in Chicago in 1928. *Tobacco Road* (1933) kept the author active for many years, for he supervised many of its traveling companies, and was the producer of three New York revivals (1942, 1943, and 1950, the last with an all-Negro cast). He also participated in the London productions (1937, 1947, 1949).

Kirkland tried his hand at adapting another Caldwell novel, *Georgia Boy* (1945), which closed in Boston during its pre-Broadway tryout. He has adapted other works for the stage:

John Steinbeck's *Tortilla Flat* (1938), Pat Frank's *Mr. Adam* (1949), Nelson Algren's *The Man with the Golden Arm* (1956), and Kyle Onstott's *Mandingo* (1961). For most of these he also acted as producer and director. As these titles indicate, he has turned to popular, somewhat sensational stories for his materials. Like *Tobacco Road*, many of these deal with downtrodden country people; others portray big-city derelicts.

Erskine Caldwell is one of the all-time best-selling American authors, particularly in paperback editions. Some of his titles, particularly *Tobacco Road* (1932) and *God's Little Acre* (1933), have had enormous sales in Russia and other Communist countries because they have been read as an indictment of capitalist exploitation of the poor. In most of his fiction, comprising more than thirty titles starting with his first novel, *The Bastard* (1929), Caldwell has drawn his subject matter from the life of the poor Negroes and whites among whom he grew up. Though few have seriously questioned the accuracy of the details in his stories, serious readers agree that he has overemphasized the sensational and salacious. Many critics feel, in fact, that Caldwell betrayed his own considerable talent, preferring to write according to a surefire marketable formula.

Three Men on a Horse

by

JOHN CECIL HOLM (1904–   ) and
GEORGE ABBOTT (1887–   )

The Characters

Erwin Trowbridge—a meek, henpecked writer of greeting-
card verses.
Audrey Trowbridge—his pretty, silly wife.
Clarence Dobbins—her brother, a blustering bully.
Harry—bartender at the Lavillere Hotel.
Charlie and Frankie—horse players.
Patsy—another horse player, somewhat tougher and smarter
than the others. They regard him as their leader.
Mabel—his mistress, an ex-Follies girl, grown a bit pudgy but
no smarter.
Mr. Carver—Erwin's employer, a brusque, no-nonsense busi-
nessman.

The Setting

Although the Trowbridge home in Ozone Heights, New
Jersey, is one of Clarence's jerry-built development houses, the

builder is dismayed that his brother-in-law does not appreciate the fact that they are all exactly the same. Audrey has decorated her living room in equally standardized style. The other setting is the bar and rooms of the Hotel Lavillere, in New York, a third-rate hotel patronized by gamblers, dingy and anything but homelike.

The Story

Erwin is eager to get to the office to meet his deadline for Mother's Day verses. Audrey, in going through his suit before sending it to the cleaners, comes across a mysterious notebook full of girls' names. She promptly calls her brother and when Clarence arrives they both attack Erwin for cheating on his wife. Erwin explains that these are the names of horses. On the bus to and from the city, he dopes out the races, and on paper he has been having extraordinary success. His brother-in-law is sure Erwin has a pile of winnings hidden away. The two men quarrel. Delivery of some expensive dresses which Erwin must pay for with his vacation savings angers him even more, and he leaves in a rage.

That afternoon, having stayed away from work, sulking, Erwin wanders into the bar of the Hotel Lavillere. He overhears some gamblers trying to decide how to bet their last few dollars, and he suggests some horses. They think he is crazy and ignore him until his choices begin to win. Then, plying him with more drinks, Patsy gets the befuddled young man to agree to a 10-percent commission if he sticks with them. Erwin is still concerned about his Mother's Day deadline and keeps scribbling away until he is thoroughly drunk.

The next morning, Erwin awakes in Patsy's hotel room. The verses are completed; though written during the night in a drunken haze, they are splendid. Erwin is still eager to get to work. Patsy agrees to get the verses delivered if Erwin will stay and dope out the next set of races. The gambler is so impressed by the verses that he decides to get Erwin a better salary. He calls Carver, claims to be the poet's agent, and demands higher rates. When Carver refuses, Patsy has the verses taken to a printer friend. They will go into business for themselves.

When Erwin discovers what has been happening, he is upset, and cannot concentrate on the races. Everyone goes off to locate Erwin's poems. Patsy leaves Mabel with Erwin to see that their treasure does not escape. While alone, Erwin is inspired to write a Valentine verse which enraptures the dumb blonde. She tells Erwin about her past and begins to demonstrate her Follies dance. She takes off her dress and goes into a high-kicking routine. But she is out of practice and is soon panting. Erwin, always the gentleman, tucks her into bed to rest. At this moment, Patsy returns with the verses, jumps to the wrong conclusion, orders Mabel to her room, and violently tears up the verses.

When Erwin and Mabel prove their innocence, Patsy contritely agrees they will copy the verses if Erwin sits down and works on the races. The young man tries, but the one name he comes up with, Equipoise in the fourth race, he feels sure is wrong. He can do this work only on the bus to and from Ozone Heights. So Mabel and Frankie hustle him off to the bus terminal.

Meanwhile, his wife has reported Erwin's absence to the police. She and her brother, harrassed by reporters, wait for news. Mr. Carver storms in and imperiously demands to know where Erwin is hiding out while working for a rival firm. When Erwin arrives, Mabel and Frankie call in the suggested names for the first four races. After a bewildering conversation with Audrey, Erwin is once more rushed off to complete his work on the bus back to New York.

In the hotel room, all the gamblers work furiously but inefficiently at reconstructing the Mother's Day verses. By the time Erwin returns, the first three races have ended as he predicted. They bet everything they have won on Mr. Khayyam in the fourth, but Charlie is still worried about Erwin's initial choice of Equipoise, who should be the better horse. To convince them he is not attempting a doublecross, Erwin bets all his earnings on Mr. Khayyam. They listen to the race on the radio, and Equipoise wins. Patsy, infuriated, starts beating Erwin, but turning on the radio again they discover that Equipoise was disqualified, and Mr. Khayyam wins. With renewed confidence, Erwin takes a swing at Patsy, who retreats. He then orders the others about and threatens to hit Clarence, who runs away. Audrey is cowed by this display of masculinity and humbly begs him to listen to Mr. Carver, who promises him a new office and a substantial raise.

The gamblers want Erwin to stay with them, but he explains that now that he has actually made a bet, his gift has deserted him. To top off his victory, he develops a horse-race image into a new Father's Day verse.

Critical Opinion

The typical nineteenth-century French farce (still a lively genre) deals with a sex triangle, and involves hasty, ludicrous disguises along with much rushing in and out of bedrooms. The British drawing-room comedies until recently specialized in witty talk about adultery. In both the French and English forms, the participants are most likely to be articulate, upper-class sophisticates only temporarily discomfited by the predicaments they find themselves in. In the years between the World Wars, the Broadway theater developed a distinctively American farce, of which *Three Men on a Horse* is an excellent example. George Abbott more than any other person was responsible for the refinement of this type of play.

The American farce plays on the naïveté of its characters. Erwin, the poor innocent, is the victim of everyone because he has no idea of his own strength and his own value. All the others are dopes, too, only they foolishly overestimate their knowledge and their wickedness. The gamblers are not very bright about their "profession," and they are awestricken by Erwin's vapid poems. Though they play at being tough guys, they are clearly harmless. Mr. Carver sees himself as the tycoon of the greeting-card industry, and any time a telephone rings, anywhere, he announces he is in conference; of course, he is only bolstering his ego and he would be lost without Erwin. No matter how often he is proved wrong, Clarence never hesitates to find a sinister interpretation for his brother-in-law's bland behavior. The pattern is completed in the end when the worm turns, and the "bad guys" are revealed as cowards.

The action of the play is similarly innocuous. Suspicions of sexual immorality are one source of laughter because they are always groundless, involving a misreading of what appears to be solid evidence of adultery. Erwin standing in his underwear next to the bed in which Mabel is lying in her underwear could be a scene from a French farce. This is how Patsy interprets it, and the fun lies in the complete inaccuracy of his deduction. The rest of the humor depends on the ingenious elaboration of confusions built on a single, preposterous premise: Erwin's inexplicable clairvoyance. Though inexplicable, it is nicely moral, for it cannot profit its possessor directly—in fact, he agrees to his commission only when he is drunk and is never quite clear about why he is receiving so much money. In addition, the gamblers lose their source of riches because they grow suspicious, it serves them right.

Add to this farcical pattern Abbott's great skill as a director, visible even in the printed stage directions. The simple-sounding trick of comedy staging is pace, speeding and slowing the action so that each possible laugh is well-focused while the overall effect is a rapidly accelerating movement toward some bigger and more hilarious comic climax. Purely situational comedy of this variety has gone from the stage to the movies, thence to television, where briefer programming and technical ingenuity compensate for lack of substance.

Writers for the stage today are concerned that their plays should reflect more accurately the society around them, and a skillful farceur like Neil Simon is far more sophisticated than Abbott and Holm were in 1935. Few light plays now are without some social commentary or satire. Yet, like the thinnest television skit, they owe much to the work of Abbott and other writers and directors of his time, who created a distinctly native play form.

The Authors

George Abbott has had a Broadway theater named for him, but this honor, usually reserved for elder statesmen of the entertainment world, is not a sign of his impending retirement. After more than sixty years in the theater, he is still going strong.

Born June 25, 1887, in Forestville, New York, Abbott began his theatrical career by writing and producing a one-act play at Harvard in 1912. He made his professional debut as an actor the following year, and for the rest of the decade continued to work in that capacity. In the early twenties, he collaborated on a number of quickly forgotten scripts. In 1926 he helped Philip Dunning revise a play about backstage life at a nightclub, and then directed the first production. *Broadway* was a resounding success. It contained almost all the ingredients of an Abbott production: a cast of colorful characters, including a number of New York underworld types who are tough but not dangerous; a plot with a rich assortment of farcical, melodramatic, and romantic complications and a frankly sentimental ending; dialogue enlivened with wisecracks and the rich argot of the theater and the criminal; and in performance, rapid but carefully controlled pace and endlessly inventive stage business. Though the original idea was Dunning's, it was Abbott who gave the work its final shape and virtually created a school of American comedy of which he is the leading exponent.

By their very nature, most of the plays with which Abbott has been connected have been ephemeral. Often it is difficult to determine Abbott's contribution to the work, since he has been not only the director of scores of plays but their "play doctor" as well. For such resounding successes as *Brother Rat* (1936) and *Room Service* (1937), Abbott was listed only as director, but there seems little doubt that his role was larger than that. Yet *Three Men on a Horse* (1935) is the only outstanding farce besides *Broadway* on which his name appears as coauthor.

Other plays credited at least in part to Abbott are mostly musicals, including *On Your Toes* (1936), *The Boys from Syracuse* (1938), *Where's Charley?* (1948), *Pajama Game* (1954), and *Fiorello!* (1959). He also directed all of these, as well as many other musicals, comedies, and films. The sheer volume of his work would in itself be remarkable, but the level of its success is even more amazing. Very few productions in which he had a hand as director have been utter failures.

John Cecil Holm, like Abbott, began his theatrical career as an actor. Though he has done some directing as well as writing, his main connection with the stage has been as performer. Holm's only other successful plays have been *Gramercy Ghost* (1951), a light comedy, and *The Southwest Corner* (1955), a bittersweet story of an old lady's last few months of life.

One-Third of a Nation

by

ARTHUR ARENT (1904–   )

The Characters

The Voice of the Living Newspaper, heard over the loudspeaker, is narrator and commentator.
The Little Man (Mr. Buttonkooper)—a slum dweller who appears from the audience.

The other characters appear briefly, usually in no more than one scene. Some are historical figures, others are fictitious. Most of what they and Voice of the Living Newspaper say is drawn from histories, reports, encyclopedias, and other printed sources.

The Setting

The stage is occupied by a cutaway view of a tenement building with cramped cubicles and narrow, steep stairways. At times, a curtain is lowered to conceal the setting while action and discussion proceed on the stage apron. Maps and photographs are frequently projected onto the curtain.

The Story

A fire starts in the tenement and spreads quickly. In the excitement and panic, lives are lost and most of the tenants' belongings are destroyed. The loudspeaker explains that the scene, set in February of 1924, could have happened in any one of a number of places in New York.

In the course of an investigation of the fire, it is pointed out that the building, built in 1884, was an old-law tenement. Therefore, it was not subject to most of the regulations passed in 1901. The building was inspected six months before, after a complaint about roaches, and no violations were discovered. Legally, there is no one to blame for the hazardous state of the property. The landlord justifies his failure to maintain the property, pointing to the rising costs he cannot meet. If he renovated the building he would need to raise the rents. This would drive away the tenants. However, when it is suggested that he sell his property, he refuses, for the land it stands on is the real investment, one that can never go down in value.

The action shifts to 1705, when a grant of land was made to Trinity Church, which promptly leased most of it. As time moves on, Trinity receives more land, the price of leases goes up, and efforts to control the church's income fail. More time passes, and a landowner with a small property begins to rent it in smaller and smaller pieces for ever higher rents as the population grows. With the beginnings of mass immigration in the mid-nineteenth century, the pace of land speculation increases. Many of the great New York fortunes are identified with booming land values.

At this point, the Little Man interrupts. He has been trying to get into a new housing development for years, but always the number of applicants far exceeds the number of available spaces. The narrator tries to explain the situation by continuing the history of land speculation. The first multiple dwelling is described, and the psychological and moral erosion created by dirty, crowded tenements is vividly dramatized. Young people take to crime. Disease, especially cholera, sweeps through the slums. Investigations and proposals always tell the same story, and law after law is passed, but conditions improve little if at all. The landlords, including Trinity Church, argue against the burdens imposed on them, and the laws are always weakened or subverted.

It is now 1933. The Little Man suggests that the old-law tenements simply be torn down. But then the residents would move on to crowd the remaining tenements worse than ever, thus breeding more crime and disease. What solutions are possible? Rent strikes help some, but not enough. New building is extremely costly and it results in new slums if rents must be kept low. Government housing is probably the only answer, but when it is not condemned as socialism, it is hamstrung by inadequate appropriations.

The pattern of speculation, crowding, deterioration, and inadequate legislation is not broken. However, the narrator argues that by continuing to demonstrate the true cost of slums in crime and illness, the people should be able to influence the lawmakers. The audience is exhorted to demand reforms and significant increases in government-supported housing.

Critical Opinion

In August of 1935, the Federal Theatre Project was set up as a branch of the Works Progress Administration. As with projects created to employ writers, painters, and musicians (along with the larger and better-known construction programs), the Federal Theatre was designed to provide income for at least a fraction of the vast number of people on relief rolls during the Depression. The project lasted until the summer of 1939, but in its brief lifetime the Federal Theatre, under the dynamic direction of Hallie Flanagan, provided a wide range of theatrical experiences for millions of people all over the country. Works produced included classics like *Dr. Faustus,* noncommercial contemporary works like T. S. Eliot's *Murder in the Cathedral,* children's plays, dance drama, radio drama, and variety shows. Performances took place not only in theaters but in tents, in parks, on trucks, and in every conceivable type of hall. The Federal Theatre provided a training ground for many writers and performers.

From the start, the Federal Theatre was dedicated to experimentation and contemporaneity in its effort to attract new audiences and to provide what the commercial theater was not interested in or could not afford to try. Such productions as an all-Negro *Macbeth* were startling and successful. But in time Congress became disturbed by the polemical nature of many of these works. The Living Newspaper, the most frankly propagandistic of the forms developed, was defended by Mrs. Flanagan as part of a "pioneer theatre" dedicated to a "tremendous rethinking, redreaming, and rebuilding of America." Since this involved considerable criticism of the government, the church, and other American institutions, most Congressmen found it impossible to sponsor the Federal Theatre any longer. Supporting funds were discontinued. The hope of establishing a subsidized theater comparable to those in most European countries was dashed.

One-Third of a Nation (1938) was one of the most effective of the Living Newspapers and clearly demonstrates the nature of these forms. Influenced by the flexibility of movies and taking advantage of the large number of available actors, the Living Newspaper analyzed a social problem in a series of brief scenes, each based on factual material adapted to underscore a central point. The term "Newspaper" is something of a misnomer. Actually, it more closely resembles the pamphlet or broadside. New statistics and details were added, depending on the time and place of production. The writer in charge was usually referred to as the editor, reflecting both the newspaper analogy and the group participation in its creation.

The title of *One Third of a Nation* was drawn from President Roosevelt's Second Inaugural Address (1937), in which he charged that one-third of the nation was "ill-housed, ill-clad, ill-nourished." The play took shape during that summer, and the printed text includes news items from early 1938. It is distressing to realize that much of the play still seems fresh and accurate today.

Some other powerful Living Newspapers were *Triple-A Plowed Under* (1936), a study of agricultural depression and the brief life of the Agricultural Adjustment Administration, and *Spirochete* (1939), about syphilis.

The Author

Arthur Arent was born in Jersey City, but his family later moved to New York City and he completed his public-school education there. He attended Lafayette College and New York University, but did not complete his degree. Before joining the Federal Theatre Project, Arent had some experience writing musical-revue sketches.

Although the Living Newspapers were collaborative productions, Arthur Arent most frequently appears as author, co-author, or editor, indicating that his hand was the decisive one. In addition to *One-Third of a Nation,* he wrote *Triple-A Plowed Under* (1936), *Injunction Granted* (1936), and *Power* (1937). In 1943 he used the Living Newspaper approach in a script commissioned by the Department of Agriculture, *It's Up to You.*

During the thirties, many groups took to the stage as a way of arguing their social ideas. One of the most interesting of these companies was the amateur recreational theater company of the International Ladies Garment Workers Union. In 1936 they produced a lively musical revue entitled *Pins and Needles,* in which propaganda, satire, and entertainment were effectively fused. With frequent revisions to keep it topical, *Pins and Needles* was performed one thousand times before closing in 1940. Arent was one of the collaborators, once again demonstrating his skill in dealing with contemporary issues.

Since the demise of the Federal Theatre, Arent has been an active writer for films, radio, and, in most recent years, television. His abilities as an adapter are evident in the many scripts he wrote for the popular Theatre Guild on the Air.

Awake and Sing!

by

CLIFFORD ODETS (1906–1963)

The Characters

Jacob—a barber, in his late 60s. An idealist and romantic, he
reads Marx and listens to Caruso records, but is too old and
too gentle to put any of his ideas into action.

Bessie Berger—his daughter, near 50. An energetic, overbearing woman who manages all the lives around her, she fears
poverty and disgrace and is always alert to dangers.

Myron Berger—her husband. A sweet, somewhat dreamy man
who hardly objects to his wife's managing, he sometimes
feels that life has passed him by.

Hennie—their daughter, 23, proud and defensive, with much
of her mother's energy and fear of being taken advantage
of.

Ralph—their son, 21, a young man with his grandfather's
dreams, trying to escape the wrangling and pettiness of his
family but baffled by the barriers he finds all around him.

Uncle Morty—Bessie's brother, a successful dress manufacturer, superficially hearty and generous, but actually intolerant
and insensitive.

Moe Axelrod—a veteran who lost a leg in World War I, bitterly cynical, constantly fighting his sympathies, and determined not to get involved in other people's lives.

Sam Feinschreiber—a young immigrant, a timid, self-conscious man eager to have a home and family.

All these character are Jewish. Jacob is an immigrant; his children and grandchildren were born in America. Their speech indicates the degree of assimilation. Jacob has a heavy accent. His children handle English awkwardly. Ralph and Hennie are the products of public education in the Bronx.

The Setting

The front room and dining room of the Berger apartment in the Bronx are conservatively, rather gracelessly furnished, but the housekeeping is conscientious. Jacob's room opens off the front room. It is the mid-1930s, in the depths of the Great Depression.

The Story

At supper, the Berger family conversation centers on money, as usual. Ralph complains about his meager salary and his frustrated ambitions. Jacob recommends revolution, while Myron daydreams about winning the Irish Sweepstakes. Bessie praises Sam Feinschreiber as a possible husband for Hennie, but the girl vigorously rejects the immigrant. Restless, she invites her parents to the vaudeville theater. As soon as they are gone, Ralph prepares to go out, telling his grandfather that he has a girl friend, Blanche, an orhan who lives with an uncle. He wants to keep his romance from his mother, who would object to the loss of his income as well as to his choice of a penniless bride.

Moe Axelrod arrives to deliver some track winnings to Myron and to ask for a date with Hennie. He is furious that she has gone out, but pretends indifference, sending Ralph off with sarcastic advice about women. The rest of the family return because Hennie has taken sick. She refuses to see a doctor. While Moe is out, Bessie begins to fathom Hennie's evasive statements and realizes with horror that the girl is pregnant.

The father has disappeared. Immediately taking matters into her own hands, Bessie instructs Myron to invite Sam for dinner the next night. When Moe returns, Bessie tells him that Hennie is engaged. When Moe indicates his own interest, Bessie tries to shift ground, but to conceal his love, the veteran wisecracks and brushes off any suggestion of marriage.

A year later, Moe has become a boarder, living in Hennie's old room. Uncle Morty comes to dinner and to have his father cut his hair. He merely laughs at the old man's criticisms of capitalism. When Ralph angrily confronts his mother with evidence that she has been doing everything she can to break up his romance, she insists she is acting in his best interests. Ralph rushes out to see the girl when he learns her uncle is sending her to Cleveland.

Later that night, Ralph returns, despondent. A few minutes later, Sam rushes in, utterly distraught, demanding to see his mother-in-law. Hennie, in a particularly ugly mood, has told him the baby, to whom he is devoted, is not his. Bessie consoles him, inventing evidences of Hennie's deep affection. She gets him to go home. Myron lets slip the fact that Hennie has told the truth. Ralph is stunned. In his fury, he not only condemns his parents for using Sam, but he also turns on his grandfather for condoning the action. Bessie's rage also focuses on her father, and she smashes his beloved Caruso records. Jacob quietly leaves to take the dog up on the snow-covered roof for some air. A few moments later, the janitor rushes in to tell them the old man has fallen off the roof to his death.

A week later, Morty, Bessie, and Myron plan how they will get Ralph to sign over the insurance money Jacob left him. Moe intercepts the boy when he comes home from work and tells him of the plan. When the insurance adjuster rings the bell, Moe claims to have a suicide note, which cuts short the scheme. The "note" is actually a blank piece of paper, but Ralph has already decided that his grandfather did commit suicide so that the grandson would have the funds to help him escape.

While Ralph is going through Jacob's books and trying to get his thoughts in order, Moe proposes to Hennie that they run away together. At first, she continues denying her love for him, but then she capitulates. Ralph encourages Moe and Hennie. He tells them he has decided to give his parents the money.

He will work to fulfill his grandfather's ideal that life should not "be printed on dollar bills."

Critical Opinion

No other American play of the 1930s so fully embodies the despairs and the hopes of that terrible period as does *Awake and Sing!* Odets begins his description of the cast of characters by saying that they "share a fundamental activity: a struggle for life amidst petty conditions." Though the play focuses on the problems of a single family, it is permeated with the economic and social problems of the time.

Bessie embodies the deepest fear of financial insecurity. She despises her father because his radical attitudes have lost him one job after another; ideas have no cash value. Her brother is a coarse braggart, but because he is successful she fawns on him. She marries her daughter off to the first responsible man she can find. When Moe seems interested, she is willing to change plans, not for reasons of sentiment but because his pension provides even greater security. Her attitudes toward her son's sweetheart are even more frank. He simply cannot be permitted to marry a poor orphan. Even under the best conditions, Bessie would never be a quiet, gentle creature, but throughout one feels her energies and her sympathies have been channeled in one direction. For her, life *is* printed on dollar bills. However, because her concerns are so deeply sincere and her fears so solidly founded, Bessie emerges not as a monster but as a character who commands our respect and compassion. Her feeling that the family would disintegrate without her is only a slight exaggeration.

The other characters illustrate varying points of view. Moe is less concerned about money, but scorns the society for which he suffered. The war in which he fought seems now to be a gigantic fraud, and the world seems to be rushing to its doom anyway. Like Bessie, he also suspects emotions, for he feels they may lead to disaster. Jacob's feelings lead him to a faith in Marxism, but also to frustration, for no one respects him and he knows he is ineffectual. Hennie and Ralph struggle to escape the net they feel enclosing them, but the options are almost nonexistent. All his life Ralph had wanted a pair of brown-and-white shoes—such a modest desire, yet it has never been realized.

Odets creates this microcosm of a period out of a group of overwhelmingly real people. He has a marvelously acute ear for the idioms, the clichés of these urban, lower-class Jews. Never before had they been heard on the Broadway stage in a serious play.

At the end, Ralph sounds a triumphant note, repeating his grandfather's favorite quotation form Isaiah: "Awake and sing, ye that dwell in dust." What he intends to do is unclear, but the call to action is unmistakable and clamorous. Here, too, Odets captures a key mood of the period, particularly among the young and socially committed. Spurred by the New Deal, the growth of the labor unions, the spread of Marxist ideas, and the horror of fascism abroad, they put aside despair and demanded social change. And though life might be bleak, belief in a new world could be exhilarating. Odets, in telling of one family, dramatizes both the bleakness and the optimism of the thirties, the sense of a whole era.

Awake and Sing! is more than just a document of its period. It is a superb example of realism, which many playwrights of the period and since have found both a model and a challenge. Odets is fascinated with the rhythms and details of everyday life. The simplest moments are often like discoveries, as both author and audience recognize the familiar in a bright, new light. Much of the strength of realistic drama has depended on this "shock of recognition," from the mid-nineteenth-century experiments of Antoine in Paris to the most recent revelations of ghetto conditions in the plays of angry black writers. Mere novelties, of course, only startle and then become banalities, but when the dramatization achieves the three-dimensional solidity of the characters and settings of *Awake and Sing!*, the play remains alive even when the immediacy of its message has faded somewhat. Of all Odets' plays, only this one has retained most of its original vitality, compassion, and feeling for the ordinary.

The Author

The setting and the idiom of *Awake and Sing!* are those of Odets' own youth. He grew up in Philadelphia and in the

Bronx in a family where poverty was always a terrifying possibility. In his teens he began working in vaudeville, and before he was twenty he was employed as a reader of stories and poetry on radio. His good looks and deep voice helped him get roles in stock companies and with touring productions of the Theatre Guild. In 1931 a number of Guild associates started a separate company, the Group Theatre, devoted to producing plays of social significance. Clifford Odets was one of the charter members; most of his best work was written for the Group and reflects its special skill in realistic, ensemble acting.

The first of Odets' plays to be produced was *Waiting for Lefty* (1935), entered in the contest run by the New Theatre League. It was promptly added to the Group program. A long one-acter, *Waiting for Lefty* presents a meeting of cab drivers discussing a possible strike. While they wait for Lefty, their leader, the drivers act out their reasons for a strike. At the end, news arrives that Lefty has been shot, and union members (as well as many in the audience) cry, "Strike! Strike!" The power of the play, as in *Awake and Sing!*, produced the same year, lies in the brilliantly realized details of lower-middle-class life and in the force of its social protest.

In 1937 Odets saved the Group from bankruptcy with another fine work, *Golden Boy.* Joe Bonaparte is a talented violinist and also a fine boxer. He takes the road to quick success, and becomes a rich and famous fighter, but also damages his hands so he cannot play music any longer. When he kills a man in the ring, he tries to run away, but dies in an automobile crash. An allegory of the conflict between the artist and a materialistic society and between sensitivity and brutality, *Golden Boy* achieves a sense of tragic inevitability. Other Odets plays produced by the Group were *Paradise Lost* (1935), *Rocket to the Moon* (1938), *Night Music* (1940), and *Clash by Night* (1941), all solidly based realistic studies of personal and social problems.

For most of the late thirties and forties, Odets lived in Hollywood, working very profitably as a film writer. In 1949, however, he returned to the stage with *The Big Knife,* a rather melodramatic attack on Hollywood's corruption of artistic integrity. In 1950 he produced *The Country Girl,* an effective psychological study of an alcoholic actor, his loyal wife, and an idealistic director. In 1954 *The Flowering Peach,* a retelling of the story of Noah in a Bronx-Jewish idiom, combined Odets' old interest in the family with a symbolic warning of universal destruction. Odets died in 1963 while working on a musical version of *Golden Boy*.

Dead End

by

SIDNEY KINGSLEY (1906–   )

The Characters

Tommy ⎫ a neighborhood gang, all about 15. Tommy is more
T. B. ⎪ or less the leader; Spit is the bully, reined in only
Dippy ⎪ by Tommy's strength and the gang's loyalty to
Angel ⎬ their leader. Poor, uneducated, amoral, they live
       ⎪ only for the paltry pleasures of the moment. T. B.
Spit ⎪ has already spent time in reform school, a fate that
Milty ⎭ lies in wait for the rest of the gang.

Gimpty (Pete)—in his late 20s. An idealistic architect, but unemployed, a product of the slums who knows something of the world outside, he tries to maintain a balance and avoid bitterness. Most people call him by the name that identifies his leg withered by rickets.

Kay—the girl he loves. A sleek, beautiful young woman, mistress of wealthy Jack Hilton, she is terrified of returning to a life of poverty and struggle.

"Baby-Face" Martin—same age as Gimpty. A product of the neighborhood, now one of the nation's most wanted criminals, he is vicious but slightly, inexplicably sentimental.

Drina—Tommy's older sister. Desperate to escape the slums, she finds a faint ray of hope in the labor movement.

Francey—Martin's boyhood sweetheart, now a cheap, ravaged prostitute.

The Setting

The dead end of a Manhattan street as seen from the East River. At one side are the terrace and back door of an expensive, new riverside apartment house. The rest of the neighborhood is a cluster of dilapidated tenement buildings with rusty fire escapes, filthy, uncurtained windows, ragged laundry, and sickly plants. The street is full of paper and other litter. Narrow alleyways provide a fragmented view of Rockefeller Center and the Empire State Building. The effect is one of utter squalor made more intense by contrast with the exclusive apartment house.

The original production by Norman Bel Geddes was a landmark in naturalistic staging.

The Story

It is a hot summer day in the early 1930s. A gang of boys are swimming in the filthy river, pitching pennies, and squabbling. They enjoy making fun of the apartment residents, who are using the back door to their building because the street in front is torn up for repairs. To one side, Gimpty sits sketching, lost in his work. The boys are particularly irritated by Philip Griswald, a boy from the apartment house who scorns their taunts. They hardly notice the two men who come in and stand watching, but Gimpty is struck by one whom he recognizes as "Baby-Face" Martin despite the gangster's plastic surgery. Martin, after Gimpty has identified himself as an old schoolmate, explains that he has come back to the old neighborhood after seven years to see his mother and his old girl friend. At the moment, since his companion is having no success in locating either one, Martin plans to stay around for a while.

Drina comes to find her brother, and stops to admire Gimpty's sketches for community housing. Neither Drina nor the architect is optimistic about the chance of escaping the present environment. They are interrupted by Kay, cool and elegantly dressed, a visitor from another world, who comes to give Gimpty a letter of introduction to a major architectural firm. He tries to convince her to leave Hilton, but she evades his questions about love. Meanwhile, the boys, once more insulted by Philip, plan their revenge.

The next day, the boys gather again to plot, to swim, and to play cards. Martin, waiting for his mother, cynically advises the boys to ignore all promises and codes if they want to win in a fight with a rival gang. He persuades Tommy that the leader needs a weapon, and Angel reluctantly gives up his new, treasured knife. Philip arrives again. The boys entice him into a tenement entranceway, beat him, and steal his watch. He runs home to get his father. Kay comes to ask Gimpty whether his interview was successful. Bitterly he tells her that the firm she sent him to cannot possibly afford any more employees. He begs her again to break with Hilton. She refuses, explaining that a visit the evening before to Gimpty's poor flat had frightened and depressed her. She is leaving that night for a long vacation with Hilton on his yacht.

Mrs. Martin is brought in by Martin's henchman. An exhausted, bitter old woman who can hardly bear to talk to her son, she slaps him, curses him, and refuses to take money from him. As she leaves, Mr. Griswald comes rushing in to punish the boys who hurt his son. He succeeds in catching Tommy and sends for the police. The boy panics, struggles, then draws the knife and stabs Mr. Griswald in the wrist. The policeman who arrives after Tommy gets away questions the bystanders, but they all deny knowing the boy, and leave to avoid further questioning.

Alone once more, Martin receives a visit from Francey. At first he welcomes her as if neither of them had changed, but she forces him to recognize the obvious signs of her profession, and tells him she is diseased. Disgusted, he gives her money and sends her away. With his henchman, he prepares to leave, but is surrounded by G-men, who shoot him down. Desperate for some money, some way of getting Kay to stay with him, Gimpty has informed the police about Martin's visit. At the same time, Spit, identified by Philip as one of the boys who attacked him, agrees to show the police where Tommy lives.

Later that night, all the boys except Tommy gather around

a fire to cook some stolen potatoes. Milty knows where Tommy is hiding and reluctantly agrees to lead Drina there. Spit decides to follow, and most of the other boys go off to find more wood. Tommy, who has been hiding in the shadows, tells Angel to help him trap Spit into revealing that he has been an informer. When the boys return, Angel works the trick and Tommy jumps on Spit, threatening to cut his face. Drina and Gimpty prevent it and get him to hide. However, rather than face a few years in reform school, Tommy decides to give himself up to Mr. Griswald and ask for mercy. But Griswald will not be moved, even by Gimpty's forceful argument that prison can only succeed in transforming Tommy into a vicious criminal. Tommy is led off, and the boys, fatalistically shrugging off their loss of a friend, watch the departure of Hilton's yacht, cheerfully responding to Kay's farewells.

Critical Opinion

Naturalism, the re-creation on stage of a specific place, complete with the grime and myriad details of actuality, has had few exemplars in American drama to compare with *Dead End*. In production, the illusion of the riverfront scene, with wharves and the dirty waters below, must be complete to give full force to the drama. The setting is itself the main character. *Dead End* was adapted into a highly successful film in which the camera was superior to the most skillful stage designer in creating the naturalistic illusion.

In *Dead End* Sidney Kingsley is concerned with portraying slum life and the sharp contrasts between the lives of the very rich and the very poor. In the process, he allows the plot and the characterizations to slip into stereotypes. The scenes involving "Baby-Face" Martin are reminiscent of too many gangster movies, though there is force in the scenes with the mother and the old girl friend. Gimpty, the idealist crippled both literally and figuratively by his background and by the Depression, is a familiar figure out of the liberal drama of the thirties. Making him an unemployed architect with brilliant ideas about public housing is underlining an already obvious point. Kay, the poor girl who becomes the rich man's mistress and can no longer turn back, is one of many characters treated as parts of a diagram rather than as individuals. The plot relies heavily on coincidences and parallels.

Kingsley, however, rises above the clichés of protest drama in the portrayal of the adolescent gang. Each is an individual carefully and convincingly developed. As a group the gang is imbued with a profound sense of waste, of the "dead end" that awaits them so long as conditions remain unchanged. Vital, ingenious in inventing pleasures, precocious in their knowledge of the world's vices, with only remnants of a private code of behavior, they are on the verge of total corruption. Kingsley's portrayal of the boys is fascinating, at once funny (they do have a good time) and terrifying. At the end, brushing aside Tommy's arrest and Spit's defection, they gaily sing the song T. B. learned in reform school, "If I Had the Wings of an Angel," a bitterly ironic finale. The boys who created the roles on Broadway went on to play the same parts in the film. Then, as the Dead End Kids, they made a few more films exploiting the impact of their first appearance, surely a tribute to the author who created them.

Dead End (1935) remains a powerful document of the Depression. The relationship between poverty and crime is forcefully presented, and the despair of those trapped in their narrow lives is painfully explored. The contrast between the haves and the have-nots may seem a bit oversimplified today but it still speaks dramatically of the basic attitudes of the time. Finally, Kingsley's own profound concern for the poor and the disenfranchised speaks eloquently for his fully awakened social consciousness.

The Author

Many of the American playwrights who came to prominence in the 1930s were fascinated by the problem of capturing on the stage the details and rhythms of big-city life. Elmer Rice's *Street Scene* and Clifford Odets' *Awake and Sing!* are significant examples. But only Sidney Kingsley effectively made the realistic settings and background the very core of his work. As a native of New York City he was dealing with familiar terrain.

In his first play, *Men in White* (1933), the details of hospital life occupy the center of his attention. In *Detective Story*

(1949) the comings and goings in a grimy police station over-
shadow the tale of a detective's struggle with his conscience.
However, in *Night Life* (1962) the method fails, perhaps
largely because the picture of behind-the-scenes corruption in
a nightclub is too familiar to capture and hold our interest.

The same concern for background detail helped Kingsley to
adapt Arthur Koestler's novel *Darkness at Noon* (1951). Using
a cutaway view of a Russian prison cellblock, he created a
powerful sense of prison claustrophobia pressing in on the
play's hero, an old revolutionary condemned in a purge and
trying to reconcile his fate with his past and his faith in the
party. Kingsley also staged the play, bringing to bear on it
all his theatrical powers to illuminate Koestler's ideas.

Other works by Kingsley include *The Patriots* (1943), a play
about Thomas Jefferson that owed much of its interest to its
reflection of the national mood during World War II; and
Lunatics and Lovers (1954), a farce about Times Square con
men and tarts.

The Little Foxes

by

LILLIAN HELLMAN (1905–   )

The Characters

The Giddens Family:

Horace—about 45. Intelligent and sensitive, he struggles to retain some humane values and self-respect even though his wife despises him as a weakling.

Regina—his wife, born a Hubbard, about 40. A handsome woman, ambitious and frustrated, she is determined to be richer than her brothers and to dominate the world around her.

Alexandra—their daughter, 17. Sweet, innocent, drawn to her father and her gentle Aunt Birdie, she is becoming aware of the cruelty in her mother and her uncles.

The Hubbard Family:

Benjamin—about 55. Unmarried, he is devoted to nothing but making money. Always alert to the nuances of every situation, he is rarely caught unprepared. Although ruthless, he is ironically self-aware.

Oscar—about 50. Brutal and coarse, much slower-thinking than his brother and his sister, he thinks he can outsmart them.

Birdie—his wife. Many years of browbeating have left her frightened and timid and an alcoholic.

Leo—their son, about 20. A lazy, stupid boy, he has inherited much of his father's brutality, none of his mother's generosity.

The Setting

The living room of the Giddens house in a small Southern town is expensively furnished, but without much charm or taste. It is spring, 1900.

The Story

The Hubbards have gathered for dinner at Regina's house. Their guest is Mr. Marshall, an important industrialist from Chicago who has just agreed to invest considerable money in cotton mills which the Hubbards will control. For the brothers it represents the end of many years of scheming and planning, and the chance to become enormously wealthy. Regina is exhilarated even more because she sees in Mr. Marshall and his socialite wife the entrée into high society once the great profits begin. But when their guest has left for the station, Ben reminds Regina that her share is by no means certain. Horace, who has been in a Baltimore hospital for five months with a heart condition, has ignored their letters. Regina uses her husband's silence as a bargaining point. Since Ben and Oscar are unable to supply the entire sum needed and are reluctant to let outsiders into their game, she argues that she and Horace should have double the share proposed. Ben immediately suggests that the difference be subtracted from Oscar's portion. Accustomed to being dominated by his older brother, Oscar reluctantly agrees, after extracting a promise from Regina that she will think seriously about a marriage between Alexandra and Leo. To Oscar this means that his family's share will eventually be the largest. Since quick action is necessary, Regina dispatches Alexandra to Baltimore to bring her father back.

A week later, they wait impatiently for Horace to arrive. Leo, who works in Horace's bank, proudly tells his father that he has been looking into Horace's safety-deposit box and knows there is $85,000 worth of bonds there that Horace looks at only when he clips coupons. Horace arrives, exhausted from his trip, and tries to postpone discussing business. Regina, however, is insistent. Horace soon confirms his suspicion that the brothers plan a ruthless exploitation of the poor white and Negro laborers. Then, even worse, he discovers the suggestion about his daughter's marriage and flatly refuses to cooperate.

Oscar tells his brother about Horace's bonds, and the brothers arrange for Leo to "borrow" the securities for a few months, long enough to get contracts signed and money borrowed on the strength of Mr. Marshall's signature. They plan to return the bonds before Horace misses them.

Horace knows he is dying, and sends for his bank box to review his holdings, because he plans to rewrite his will. When he discovers the bonds are missing, he realizes at once what has happened, but tells Regina that he will maintain the pretense that he lent them to Ben. In his new will, Alexandra will get almost all his property, Regina only the bonds and the income they will provide. This is more than she can bear; another opportunity is gone and Horace is about to triumph, for she sees their relationship as a continual battle for supremacy. She becomes vituperative, viciously insulting him, pouring out all her contempt, her hatred of his sexual demands and of his generosity. She taunts him with the lies she invented so that he would not sleep with her, then blames his infidelities for his illness. Horace is deeply disturbed and has a heart seizure. He drops and breaks the bottle of medicine, but when he asks Regina to get the extra bottle from upstairs, she ignores him. Desperate, he leaves his wheelchair and tries to get up the stairs. Halfway up, he collapses. Regina calls the servants to carry her husband to his room.

Ben, Oscar, and Leo arrive, having learned that Horace has been examining his safety-deposit box. Regina tells them of Horace's plans, which suit them perfectly. At that moment, Alexandra enters with the news that Horace is dead. The brothers are immediately reduced to meeting Regina's demand for a 75-percent share.

For all her delight, Regina's victory is incomplete. Ben ponders Alexandra's question: "What was Papa doing on the staircase?" And when Regina tells her daughter how they will go

off to Chicago and the grand life, Alexandra refuses. She has
learned too much about the cannibalistic world of her mother
and her uncles and intends to make her own way.

Critical Opinion

The subject of *The Little Foxes* (1939) is the growth of
ruthless capitalism, on the one hand destroying the old aristoc-
racy and its humane values, on the other exploiting the poor,
particularly the Negroes. The title is drawn from a passage in
the Song of Songs: "Take us the foxes, the little foxes, that
spoil the vines; for our vines have tender grapes." The Hubbards are the foxes, and by no means little ones, devouring the
fruits planted and nurtured by others. Ben makes the point
clear when he consoles himself at the end: "The century's turning, the world is open. . . . After all, this is just the beginning.
There are hundreds of Hubbards sitting in rooms like this
throughout the country. All their names aren't Hubbard, but
they are all Hubbards and they will own this country someday."

Each character fits into the pattern illustrating the rise of
brutal capitalism. Birdie is a last fragile remnant of a fine family, married by Oscar in order to obtain land and status. He
has destroyed her almost as completely as the birds he shoots
every morning and then throws away, not even allowing the
Negroes to have them for food. Horace, too, represents the
past. Once he played duets with Birdie, and as a banker he
tries to live according to gentlemanly ethics, but in the war
with Regina and the Hubbard juggernaut he is doomed to
lose. Only Alexandra offers some hope, already looking forward to the struggle against the evil represented by her uncles
and her mother.

This theme of rampant greed gives the play its shape and
drive, but the drama owes its essential power to its magnificent characters. Half a decade after the production of *The
Little Foxes*, Miss Hellman demonstrated what a hold the
Hubbards had over her imagination by writing *Another Part
of the Forest*, a play about the earlier days of the Hubbards,
when their parents were still alive. The second play was almost
as successful as the first. The development of these evil but
fascinating people is a source of great theatrical power.

Dominating both works is the figure of Regina, one of the most brilliant characters in American drama. As a young girl she is Papa's pet, already competing with her brothers, learning to despise weakness, eager to be a man but skilled in using her femininity to get her way. As a woman she lives in a state of almost continual tension, desperate for triumph, her rage against life ready to erupt at any moment. It is her desperation and her rage that make her something other than a simple villainess. In fact, we cannot help sharing her angers, her contempts, her cruelties, for there is nothing petty about her. As with Cleopatra or Hedda Gabler, the behavior that would normally make a Regina despicable becomes so infused with her passion that it evokes a sense of cosmic, tragic evil, not to be confused with the stupid greed of Oscar or the cold calculations of Ben. When Marc Blitzstein used *The Little Foxes* as the basis for an opera, he aptly named his version *Regina*.

The Little Foxes is a finely honed melodrama. The social issues now seem oversimplified, but the plot is solidly constructed, with scrupulous attention to detail. Theatrical prophets frequently announce the end of the well-made play, but a recent revival of *The Little Foxes* has demonstrated that such announcements are premature. The actors were delighted to undertake such bravura roles, and the audience was gripped by the suspense and the clash of personalities.

The Author

A meticulous craftsman, Lillian Hellman has produced only a dozen plays in more than thirty years of writing. Although not always box-office successes, they have all combined serious, intelligent thought with stirring theatricality. A native of New Orleans, she has frequently set her plays in the South. The themes, however, are universal.

Miss Hellman's plays have always been humanitarian, profoundly concerned with the struggle between the gentle and kind on the losing side, usually, and the callous and mean-spirited: the life-bringers against the destroyers. In her first play, *The Children's Hour* (1934), the pattern is clear. A malicious child invents a story of unnatural relations between two women teachers and starts a chain of events that damage everyone, even though the teachers are eventually vindicated.

In *Watch on the Rhine* (1941) and *The Searching Wind* (1944), the threat of evil is even more explicit, for fascism is under attack. In adapting Jean Anouilh's play about Joan of Arc, *The Lark* (1955), Miss Hellman once again chose to dramatize spiritual victory over worldly evil. Perhaps her most interesting treatment of this theme was in her book for the musical version of *Candide* (1956), with a score by Leonard Bernstein.

Although Joan of Arc and an anti-Nazi agent make vivid subjects for drama, Miss Hellman has done best with studies of domestic conflict, as in the two plays about the Hubbard family. Her subtlest play is *The Autumn Garden* (1951). Dealing with a group of people, most of them middle-aged, spending some weeks in an elegant old mansion converted into a summer guesthouse, the play explores various struggles for dominance, the fear of death, and the abrasive effects of both wealth and poverty. Though nothing spectacular happens, the play ends with all the characters changed by the need to examine and face themselves. In *Toys in the Attic* (1960), Miss Hellman returned to a more melodramatic approach in showing a young man's struggle to break away from the too-loving grip of his sister.

Lillian Hellman's autobiography, *An Unfinished Woman*, was published in 1969.

The Time of Your Life

by

WILLIAM SAROYAN (1908–   )

The Characters

Nick—the saloon owner. He maintains a tough, businesslike air, but is generous, concerned, deeply responsive.

Joe—a wealthy young man who spends most of his time drinking champagne and observing life. Intelligent but puzzled, wise but frequently surprised, he is trying to live without surrendering to a materialistic, inhumane society.

Tom—about 30, Joe's errand boy. Despite his years, he is an innocent, clumsy boy.

Kitty Duval—a prostitute, in her 20s. Tough and bitter when on the defensive, she is a lonely girl trying to recapture the dreams of her youth.

Blick—head of the Vice Squad. An arrogant, puritanical, much-hated man who sadistically uses his power for petty persecutions.

"Kit Carson"—an old man dressed like a frontiersman, full of wildly implausible stories of his past adventures.

Some other saloon regulars:
Willie—the pinball-machine addict.

Wesley—a young, unemployed Negro, delighted to learn he can make money playing the piano.

Harry—a self-proclaimed comedian and dancer looking for a chance to break into show business.

The Arab—a gloomy old man, oracularly commenting on the sad state of society.

The Setting

"Nick's Pacific Street Saloon, Restaurant and Entertainment Palace" is near the docks in San Francisco. A honky-tonk place, but not too garish, it attracts a wide variety of customers, including wealthy people who like to go slumming. For one scene, part of the stage represents a shabby room in the New York Hotel, nearby. The time is October, 1939.

The Story

After three years of working for Joe, who saved him from starvation, Tom is still bewildered by the errands he must run. Today he is sent off to buy a few dollars' worth of toys. As he starts to leave, Kitty Duval enters. Instantly, Tom falls in love, not with the prostitute but with the lovely, sad girl he recognizes beneath the professional façade. Joe sends him away and invites Kitty to join him for champagne. At first suspicious, she relaxes and tells him of her career in burlesque and of her childhood on a large farm, both stories transparently false. Meanwhile, others drift into the bar. Nick lets Harry try out his comedy act, but the young man's routine consists of long, detailed monologues which focus on the absurdity of life without being amusing in any way. As a dancer, however, he shows great promise. When Tom returns, Joe gives him some money and sends him off with Kitty. Luckily, they are gone when Blick storms in to threaten Nick with prosecution if prostitutes are ever caught in the saloon.

Joe continues drinking champagne, observing and dreamily chatting with people who stop by. Tom returns heartbroken to say that Kitty is in her room crying. Without explanation, Joe sends him out to buy a map of Europe and a good revolver. He is also to take the toys to Kitty; perhaps they will distract her. While he waits, Joe is joined by "Kit Carson," who launches into a series of disconnected, preposterous stories, including his falling in love with a thirty-nine-pound midget, and his herding cattle while riding a bicycle in Toledo, Ohio. Joe listens fascinated. When Tom returns, Joe decides to go with Tom to Kitty's room.

At the New York Hotel, Joe encourages the girl to think of marrying Tom, but the arrival of a customer breaks the spell. Joe takes Kitty to an elegant hotel, pays her rent, gives her money for clothes, and then returns to Nick's to figure out a way for Tom and Kitty to marry. He sends Tom out to check on a job as a long-distance truck driver. Kitty returns to say that she is afraid to leave her present job, much as she hates it, and to make a new life with innocent, trusting Tom. While Joe tries to persuade her to follow her dreams of love and respectability, Blick comes in again to check on streetwalkers. He torments Kitty, and brutally attacks Wesley when the young Negro tries to protect her. Tom returns during the fight, and Joe briskly orders Kitty to go off with the young man at once; they will go in the truck to San Diego, and will be married there. Then Joe tries to shoot Blick with the revolver Tom has bought, but he does not know how to operate the weapon.

Nick gets Blick to leave, and almost at once two shots ring out. Blick has been killed. Even the police hate him so much that they do not plan to investigate. "Kit Carson" swaggers in to tell his new story, about shooting a man once—"In 1939, I think it was. Fellow named Blick or Glick or something like that." Joe gives the old man his revolver and leaves, almost certainly not to return. Life in the saloon returns to its normal routine.

Critical Opinion

In a brief epigraph to *The Time of Your Life,* Saroyan says:

Have no shame in being kindly and gentle, but if the time comes in the time of your life to kill, kill and have no regret. In the time of your life, live—so that in that wondrous time you shall not add to the misery and sorrow of the world, but shall smile to the infinite delight and mystery of it.

The sense of that "wondrous time" and of the "infinite delight and mystery" of life permeates the play. Every moment is infused with overtones. Music and lighting enhance the poetic atmosphere. Saroyan's finest effects, however, are achieved through the use of simple but carefully developed realistic details. For example, Nick's little daughter comes to visit. She watches her father for a few moments, then says proudly, "That's my father." Nick notices her for the first time, becomes angry, and sends her home. A moment of love, childhood innocence, and pride has been created. At another point, Nick's mother visits the saloon, and they just chat warmly in Italian. Somewhat more significant is the Arab, who morosely mutters that there's "no foundation. All the way down the line." His statement becomes something like a musical motif, reappearing with slight variations and acting as a tragicomic chorus. Or on the more farcical level, there is the pinball machine. When Willie finally hits the jackpot in the closing moments, it plays patriotic music and unfurls an American flag. The sense of life's wonder comes through these details and through the brief moments when the characters reveal their dreams and their natural sweetness.

Not only is life wonderful, mysterious, and beautiful, but imagination can make it even better. When Joe is asked why he drinks so much, he answers that only when drunk does he feel truly awake and alive. When "Kit Carson" is startled because Joe believes his fantastic stories, the young man replies, "Living is an art. It's not bookkeeping. It takes a lot of rehearsing for a man to get to be himself." The wealthy couple who come slumming in the last act provide a vivid contrast. Their imaginations deadened by convention, the unusual frightens them.

Yet below the surface lies a deep melancholy. The date, 1939, has much to do with it, for the coming war is always casting a shadow. Harry's monologues usually end with war, the ultimate, horrible absurdity, and his longest monologue ends with a vision of Hitler, and of everybody "behind the eight ball." There are also reminders of labor turmoil, of illness and death, and of grief. Unlike the easy, superficial optimism that cheapens many of Saroyan's other works, his reassertion of human worth and dignity in this play is muted and genuine. *The Time of Your Life* rises to tragic heights despite its fairytale plot. In very few of his plays has Saroyan achieved this balance between rich inventiveness, dark shadowing, and resolute cheerfulness.

The Time of Your Life was awarded the Pulitzer Prize in 1940. But with a characteristic gesture, Saroyan refused the prize because he believed that it had in previous years been denied to works that clearly deserved it.

The Author

William Saroyan was born in Fresno, California, in 1908, the child of Armenian immigrants. In his youth he knew both the urban poverty of his parents and the rural struggles of relatives who tried their hands at developing orchards and farms, often with little success. Saroyan educated himself in the public libraries of Fresno after completing his formal schooling without finishing high school, and he was busily writing before he was out of his teens.

One of the most prolific of American authors, William Saroyan has written some two dozen plays, as well as novels, short stories, memoirs, song lyrics, film and television scripts, and a wide variety of articles and essays. His "spontaneous" methods, his failure to revise carefully, have focused criticism on his stylistic carelessness and wastefulness. However, his best work and his worst spring from the same impulses; if he is sloppy and tawdry in some places, he can be inspired and delicate in others. Unfortunately, the unevenness of his dramatic writing has deterred producers and it may well be that something valuable has been lost to the theater.

The first enthusiasm for Saroyan as an untutored genius quickly diminished when it was realized that his themes did not change much and that his sensitivity could become maudlin. There was even a period when he was written off as not worth discussing. Saroyan's reputation is a fascinating case study of the alternation of overpraise and underestimation. But a number of his works have remained tenaciously alive and impressive; neither as a playwright nor as a writer of fiction can Saroyan be lightly dismissed.

Three plays that reveal Saroyan's range are *Hello, Out There* (1942), *My Heart's in the Highlands* (1939), and *The Cave Dwellers* (1957). The first is a one-act play dealing with a young man imprisoned in a small Southern town on a trumped-up charge of rape. Before he is killed by a lynch mob, he manages to awaken a sense of her own worth and a longing for freedom in a plain girl who brings him some food. Most of the play consists of an intensely lyrical dialogue between the two. *My Heart's in the Highlands* is a virtually plotless fantasy, a wish-fulfilling dream in which poor people are transformed by the powers of music, natural goodness, and selfless love. *The Cave Dwellers* is more acerbic, examining some of the agonized life of drifters who find refuge in a deserted theater. Nonetheless, Saroyan's faith in human goodness is strongly felt throughout the play.

William Saroyan's own background as a child of Armenian immigrants living in California is explicitly presented in some of his short stories and memoirs. The plays are less autobiographical, but the exuberance and the folk-tale quality of many of his works have roots deep in his past.

The Glass Menagerie

by

TENNESSEE WILLIAMS (1911–   )

The Characters

Amanda Wingfield—the mother, about 45 years old. Trained to be a pliant, adoring belle, always ready to fascinate gentlemen callers, she is caught between her memories of social success in Blue Mountain and the difficulties of survival in St. Louis. Tragically ambivalent, by turns euphoric and practical, absurd and gallant, she confusedly tries to guide her fatherless family.

Laura Wingfield—the daughter, 24 years old. Crippled by a childhood illness, she wears a brace on one leg. She is so shy that she spends most of her time playing old phonograph records and polishing her collection of glass animals. Contact with the outside world is agonizing, and every failure and disappointment darkens the shadows of her mind.

Tom Wingfield—the son, 22 years old. He works in a warehouse, but yearns to be a poet. While his mother looks backward toward her glorious youth and his sister finds comfort in a world of crystal, Tom searches for adventure. Tom is the narrator of the play.

Jim O'Connor—the gentleman caller, 25 years old, a pleasant young man who works with Tom. Practical, sensible, and kind, he should be the ideal "gentleman caller" come to discover and cherish Laura.

Mr. Wingfield—the father. His smiling photograph faces the audience, but as a telephone man he "fell in love with long distance," and deserted his family. His phonograph records he left to his daughter; his search for adventure he left to his son.

The Setting

The action takes place in the Wingfield apartment and on the fire escape, which is the only entrance to the apartment. The Wingfields live in a poor, shabby-genteel section of St. Louis. Tom, dressed as a merchant seaman, addresses the audience in the present (i.e., 1945, when the play was first produced), but the events dramatized occur during the mid-1930s. Since this is a "memory play," neither the settings nor the events are completely realistic. In fact, Tom says that he will provide "truth in the pleasant guise of illusion." Throughout, music adds to the nostalgic, gently melancholy tone of the play.

The Story

A small apartment in St. Louis during the Depression is a far cry from the grand plantation where Amanda Wingfield grew up and where once, on a Sunday afternoon, she claims to have received seventeen gentlemen callers. Laura encourages her mother to retell stories of Amanda's youth, but Tom is irritated by his mother's romanticizing and her exaggeratedly genteel ways.

Though she keeps her spirits up by remembering the beautiful past and pretending that even greater glories await her children, Amanda also tries to be practical. She has enrolled Laura in a secretarial school, and she nags at Tom to save money by reducing his smoking and his visits to the movies. Tom, however, demands far more of life than a secure job at the warehouse, and quarrels frequently and bitterly with his mother about his desire to find adventure, even if only at the movies. He also wants to be a poet. His mother scolds him for reading D. H. Lawrence and belittles his ambitions. Laura hovers in the background, trying to act as a peacemaker, but is too quiet and frightened to succeed.

What little hope Amanda has for Laura's business career is shattered when she discovers that the girl stopped attending classes after a few days. Laura explains that she simply could not return after vomiting during the first speed test. She has spent her days since then walking in the park, visiting the zoo and the art museum, or going to the movies—anything but face her mother with the truth. Amanda is at first outraged, feels herself humiliated and betrayed, martyred by her weak, uncooperative child. All she can imagine for Laura is a future as a poor spinster barely tolerated by grudging relatives. But then, in a typical reversal, she triumphantly announces a solution: Laura must marry. Questioned by her mother, Laura admits that she once felt strongly about a boy, Jim O'Connor. However, he hardly noticed her. Laura is terrified at the prospect of meeting and attracting any young man, but Amanda blithely assures Laura that all she need do is develop her charm.

Mrs. Wingfield turns to Tom for help, insisting that he find some nice young men to bring home and introduce to his sister. This precipitates even more quarrels, but a few days later he says he has invited his friend Jim to dinner the following evening. Immediately Amanda begins planning to impress him, and shortly has convinced herself that their guest will propose and that Laura's future is settled. She buys Laura a new dress, gets new slipcovers, and spends most of the day cooking dishes which will be presented as Laura's creations. For herself, Amanda resurrects one of her own youthful gowns, slipping once more into her memory of herself as a young girl, playing the role she wishes her daughter to play, and painfully pointing up the difference between them.

When Laura discovers that the guest will be Jim O'Connor, she panics and at first refuses to see him at all. Then, unable to hide, she becomes ill and leaves the dinner table for the sofa in the living room. There she rests in a half faint while Amanda plays the charming hostess. After dinner, she arranges for Laura and Jim to be alone.

Jim remembers Laura as "Blue Roses," the name he gave her when she returned to high school after an attack of what she calls "pleurosis." In his gentle and self-confident way, he gets Laura to relax and talk. She shows him her collection of glass animals, especially the unicorn, with whose singularity she identifies. Jim tells her of his night-school work and of his ambitions. He assures her that her limp—the unicorn's horn— and his own drives help to distinguish both of them from the masses. He considers himself psychologically astute, and assures Laura that her inferiority complex is not much different from his own, and that it can be overcome easily. He even gets her to dance. They bump against the table, and the unicorn falls; the horn breaks off. Laura, in her euphoric mood, assures Jim that it hardly matters, that the unicorn is probably happier to be like the other horses. They continue to talk freely, and Jim tells Laura that she is pretty. Then, caught in the mood he has helped create, he lightly and sweetly kisses her. At once embarrassed and angry with himself, Jim tells her that he is engaged and came to dinner only because his fiancée is out of town. Laura gives him the broken unicorn as a souvenir. It is her gesture of farewell, to Jim and to the world.

Quite unaware of what has happened, Amanda rushes in. For a few moments she rides the crest of gay confidence. Then she discovers that Jim is engaged. As soon as the guest has gone, she angrily attacks Tom. They all know he has not created this situation deliberately, but Amanda's frustration has driven her beyond logic. Once more Tom storms out of the house, to go to the movies. Amanda and Laura are left to console each other.

At this point, Tom turns to the audience. While we watch his mother and sister silently comfort each other behind the transparent wall, Tom explains that shortly after his disastrous dinner party he was fired for writing a poem on the lid of a shoe box, and went off to join the merchant marine. Yet, in all his travels and adventures, he has not been able to forget his sister, as fragile as one of her glass animals. The play ends with Laura blowing out the candles, at once symbolizing the end of the story and the final darkening of her mind.

Critical Opinion

The Glass Menagerie is a much gentler play than Tennessee Williams' *A Streetcar Named Desire, Cat on a Hot Tin Roof,* or his other plays filled with grotesque characters and violent situations. Yet the group of loosely connected scenes that make up *The Glass Menagerie*, dealing with only one extended event, the visit of the gentleman caller, embodies most of the qualities which distinguish Williams as one of the finest of modern playwrights.

Technically, the use of short scenes connected by changes in lighting and offstage music has remained constant in Williams' dramas. This pattern, which reflects some movie influence, is deeply ingrained in his concepts of form and can be seen just as clearly in his fiction and one-act plays. While it gives a ragged quality to some of his work, in *The Glass Menagerie* the pattern of short scenes, often vaguely connected chronologically and frequently introduced by the narrator, creates the uniquely fragmentary, dreamlike quality of the play. The set directions call for one wall of the apartment to serve as a screen on which pictures and words are flashed to point up key ideas and moods. This device was never used, for Williams says that the skill of the actors made such emphasis unnecessary. His plan, however, reveals Williams' concern with developing a form which could heighten and yet avoid the limited photographic realism of the tightly constructed, three-act Ibsenite play.

The themes of *The Glass Menagerie* are even more closely related to Williams' more sensational plays, though presented in a minor key. The title has a multiple significance. Most obviously it refers to Laura's collection of glass animals and to her own desire to escape the demands of the crude world into a pure, isolated realm where everything is small and radiant. Like her animals, she is pure, transparent, and fragile, and at the end she has been broken as irreparably as the unicorn knocked off the table. Laura, however, is not the only glass figure, for in effect all the Wingfields, perhaps all people, are fragile. Amanda may be amusing, irritating, exasperating, even momentarily hateful as she prods and nags, but we know her also as the belle of Blue Mountain, swept off her feet by the handsome young Wingfield, and then deserted. We see her desperately trying to exploit the Southern charms designed to entertain gentlemen callers rather than support a family in the urban jungle. Tom presents himself to the audience more cynically, but we see him torn between the desire to become a writer and the need to assume responsibility for his family.

Though driven to desert them as his father did before him, he is haunted by his tragic memories. Even Jim, for all his hearty, sensible ambition, is pained when he is reminded of his faded high-school glory or when he realizes that he has hurt others. Finally, the play is full of echoes of the Spanish Civil War, of the growth of Nazi power, and of the destructive forces of the Depression in America, reminders that men are publicly as well as privately vulnerable. This concern with hurt, insecure people is central to all of Williams' writing.

The dialogue is another distinguishing element of Williams' play. Without slipping into "literary" diction, Williams infuses his characters' speech with lyrical and satiric overtones. Laura's pleurosis becomes "Blue Roses"; Amanda's sales talk for *Homemaker's Companion* becomes a rhapsody of advertising hyperbole; Tom's description of the Paradise Dance Hall evokes a picture of sad, seedy glamour. The very term "gentleman caller" grows richer in tragicomic connotations with every use. The tone slips easily and quickly from comic to pathetic, but always Williams' touch is firm. Thus a simple story is presented gently, almost tentatively, as if it were only a private memory, and captures a mood, strikes a rich, resonant chord.

The Glass Menagerie is one of Williams' finest plays. In the works he wrote later, he often achieved more sensational effects, but never more touching ones. The three Wingfields, caught in the web of their memories, fears, and desires, are among the most memorable characters in American drama. Their story, with its mingled comedy and gentle pathos, remains fresh and moving.

A Streetcar Named Desire

by

TENNESSEE WILLIAMS (1911–   )

The Characters

Blanche DuBois—on the surface fluttering, genteel, a bit silly, she tries to conceal the guilt, sexuality, fear, and loneliness that threaten always to overflow into hysteria.

Stella Kowalski—Blanche's younger sister. Passionately in love with her husband and able to forgive him anything, she is cheerfully adjusted to the world she lives in.

Stanley Kowalski—Stella's husband. A hard-working laborer, he glories in his masculinity, enormously relishing all experiences, whether poker playing, quarreling, or sex. To Blanche he seems little more than an ape, possessing none of the cultured sensibility she lays claim to.

Harold Mitchell (Mitch)—a friend of Stanley's. Awkward and shy, devoted to an ailing mother, he searches dimly for something finer than the coarseness he sees in his friends.

The Setting

The Kowalskis live in a shabby two-room flat in a run-down section of New Orleans. Nearby are the railroad tracks. The district is well supplied with bars, bowling alleys, and movie houses. Through the streets pass flower sellers, tamale vendors, prostitutes, sailors on leave, and the neighborhood residents. The audience can see both the interior of the Kowalski flat and parts of the street.

The Story

On a warm, humid evening early in May, Blanche DuBois, elegantly dressed in white summer clothes, arrives at her sister's home. She is dismayed to discover that Stella lives in what is, in her eyes, a horrible slum. But despite her airy ways, it is clear that she is desperate, has no choice but to stay. Before Stella appears, she finds a whiskey bottle and takes a long drink. Stella's arrival intensifies her feelings of disgust. Depressed by the setting, stimulated by alcohol, and infuriated by her sister's open delight in her marriage, Blanche hysterically accuses Stella of having abandoned Belle Reve, the family's old plantation home, leaving Blanche to cope with the agonizing series of deaths and debts which finally led to the loss of everything. Shaken by Blanche's story and her nervous condition, Stella assures her that she can stay as long as she likes.

The next day, irritated by Blanche's patronizing attitudes and by the hours she spends in the bathroom taking long baths to settle her nerves, Stanley concludes that she has improvidently spent all the family money on clothes, thus cheating him out of his share of the family fortune. He opens her trunk, pulls out her dresses and furs, and threatens legal action. Blanche gladly turns over to him all the papers showing that there simply is no more money. Sullenly, he explains that his concern is in protecting the interests of his unborn child. The news that Stella is pregnant comes as another blow to Blanche.

Later that evening, the two women return from the movies to find Stanley and his buddies deep in a poker game. Blanche is struck by Mitch's shy, clumsy politeness, and he is impressed by her fine manners. She turns on the radio and begins to dance for him when he comes into the living room. Stanley is enraged by the interruption, storms in, and throws the radio out the window. When Stella remonstrates, he strikes her. Blanche rushes her sister upstairs, while the men hastily leave.

Stanley, shattered by Stella's absence, shouts and pleads until she returns.

The next morning, Blanche urges her sister to leave her brutish husband, referring to him as an animal. Stanley overhears the conversation. Stella rejects her sister's advice. Blanche tries to plan her escape, hoping that a clever letter to an old admirer will bring an invitation to his Texas ranch or his yacht.

A few days later, Stanley reports that someone has mentioned knowing Blanche in Laurel, but that his informant's description does not quite fit Blanche's stories. The older sister begins to panic, complains to Stella about her fading looks, her fears of the future, and confides that she would like to marry Mitch, because he represents security. Alone in the house, waiting for Mitch to arrive for their date, she admits a young man who has come to collect for the newspaper. She embarrasses him by trying to seduce him, then gently kisses him and sends him away.

Late that night, when Mitch brings her back from their date, they share confidences. He tells her of his worries about his mother; she complains of her life with the Kowalskis. Then, feeling a growing bond of sympathy between them, she tells him of her marriage at sixteen to a quiet, poetic boy whom she destroyed: discovering that he was homosexual, she told him that she knew and that he disgusted her. In despair, he ran out of the casino where they had been dancing, rushed to the lake, and shot himself. Mitch is tremendously moved, and assures Blanche that they can satisfy each other's great needs. Gratefully, she kisses him.

Some weeks later, on Blanche's birthday, when Stella has planned an elaborate party at which Mitch will be a guest, Stanley arrives from work and tells Stella the truth about Blanche. She had become notorious in Laurel for her open promiscuity, and was fired from her teaching position when it was discovered that she had seduced a seventeen-year-old. He has already told Mitch the whole story. The party, without Mitch, is funereal. Blanche attempts to remain bright, gay, and ever the charming hostess, but all her confidence collapses when Stanley gives his sister-in-law a birthday present: a one-way bus ticket back to Laurel. Before Blanche can react, Stella begins to have labor pains and must be rushed to the hospital.

Still alone, some hours later, Blanche is visited by Mitch,

drunk and bitter. He berates her for lying about her age and
for pretending virtue. When he tries to rape her, she screams
and he leaves. Later, Stanley returns from the hospital to find
Blanche drunkenly packing. She says that she has suddenly received an invitation to a cruise. He leads her on to creating
ever more preposterous stories, all the while enjoying her dis-
comfiture. Frightened by his domineering behavior, she threatens him with a broken bottle, but he is even more aroused by
her resistance. He easily disarms her and carries her into the
bedroom.

A few weeks later, Stanley and his friends are again playing
poker, while Stella and her neighbor help Blanche pack for
what she believes is a cruise but is actually a trip to the asylum
where Stella and Stanley have had her committed. Stella explains to her friend that to believe her sister's story about Stanley would destroy her marriage. Blanche is easy to discredit
because she is obviously disoriented, possibly schizophrenic.
At first suspicious of the doctor and nurse who come for her,
Blanche is calmed by the doctor's gentleness. Taking his arm,
she says, "Whoever you are—I have always depended on the
kindness of strangers," and they walk out. Stella is left sobbing
in Stanley's arms.

Critical Opinion

To reach Stella's house, Blanche took a streetcar named
Desire, transferred to one named Cemeteries, and got off at
Elysian Fields. These are not only accurate directions for a
trip in New Orleans, but they supply a diagram of Blanche's
doom. It is desire that starts her on her trip toward insanity,
desire first in the form of her love for Allan, the boy she married. But for Blanche, desire is often followed by cemeteries,
for her disgust led her husband to suicide. In the same way,
the desires of the DuBois ancestors led to dissipation and
debts that destroyed Belle Reve (Beautiful Dream), and
Blanche's last few years in Laurel were spent attending the old
as they sickened and died. Desire, fed by guilt, by advancing
years, and by loneliness, turns Blanche toward nymphomania
and loss of what little security she has as a teacher. Now she
comes to seek a haven with her sister in Elysian Fields, but the
fateful pattern is once more repeated: desire, catastrophe, and

a further search for peace, this time in an asylum. For Blanche, the Streetcar Named Desire can only carry her to disaster, though others, like her sister, ride to fulfillment and happiness.

At issue between Blanche and Stanley is a conflict between complex, introspective idealism and open sexuality, between an overrefined gentility and a deliberate coarseness. Williams portrays the conflict in richly ambiguous terms, but he supplies no simple answers, nor does he indicate whose side he is on. To Stanley, Blanche is a fraud, her every ladylike gesture an affront to his conviction that animal appetite alone is real. The truth about her life in Laurel and the ease with which he destroys her seem to confirm his view. Yet, in all her evasions, her flutterings, her pathetic attempts to beautify her surroundings, Blanche represents many of the respected values and aims of civilization. While Stanley's victory calls into question such ideas as love, sensitivity, and culture, it also demonstrates how necessary they are. Blanche's instability does not show that sensitivity is useless, only that it cannot survive without an awareness of physical desire; civilized behavior must be more than a veneer. Nor is Stanley invulnerable, though he sees himself as the masterful realist. He is equally the victim of his desires. When Stella leaves him after their quarrel, he becomes desperate, expresses himself only in violence and abject pleading, and is reduced to being a frightened little boy. At the climax of the play, left alone with Blanche, he violates her almost as a reflex action, driven by a need to demonstrate his masculine dominance. After that, only Blanche's madness saves his marriage, though he acts as if nothing had happened.

The power of the play lies in the fullness with which Williams dramatizes this conflict. Once again he demonstrates his ability to select and intensify language; this is most apparent in the names—Elysian Fields, Belle Reve, Moon Lake Casino, Blanche (white), Stella (star), and, most powerful of all, that streetcar named Desire. He also uses to splendid effect the shifts between life in the street and in the Kowalski apartment. The flower sellers and the prostitutes, the flashing lights and the smoky jazz outside the apartment, frame the struggle within. Brilliantly outlined against this chiaroscuro background, the phantasmagoria of the hot, crowded, noisy streets, stand Blanche and Stanley, near-mythical figures. She is all bogus Southern lady; he is all sweaty stud. Each small, realistic detail takes on symbolic value. For example, for Blanche the bathroom is a refuge for soaking in the tub, washing her hair, putting on makeup, hiding from the brute world; to Stanley the bathroom is just a place for emptying his bladder after a couple of beers. A paper lantern over a naked light bulb is for Blanche a screen against ugliness, for Stanley an insult to truth. At every level, the battle is joined, the theme enriched.

The Author

Thomas Lanier Williams was born in Columbus, Mississippi. His mother was the quiet, ailing daughter of an Episcopal clergyman. He spent the first years of his life near the home of his maternal grandparents. His father was a shoe salesman, a robust kind of man, who moved his family to St. Louis when the boy was eight. The contrast between the urban, commercial world and the pastel-colored world of Southern ladyhood is implicit in all his works, most vividly in the conflict between Stanley and Blanche in *A Streetcar Named Desire,* most autobiographically in *The Glass Menagerie.*

Williams says he began writing when he was fourteen, and he continued during high school, two years at the University of Missouri, and two more working in a shoe warehouse. Following a nervous breakdown, he attended a number of other schools and drifted around the country doing odd jobs. Then, in 1939, some of his one-act plays won a prize in the Group Theatre's playwriting contest and he attracted the attention of a literary agent, who helped arrange for his first productions.

The Glass Menagerie (1944) won the New York Critics' Circle Award, and *A Streetcar Named Desire* (1947) and *Cat on a Hot Tin Roof* (1955) both won Critics' Circle and Pulitzer awards. Other Williams plays which are very highly regarded include *Summer and Smoke* (1948), *The Rose Tattoo* (1951), and *Sweet Bird of Youth* (1959). In *Camino Real* (1953), he attempted to develop a symbolic, nonrealistic play mingling historical characters, such as Lord Byron, famous literary figures, such as Don Quixote, and newly invented characters, such as Kilroy, the embodiment of American innocence. Although it confused many who could not adjust to its fantastic style, the play is a fascinating variation on Williams' favorite subject, the conflict between the insensitive and the gallant though damaged idealist.

In addition to his plays, Williams has published numerous short stories and one novel, *The Roman Spring of Mrs. Stone*. Both his drama and his fiction have been turned into movies, on many of which he collaborated. However, in very few instances have the movies based on his work captured the full richness of his imagination, particularly the lyricism of his dialogue.

A Streetcar Named Desire is Williams' most powerful play, as *The Glass Menagerie* is his most lyrical one. Together they establish Williams as a poet of the theater. He combines music, setting, vivid characterization, and a dialogue of heightened realism as he sympathetically portrays the struggle of sensitive idealists trapped in a brutal world. In subsequent works, he developed variations on this theme with varying success, but the essence of Williams as dramatist, philosopher, pyschologist lies in these two early plays.

Tennessee Williams has achieved a truly international reputation. Productions of his works in translation along with the many successful films based on his plays and stories have reached an enormous audience all over the world. His work has also exerted a direct influence on many writers, such as William Inge and Edward Albee.

Born Yesterday

by

GARSON KANIN (1912–   )

The Characters

Harry Brock—a wealthy junk dealer. A crude, loud bully, he regards everyone as a purchasable tool for his grand ambitions. He can explode into volcanic rage whenever he is even slightly thwarted.

Billie Dawn—his mistress, a former chorus girl, "breathtakingly beautiful and breathtakingly stupid," though actually she has never known that she has a brain.

Paul Verrall—a member of the *New Republic* staff, a handsome, intelligent young man, a crusader with a sense of humor.

Ed Devery—Brock's attorney, once a brilliant young lawyer, now a cynical, corrupt operator who tries to remain drunk most of the time.

Senator Norval Hedges—a distinguished-looking gentleman, but a cowardly, dishonest man.

The Setting

Suite 67D is one of the most exclusive hotel apartments in Washington, D.C. As Harry Brock is fond of pointing out, the rent is $235 a day, and the lavish furnishings are ostentatiously expensive.

It is late in 1945, shortly after the end of World War II.

The Story

Harry Brock and his entourage move into Suite 67D. Harry is in an expansive state, confident that his attorney and Senator Hedges will help him complete the big deal he has been dreaming of. Devery encourages him to grant an interview to Verrall, whose goodwill is valuable. With the writer, Brock is in great spirits, joking and nimbly avoiding embarrassing questions, setting a tone of cheerful camaraderie. He boasts of his rise from newspaper boy to the biggest junk dealer in the country, frankly confessing to dishonesty and conniving along the way. He jovially tells Verrall that he welcomes bad publicity, which can be more useful than flattery.

After Verrall leaves, Brock prepares to meet Senator Hedges and his wife. Devery asks Billie, in her capacity as corporation officer, to sign a number of legal papers, and warns her to behave properly when the Senator arrives.

The visit from the Hedgeses is awkward. Brock is self-conscious about his profanity and rough ways, but he is even more bothered by Billie's total lack of social grace. Everything she says is either stupid or faintly off color, and she is completely unaware of being out of key. Brock does, however, get through to the Senator that in return for a large campaign contribution he expects swift federal action to allow him to create an international scrap-metal combine that will handle all abandoned war material.

After the guests leave, Brock worries that Billie will ruin his contacts. Devery suggests that Brock should marry her to gain some respectability and a surer control over the properties in her name. Harry will have none of that; a wife demands things, while a mistress is always grateful for favors. Still, something must be done. Brock is inspired. How about hiring Verrall to be a kind of teacher?

Verrall, who lives in the same hotel, is intrigued with the suggestion, and attracted to Billie. He agrees. She does not at first think much of the idea, though she would like to speak more grammatically. Verrall's politeness and his growing infatuation soften her, and she agrees to tackle some books and newspapers he leaves with her.

Two months later, Billie's education has progressed significantly. She has become addicted to books, though she is in despair about how little she understands and how much there is to read and see. She is also discovering that the ideas she reads about are at variance with the simple materialistic philosophy she and Harry have shared. She is also bewildered by Paul's refusal to sleep with her. He clearly is attracted, but believes that sex, love, and marriage go together—a new notion to Billie.

For Harry, things have not been going well. Billie's growing knowledge and sophistication make him uncomfortable, and much as he hates to admit it, Verrall makes him feel inferior. Furthermore, Devery and Hedges are not moving fast enough. When Billie refuses to sign some papers until she has had a chance to read them, Harry's fury erupts. He slaps her viciously and shoves her over to the desk. When she has signed, he tells her to get out until she is ready to behave.

Very late that night, Billie has not yet returned, and Brock is worried. Devery finally persuades him to marry the girl, if only for business reasons. Brock not only agrees, he even tries to read a book to see if he can catch up with her somewhat. But it's no use. He buys and sells people who have ideas; he doesn't read them.

When all the men have left the living room, Billie and Paul slip in, and she gives the reporter papers which will provide evidence of Brock's conspiracy. Paul proposes marriage before he leaves, but Billie is hesitant.

Brock tries to be magnanimous, proposing marriage and minimizing his brutal treatment. When Billie refuses, he threatens her with a beating, but she is no longer afraid of him. When she tells Brock and Devery of the papers she gave to Paul, they call the reporter in and try to buy him off. When that fails, Brock becomes violent and tries to strangle the other man. He only succeeds in ending Billie's hesitation about marrying Paul. Though a discussion of democratic principles has no effect on Brock, he is finally tamed when Billie says she will return the property in her name, one junkyard per year so long as he behaves himself.

Critical Opinion

Born Yesterday is a clever variation on the Pygmalion and Galatea theme. Paul is the creator of a new person, the thinking Billie Dawn with whom he falls in love. The author plays lightly with ideas of birth and awakening. The title has its origin in the wise-guy comment that he "wasn't born yesterday," but in Billie's case the opposite is true; she is figuratively born when Paul encourages her to read and to use her mind. Her name, Dawn, is that of a cheap showgirl, but it also becomes ironically true. As with Shaw's Professor Higgins (of *Pygmalion*), Paul's initial task is to improve the girl's speech and social conduct, and like Shaw's Eliza Doolittle, Billie outdoes her teacher.

Kanin is also interested in another kind of birth or metamorphosis. The play was written just after the Second World War. The author is angry about the profiteering the war produced, and he is worried about the spread of greed and corruption in the postwar world. Brock embodies a cynical materialism that ruthlessly uses the law and the government to serve its ends. The demands of war have given him a momentum which it is difficult to stop. (He is symbolically interested in cornering the market on damaged war materials, since he cares nothing about the principles at issue in the war. If his philosophy prevails, what then was the war but a gigantic producer of junk?) In his blunt, unsubtle way, Brock represents the belief that only money matters, and that money can buy anything, including legislation. The transformation of Billie Dawn symbolizes, in part, the growing American rejection of the business-as-usual ethic of the prewar world. As Billie changes from a dumb chorus girl to a thoughtful citizen, so Brock changes from a hearty, expansive, even likable slob, completely frank about his love of money and contempt for intellectuals, to a destructive savage. In the end, he might well deserve Billie's label of "fascist." With the war over, the Brocks have become the enemy.

Although Kanin's theme is serious, the play is never solemn. The author almost never preaches. He is master of the scene that is at once funny and embodies a crucial idea. For example, when Brock and Billie first meet Senator and Mrs. Hedges, there is a farcical confrontation between Brock's coarseness and Billie's rather crude outspokenness on the one hand, and the practiced, old-society coolness of Hedges and his wife on the other. Through the laughter, however, one can see that Hedges' corruption differs very little from Brock's. Billie's ignorance of etiquette, however, betokens a healthy innocence. Throughout the play, Kanin expresses his criticisms and ideas through comic character and situation. As a result, *Born Yesterday* is always entertaining, but never trivial.

The Author

Although Garson Kanin has been active in the theater and films since he was in his early twenties, *Born Yesterday* (1946) was his first produced play, and the only one that has had a significant success. Following study at the American Academy of Dramatic Arts, he entered the theater as an actor, but his most important work has been as a director. George Abbott was in effect Kanin's teacher, for he assisted Abbott in the production of *Three Men on a Horse* (1935), *Boy Meets Girl* (1935), *Brother Rat* (1936), and *Room Service* (1937), all clever farces which demonstrated the director's skill with pace and inventive stage business. These skills Kanin first employed in Hollywood, where between 1938 and 1945 he directed a number of sophisticated comedies including *Bachelor Mother* (1939) and *Tom, Dick and Harry* (1940). He also worked on serious films, notably *They Knew What They Wanted* (1940) and *The True Glory* (1945).

Following the success of *Born Yesterday*, Kanin began moving back and forth between California and New York, employing his talents as writer and director in both areas. With his wife, Ruth Gordon, he has written screenplays. He directed Miss Gordon in her own play, *Years Ago* (1946). Like so many people in the contemporary theater, he has also worked with musicals, as a writer-director (*Do Re Mi*, 1960) and director (*Funny Girl*, 1964). Other plays he has written, or adapted, have fared poorly.

Garson Kanin was born in Rochester, New York. Garson's older brother, Michael, has followed a similar career as writer and director. He also married an actress-writer, Fay Mitchell, and they have collaborated on plays and film scripts. A sister, Ruth Kanin Brown, is a designer and writer.

Come Back, Little Sheba

by

WILLIAM INGE (1913–   )

The Characters

Doc Delaney—a chiropractor, about 40. A deeply disappointed
  man trying to adjust to a dull, empty life, he is polite and
  gentle when in control of himself, but violence lies just below the surface of his careful behavior.
Lola—his wife. Dumpy, slovenly, bored, she shows only faint
  traces of the pretty girl she once was.
Marie—a college student boarding with the Delaneys. A pretty,
  friendly girl, compliant and eager to avoid hurting others,
  she rarely probes beneath surface appearances to understand
  those around her.
Turk—Marie's college boyfriend. A topnotch athlete, he is
  proud of his body and of his attractiveness to women.

The Setting

   The Delaneys' living room and kitchen differ from those
of their neighbors only in their signs of neglect; the cheap,

ordinary furnishings are shabby and soiled. Otherwise, their
small house is typical of a Midwestern city sometime in the
late 1940s.

The Story

Doc comes down early to prepare breakfast, as he has been
doing for the past year. He is delighted to be joined briefly
by Marie, who stops to have a glass of juice before her shower.
To Doc she is something clean and precious, at once a daughter
he wants to protect and a girl he would like to marry. His wife
is a shattering contrast, frumpy and slatternly. In her self-pity-
ing manner, she tells him about her dream, again about her
fluffy white puppy, Little Sheba, who disappeared two weeks
before. She asks if he has said his prayer, and their talk reveals that it is now almost a year since he joined Alcoholics
Anonymous. In fact, this evening he will be busy working with
other AA men.

After Doc goes off to work and Marie to school, Lola listless-
ly tries to work around the house. She calls shakily for Little
Sheba; she chatters desperately with the postman, the milkman, and her neighbor; she listens to the radio, caught for a
moment by the dream of romance in a popular song; but time
passes very slowly. Her spirits revive when a telegram arrives
for Marie. Without hesitation, she steams it open and learns
that the girl's fiancé, a young businessman, is arriving the next
day. She is interrupted by the arrival of Marie and Turk, who
ask to use the living room as a studio; he will pose for a drawing Marie is working on. Lola, vicariously enjoying the ideal
romance she believes she sees flourishing between the two,
conceals the telegram and only gives it to Marie later in the
afternoon.

The news that Bruce is coming makes Lola aware of her role
as housewife. She cleans and tidies up the house, planning a
grand dinner for the next evening. Doc is disturbed by Marie's
apparent lack of conscience in having two boyfriends at once.
He is too easily reminded of his own experience with Lola—
a hasty marriage because of her pregnancy. The child was
aborted and Lola made sterile. Financial obligations prevented
him from completing medical school. Lola helps him brush
aside his concerns, at least for the moment, and sends him off

to his AA meeting. While Lola and Doc are out, Turk persuades Marie to let him sneak into her room that night, as he
has done before.

The next morning, Doc deduces that Turk has spent the
night. Overwhelmed, he takes a long drink, then conceals the
bottle in his coat and leaves as if going to work. Lola, unaware
of what has happened, prepares the dinner party. When
Bruce arrives, she offers cocktails, only to discover that the
bottle of whiskey is gone. She realizes that Doc has relapsed,
calls an AA member to help, but pretends to her guest that her
husband has been detained.

Doc does not return until dawn the next day, very drunk
and belligerent. When Lola tries to comfort him, she only succeeds in releasing his accumulated hatred: his anger at having
been trapped into marriage, his disgust with Lola's sloppiness
and stupidity, his feeling that she has encouraged and voyeur-
istically enjoyed Marie's promiscuity. Angered by Lola's
denials, he snatches up a hatchet and chases her until he collapses. Two AA men arrive and decide to take him to the city
hospital. Somewhat revived, Doc tries to escape, for the idea
of the hospital, sharing a ward with other alcoholics and with
mentally disturbed patients, terrifies him. The AA men must
drag him off.

Lola has only begun to take all this in, when Marie and
Bruce burst in and announce that they are leaving at once for
Cleveland to be married. Without noticing that Lola is upset,
they pack up a few of Marie's clothes, ask Lola to send the
rest on, and rush out. Utterly alone and frightened, Lola telephones her parents to ask whether her father might relent and
let her come home for a while. The answer is no.

A week later, Doc returns, thoroughly humbled. Frightened
at first, Lola becomes warm and comforting when she realizes
how desperate he is for reassurance and support. Bustling
busily about to prepare his breakfast, she reveals that she has
changed, too. Her most recent dream has convinced her that
Little Sheba must be dead, and she will call the dog no longer.

Critical Opinion

Come Back, Little Sheba is mainly a play of revelation. The
plot complication is negligible; most of it is prompted as well

as explained by the history of the Delaney marriage. Inge's finest achievement lies in the three-dimensional fullness of the Delaneys and their daily lives.

Why is Doc an alcoholic? Why is Lola a slattern? They see their life together as a failure, but they are not prepared to come to terms with themselves and find a solution. Instead, each substitutes a new dream for the one that has been lost, and tragically they project their dreams onto Marie. To Lola, the love she has missed and tries to share vicariously is what she thinks she sees in Marie's affairs, a glorious paganism as defined in popular music. The radio program Lola enjoys most is "Taboo," which combines a voluptuous-voiced announcer speaking of island paradises and romance under the stars with lush orchestrations of love songs. To Doc, Marie is a kind of vestal virgin. Listening to the radio, he is entranced by Schubert's "Ave Maria." Lola and Doc also avoid fully dealing with their problems. Lola clings to the hope that her dog will return, and with it, somehow, happiness. Doc acts as if imposing a cold routine on himself is enough to ward off evil.

Doc's relapse and Marie's departure combine to make a new life possible for Doc and Lola; if both are hurt, crippled, perhaps they can finally help each other. This conclusion is, however, far less important than the unfolding of character and the flurry of powerful action at the climax. Doc will probably have relapses, and it is too much to hope that Lola will suddenly find fulfillment in housekeeping. Still, a change has taken place, a more hopeful relationship achieved.

The oversimplified love-as-cure moral that disfigures so much contemporary drama is not sharply underscored.

Inge's skill in dramatizing the details of a meager life is most evident in the first act. While virtually nothing happens to move the plot forward, the audience's attention is held by the slow accumulation of details that reveal the characters and their plight, and form a firm foundation for what is to follow. Doc making breakfast and happy to have a moment alone with Marie; Lola naïvely admiring the milkman's physique or turning an offer of a drink of water into an opportunity to make conversation with the postman—from these fragments Inge extracts a sense of two rather ordinary people adrift, reaching out for help but not in the right direction. Though his solution to their problem is incomplete, the playwright forcefully lodges his characters in our memory. Their reality transcends the play itself.

The Author

William Inge was born in Independence, Kansas, and from childhood he was interested in the theater. Some of his mother's relatives were actors, and William decided to follow their example. He majored in drama at the University of Kansas, and was working with stock companies even before his graduation. An M.A. from George Peabody Teachers College and a few years of teaching preceded Inge's job as drama critic for the St. Louis *Star Times*, starting in 1943. Unlike Bernard Shaw, who used his reviews to attack the prevailing fashions in drama and to prepare the way for his own iconoclastic plays, Inge developed a respect for careful shaping and a desire to emulate the best examples before him. He has tended to be somewhat cautious, echoing more dynamic writers, particularly Tennessee Williams, who encouraged Inge when he began writing. At his best, he has produced a number of tightly knit realistic dramas.

Following *Come Back, Little Sheba* (1950), he had three fine plays produced in rapid succession. In *Picnic* (1953), a virile, amoral young man stops briefly in a small Kansas town and, like a rooster among hens, stirs up all the females. *Bus Stop* (1955) presents the overlapping stories of a number of people delayed in a small-town café. The most important story concerns a good-hearted, rather simple cowboy who falls in love with a tarnished nightclub entertainer. In *The Dark at the Top of the Stairs* (1957), Inge deals with a family in which each member has some fear about himself or the others, often not much clearer than the mysterious danger indicated in the title. At the end, some hope is restored through an awareness that love can help overcome loneliness and dread. In all of these plays, as in *Come Back, Little Sheba*, Inge's rather thin subjects are enlivened by well-defined characters and superbly chosen detail.

Since *The Dark at the Top of the Stairs*, Inge has not done well. In his most recent plays—for example, *A Loss of Roses* (1959)—he is still dealing with narrowly focused studies of domestic unhappiness, but the subjects have become more sensational and the touch less secure. His own comments indicate that he is searching for a new, wider angle of vision, and that in future work he will continue to struggle with the formulas which led to success but now seem in adequate.

Bury the Dead

by

IRWIN SHAW (1913–   )

The Characters

The many characters in the play are either simple stereotypes or else appear in only one or two episodes, where their personalities and points of view constitute the substance of the action. They will be identified and described in the synopsis.

The Setting

The stage is bare except for the platform toward the rear. On the platform are some sandbags and piles of loose dirt, suggesting the edge of a hastily dug trench or grave.

The time of the action is "the second year of the war that is to begin tomorrow night."

The Story

Four tired soldiers, under the direction of a tough sergeant, are digging a grave for six dead men. As they work, the soldiers gripe about the dirt, the cold, the rats and fleas—the classic discomforts of all armies. They make bitter jokes about the smell of the corpses. After the bodies are in place, two chaplains arrive—a Catholic priest and a rabbi—and after coldly chatting about the absence of the Episcopal bishop, they mechanically proceed with the funeral service. They are interrupted, however, by groans and movements from the dead men. The bored chaplains leave.

The six dead men slowly rise and stand, their backs to the audience. They plead with the soldiers not to bury them. The sergeant calls the captain, who is not surprised, since he has been expecting this to happen someday. The captain informs the generals, who accuse him of drunkenness and reject his story. They order a doctor to check the men and send them to a hospital if they are alive. The doctor carefully examines the six and finds each one is dead. His detailed, unemotional report, signed by witnesses, is submitted to the generals, who order the corpses buried. The captain asks them to visit the grave, which they reluctantly agree to do once they are assured that it is a safe distance from the front lines.

A reporter gets the story, but his editor refuses to print it because the government wants it hushed up. He orders the reporter to write a sentimental story of heroism instead.

At the grave, the chief of staff orders the corpses to lie down and be buried. He pompously evokes patriotism, duty, and scientific logic, to no avail.

The captain, who identifies himself as a student of science and philosophy in civilian life, tries to persuade the corpses that men have always died for their countries. But they announce that too many men have died for their countries and now it is time for men to recognize that they should die only for their own causes, not Caesar's. The captain then argues that the earth is too insignificant and miserable a place for anyone to cling to, but the dead insist that they have the right to decide that for themselves.

The news begins to spread through society, and everyone from businessmen to the clergy feels threatened. The captain suggests to the generals that perhaps the women of the dead men might be persuasive. The leading general sends the ladies off with a ringing, fatuous speech about how they can now serve their nation.

Private Schelling asks his wife about the farm and their son.

He tells her there is too much of nature he has not had a chance to appreciate, and he refuses to lie down.

Private Levy is visited by one of his vain girl friends, Joan, who is delighted by the war because it provides so many dances and parties. She repeats the clichés about the need to defeat the barbarian enemy. Levy dismisses her arguments and insists he deserves to stay on earth for many more years to enjoy at least the sight of women.

Private Morgan's visitor is Julia Blake, his fiancée. She pleads with him to lie down so that she can begin to forget him and stop drinking. Morgan wants more time to read and travel and write. In despair, Julia shoots herself.

Katherine Driscoll comes to see her brother, Tom, who has been a drifter for fifteen years. In death he realizes that he has things to tell people about the fight for social justice.

Jimmy Dean's mother keeps asking to see his face, but he keeps it averted because the shell that killed him had blasted away one side of his head. He tells his mother that at twenty he was too young to be cheated of life.

The last visitor is Martha Webster, whose husband, even in death, has little to say to her. Bitterly she complains of his inadequate salary and her fear of bringing a child into their shabby world. He admits he would have liked a child, and explains that his silence grows out of his shame. Now he recognizes the fault in the system and refuses to lie down until he has helped change the world.

So the women fail. Even the editor agrees that the story must be told. The bankers demand action, and the clergy attempt exorcism. Finally, one of the generals sets up a machine gun and tries to shoot the corpses down. But silently and with dignity they walk out of their graves and away from the battlefield. The live soldiers follow them, and only the general is left, slumped over the machine gun aimed at an empty grave.

Critical Opinion

Like so many protest writers of the thirties, Shaw saw war as an instrument of the ruling class, exploiting the poor and the powerless for economic ends. Disillusion with World War I, the Depression at home, and fear that growing totalitarianism abroad would soon spread to the United States all combined to create the angry mood. In Shaw's eyes, the military establishment was of course the least sensitive to the needs and rights of man, but the church's collaboration with the destructive forces of capitalism and militarism was the ultimate failure of society. Along with many other writers, Shaw abandoned leftist simplifications by the end of the decade, but in 1936, at the age of twenty-three, he found in these ideas ample grounds for an angry indictment.

Although *Bury the Dead* in many ways reflects the period in which it was written, the power of the dramatic idea and the intensity of the antiwar feelings have kept it from becoming dated. The corpses refusing burial have tremendous theatrical impact, and since the play is brief, that impact is not dissipated. No moment is as startling as the one when the corpses rise, but from scene to scene the emotional temperature mounts. The scenes with women, sharply individualized vignettes, complete the picture, ironically identifying the corpses as the truly living.

Shaw took his title from Matthew 8:22: ". . . let the dead bury their dead," Christ's curt comment to a reluctant follower. It can be taken, as Shaw does, as a rejection of an old, discredited system. When the corpses and live soldiers both leave the stage to the general, the military and economic establishment is clearly identified as dead.

Like all propaganda pieces, *Bury the Dead* is obvious and repetitious. In recent years, the author has refused to permit performances of the play, probably because he no longer accepts its ideology and perhaps because he now thinks of it as crude and naïve. It is nonetheless a valuable document of its time, and still a viable piece of theater. It is one of the few American social dramas that successfully exploit expressionistic techniques.

The Author

Irwin Shaw was born and raised in Brooklyn, and was graduated from Brooklyn College. Like so many young writers of the thirties, he was greatly influenced by the work of Clifford Odets and he gravitated toward the Group Theatre and other production companies working with plays of social analysis and protest. The Group offered to produce *Bury the Dead,* but the author was too impatient to wait for the appointed date, so the play was presented by the Contemporary Theatre, a short-lived organization. The production brought the author a considerable degree of critical attention. His next plays had little trouble finding producers.

Anger and a daring expressionistic device gave form to *Bury the Dead* (1936). However, Shaw's next productions, utilizing more traditional forms, revealed his weaknesses as a writer for the stage. *Siege* (1937), an impassioned story about the Spanish Civil War, was clumsily sensational and shrill. *Quiet City* (1939), a study of the impact of the Depression on a formerly prosperous family, and *Retreat to Pleasure* (1941), a satiric comedy about the confusions of the middle-class intellectuals in the early days of World War II, were both awkwardly written and produced. Shaw's only other play to achieve both critical and popular approval was *The Gentle People* (1939), a parable about fascism told through a story of gangsters threatening some old fishermen. Like Odets, Shaw was best at capturing the characteristic details of big-city life, but he tried to impose on his stories universal meanings they could not realistically bear.

Though he was swiftly turning out plays during the decade before World War II, Shaw was also writing the first of his excellent short stories. *Sailor off the Bremen* (1939) is a collection of stories filled with sharp details and subtly realized themes. During his years in the Army, he turned even more to fiction. In 1948, he published his first novel, *The Young Lions*, a powerful study of young men in the American and German armies. It was a great success, and Shaw has gone on to attract a far larger audience for his fiction than for his plays. In his novels and short-story collections he has found a more satisfactory form for his social and psychological concerns than he was ever able to find on the stage. Three of his recent theater works had only short runs: one a collaboration (*The Survivors*, with Peter Viertel, 1948); one an adaption from the French (*Patate*, original by Marcel Achard, 1958); and one drawn from one of his own stories (*Children from Their Games*, 1963). Though *Bury the Dead* was hailed by some critics as "better than Odets," Shaw will no doubt be best remembered for his fiction, particularly his short stories.

Inherit the Wind

by

JEROME LAWRENCE (1915–   )
and ROBERT E. LEE (1918–   )

The Characters

The play is based on the Scopes trial, which took place in Dayton, Tennessee, in 1925. The major characters are modeled on actual people, but events and names have been altered to give the play greater universality. The names of the major historical parallels are given in brackets.

Bertram Cates [John Scopes]—a biology teacher, a serious, sincere young man, not revolutionary but determined to follow his conscience.

Matthew Harrison Brady [William Jennings Bryan]—a powerful orator and politician. Three times an unsuccessful candidate for the Presidency, each time mainly supported by rural voters, he is now 65, overweight and pompous. He is renowned for his knowledge of the Bible and his unquestioning faith.

Henry Drummond [Clarence Darrow]—a lawyer famous for his skill in defending difficult, unpopular clients. He has a shrewd and ingenious legal mind. His manner is deceptively

quiet and undramatic in contrast to Brady's flamboyant the-
atricalism. He is an admitted agnostic.

E. K. Hornbeck [H. L. Mencken]—a reporter from Baltimore,
a sardonic, cynical man who considers the world a grotesque
circus.

Reverend Jeremiah Brown—a fundamentalist minister, spokesman for the town's church.

Rachel Brown—his daughter, a schoolteacher. She is in love
with Cates but frightened by ideas that contradict her
father's teachings.

Mayor, judge, townspeople—good-hearted, friendly people as
long as their cherished beliefs are unchallenged.

The Setting

Hillsboro is a small country town somewhere in the South
or Middle West. Most of the action takes place in the court-
house or in the town square. The main street is the background. Although the authors say the time is "not too long
ago," and could even be tomorrow, references to events and
details of dress and such innovations as radio indicate that
it is the early 1920s.

The Story

Never has excitement run so high in Hillsboro. For Bert
Cates's trial, none other than Matthew Harrison Brady is coming to work with the prosecution. As far as the townspeople
are concerned, the case is cut and dried anyway: there is a
state law against teaching evolution, and Cates has broken it.
What Brady will do is confirm their belief in the law. They
prepare for the trial as a combination of fair and revival
meeting.

One of the first arrivals is Hornbeck, who has come to report the trial and confirm his feelings about the medieval attitudes of rural America. He is soon followed by Brady, who
is greeted by hymn-singing and a band. Mrs. Brady is aware
that her husband should not be eating so much or exerting
himself so much, particularly in the heat; but he is in his
element, glorying in the adulation. There is a break in the

gaiety when Hornbeck announces that his newspaper has hired Henry Drummond for the defense. The name is familiar. The Reverend Mr. Brown thinks Drummond may be the devil himself. Brady, too, is briefly shaken by the news, but then greets it with pleasure, for it will magnify his victory over atheism and evil.

During the selection of the jury, Brady has the judge and the spectators on his side. Drummond can at most challenge a few legal points or make angry remarks that Brady brushes off. One very unhappy person is Rachel Brown. She pleads with Cates to confess and end the trial. She is afraid that when she is called as a witness she will be asked to repeat some of the young man's comments about evolution and religion. Cates prefers not to buy peace with cowardice.

That evening, the Reverend Mr. Brown leads a revival meeting, during which the crowd approaches hysteria. When Rachel tries to defend Cates, her father calls down the wrath of God on her as well. Even Brady finds this too harsh and brings the meeting to an end.

The trial goes well for Brady, and Cates's "heathenism" becomes public knowledge. When Drummond tries to call expert witnesses—a zoologist, a geologist, etc.—the judge refuses, arguing that the theory of evolution is not on trial. In fact, the very law Cates is being charged with breaking already forbids the kind of testimony Drummond would present. Left without a witness, Drummond calls on Brady as an expert on the Bible. Confident of victory, Brady agrees to take the stand.

Drummond has difficulty in challenging Brady or even disturbing his equanimity. Brady's ignorance of Darwin and his trust in Biblical authority are applauded equally by the spectators. The first shift in Drummond's favor occurs when Brady uncomfortably admits that a sponge might think if the Lord decided it, and Drummond demands his client's right to think, too. Brady seems to regain his assurance when he denies the claims of geology, but is trapped into agreeing that the first day of creation might not have been a twenty-four hour day, since the sun had not yet been created. In anger, he insists the Bible must not be attacked because "God tells me to oppose the evil teachings" of Darwin. Drummond pounces on this to mock Brady as a new "Prophet from Nebraska." The spectators begin laughing; Brady becomes flustered and frightened. Reduced to a childlike terror by the laughter, all he can do is recite the names of the books of the Bible.

The next day, the jury returns its verdict: Guilty. The judge, however, has been warned by the state political leaders to remove the case from public notice as quickly as possible. He fines Cates a mere hundred dollars. Drummond sees this as a victory, but still says that they will appeal. Brady is appalled and insists on reading into the record some statements he has prepared to counter the impression he gave the day before. The radio man who came to broadcast the results agrees to let Brady use the microphone, but he has barely begun when the broadcast time is ended, and Brady is once more made to look foolish when the microphone is removed. Struggling to finish, Brady is overcome by heat and frustration, and collapses. In a few moments, he is dead.

Hornbeck greets the news gleefully, but Drummond upbraids him for his inhumanity. The reporter scorns Drummond's grief as a sign of sentimental weakness.

Rachel has decided to leave home, and Cates decides to go with her. Tired and unsure of what victory he has won, Drummond leaves, thoughtfully balancing the Bible in one hand, *The Origin of Species* in the other.

Critical Opinion

In dealing with the Scopes trial, Lawrence and Lee had a ready-made confrontation between points of view and between powerful speakers. They also faced the problem of any writer dealing with such a subject: the audience not only knows the outcome but is already thoroughly committed to one side or the other. Inevitably, the struggle is between the victim and his persecutors, the enlightened and the benighted. Perhaps only Shaw in *Saint Joan* was able to rise above these limitations by giving the arguments against Joan almost more force and sympathy than those for her. To deal with this problem the authors of *Inherit the Wind* concentrate on the supercharged atmosphere and on the ambiguities and ironies of the winning side.

Hillsboro welcomes Brady as if he were a savior. He has come quite literally to renew and redeem their faith, and Brady's tragedy is in part triggered by his uncritical response to this welcome. He expands; he glows; he becomes beatific; and he oversteps the bounds of reasonable restraint. In the Greek tragic sense, he is guilty of hubris. So, in a sense, is the town itself. The revival meeting is as essential to the play as the climactic trial, for the near-hysteria of the congregation is a manifestation of the irrationality that is really on trial. The power of the Reverend Mr. Brown is also a sign of how easily the townspeople can be stirred and turned. When Drummond starts them laughing at Brady, they in effect repeat the same pattern of easy surrender they had exhibited the night before. The picture of herd behavior verges on caricature, and in a poor production could well become ludicrous, but carefully handled it conveys the idea of the town itself—a narrow-minded, unthinking society—on trial. Brady is both their spokesman and their victim, destroyed by a momentary shift in loyalties. In part the play is the story of his fall even more than it is the story of fundamentalism versus science.

Drummond's story is also more complex than it seems at first. In the past, he had supported Brady, and now it is with pain that he opposes the man, who has become inflexible and pretentious. Later, when Brady is dead, Drummond mourns him. "A giant once lived in that body," he says, but "he was looking for God too high up and too far away." Drummond senses the pain he has caused and cannot help wondering whether it was worth it. He objects to Hornbeck's determination to destroy. Though he is a defender of principle, Drummond does not lose sight of the man whose principles he abhors.

Drummond's sympathetic appraisal of his opponent occurs during the final moments of the play, and it does suggest that the issues are not as simple or as clear as they have appeared to be before. However, the overall effect of the play is melodramatic, a struggle of light against dark. Despite the authors' insistence on universality, the actual confrontation over the literal reading of the Bible puts the event in the past, and makes Brady-Bryan appear a fatuous fool, while Drummond-Darrow is a hero. There is a suggestion that the story is potentially a tragedy, but it remains only a suggestion.

The Authors

Jerome Lawrence is from Cleveland, Ohio, and Robert E. Lee is from Elyria, Ohio, but it was not in their home state that their collaboration began. During World War II, they helped found the Armed Forces Radio Service, and after the war they collaborated on the scripts for many dramatic programs on radio and, later, television. During the period between world wars, many of the finest plays were written by pairs of collaborators; however, since World War II Lawrence and Lee are virtually the only team to appear. They first appeared on Broadway as authors of the book for *Look, Ma, I'm Dancin'!* (1948), a short-lived musical. *Inherit the Wind* (1955) brought them to prominence, and is still their only successful serious work. *The Gang's All Here* (1959), using techniques similar to those employed in *Inherit the Wind,* dramatizes the corruption during President Harding's administration. *Only in America* (1960) is based on Harry Golden's memoirs of the same title, and *A Call on Kuprin* (1961) deals with Soviet-American relations. In none of these were the authors able to give their materials dramatic life. A musical entitled *Shangri-La* (1956), based on James Hilton's *Lost Horizon,* was also lifeless.

In 1956 the collaborators were immensely successful with an adaptation of Patrick Dennis' novel *Auntie Mame.* Following its appearance as a film, Dennis' story of a vibrant nonconformist reappeared as a hit musical, *Mame* (1966), again with Lawrence and Lee as authors. Their most recent work is the adaptation of Giraudoux's *The Madwoman of Chaillot* as a musical, *Dear World* (1969).

Death of a Salesman

by

ARTHUR MILLER (1916–)

The Characters

Willy Loman—60, a traveling salesman. A man who enjoys
working with his hands, he dreams of great commercial
success through personal charm and popularity. He lives
always at extremes, either where imagined success seems
just within reach or where despair waits to overwhelm him.

Linda—his wife. Her love and loyalty constitute her whole
life; she is aware of her husband's weaknesses and evasions,
but lives only to make him happy.

Biff—their son, 34. He is a man searching for identity, for a
sense of wholeness, torn by love for his father and a desperate need to escape his father's influence.

Happy (Harold)—his brother, 32. A small-time playboy, always bragging of his success with women and in business,
he is inflated with an unreal sense of his own importance.

Charley—a neighbor and friend, about the same age as Willy.
He is an unpretentious, hard-working businessman deeply
sensitive to the feelings of others.

Bernard—his son, the same age as Biff. As a boy, he was a
bookworm; as a man, he is an important lawyer.

Ben—Willy's older brother. His wealth, gotten from African diamonds and Alaskan forests, endows him in Willy's eyes with glamour and wisdom.

Howard Wagner—Willy's employer, son of the company's founder, a curt, unsentimental businessman.

The Setting

Apartment buildings loom over the Loman house, a relic of a time when the area was full of homes and gardens. Now too little sun reaches the yard for anything to grow. During the memory scenes the yard is shadowed by the leaves of the long-gone elms.

The house is transparent, or is shown in skeletal form, so that the kitchen, the parents' room, and the boys' bedroom are visible. The stage apron is used for those scenes which do not take place in or near the house.

The staging, particularly the lighting, of the play must distinguish three levels of reality: the present; the past as Willy remembers it; and the hallucinatory.

The Story

Driving to New England, his sales territory, Willy finds himself suffering brief periods of amnesia. Terrified, he turns back and arrives home late at night. Linda tries to comfort him, but he is preoccupied with thoughts of Biff, who has just returned from Texas, where he worked on a ranch. Exhausted but too overwrought to sleep, Willy wanders about the house and yard mumbling to himself, sometimes reliving moments of the past or abruptly returning to his present problems. The boys awaken, and Happy tells his older brother that their father has been acting more and more irrational. Biff determines to get a good job, settle down, and help his father, and in seconds the two brothers have dreamed up a magnificent plan for selling sports equipment. Biff will see Oliver, his old employer, and ask for backing.

In the yard, Willy relives a happy moment he experienced eighteen years before. The boys have waxed their father's car, and now Biff is practicing for the big football game. All the father's love and ambition are focused on the older boy, and he even approves Biff's "borrowing" a ball for practice. Bernard warns them that Biff may fail his math course and not graduate, but Willy can only talk about the college scholarships awaiting the boy. Alone with Linda, Willy brags of how well he has been selling, but when she asks for details he dejectedly admits that he is not doing too well. His income can just barely cover their expenses.

Back in the present, Charley comes over, ostensibly to play cards with Willy, but really because he wants to help. Charley offers Willy a job, as he has done many times, but Willy refuses though he admits he is doing badly. As they play cards, Willy begins to remember a visit from Ben, and when Charley leaves, he relives the visit in memory. Ben offers Willy a chance to make a fortune in Alaska, but Willy insists he is doing well. The boys come to see their uncle, and Willy scolds them lightly about stealing materials from a nearby building site.

Biff and Happy come down to speak to Linda. She says Willy is always bad when Biff comes home; the antagonism between father and son mingles with the father's love and his frustrated expectations. She tells them Willy is now working strictly on commission, like a beginner. Even more awful, he has been contemplating suicide; he has had a series of strange accidents, and she has discovered a length of pipe hidden near a gas outlet in the cellar. When Willy comes in, he and Biff start quarreling, but when Happy mentions Biff's plan to see Oliver, Willy plunges directly into predictions of triumph. Biff will vindicate Willy's belief that the important thing is to be not just liked, but well liked. Even Biff is caught up in his father's enthusiasm.

The next day, buoyed by hope, Willy goes to Howard to ask for a nontraveling job. Howard, enraptured by a new tape recorder, can hardly listen to the salesman, and not only denies his request but fires him. Willy goes to Charley's office. There he meets Bernard, preparing to leave for Washington to plead a case before the Supreme Court. No longer able to conceal his despair, Willy asks Bernard why Biff did not succeed. Bernard says the answer lies somehow in Biff's behavior after failing the math course. As Bernard remembers it, the boy was ready to go to summer school and repeat the work, but after visiting his father in Boston, he had refused to go back to school and never graduated. Willy angrily denies the suggestion that something happened in Boston. When Charley once more offers him a job, Willy cannot accept what he sees as charity and an admission of failure.

Happy and Biff meet in the restaurant where they are to have dinner with their father. Happy at once sets about picking up an attractive girl, and brushes off Biff's account of an awful day. (After waiting for hours, Biff saw Oliver just long enough to realize the man did not even remember him. In a spasm of anger and disappointment, he stole the executive's fountain pen.) When Willy comes, Biff tries to tell him what happened, but his father will listen only to good news. Happy willingly invents optimistic details. In disgust, Biff rushes out. Willy goes to the washroom, and there the worst of his memories finally overtakes him: Biff, running to him for help after failing the math course, had discovered his father with a woman in a Boston hotel room.

Later that night, Biff and Happy return home, drunk. Linda furiously scolds them for abandoning their father at the restaurant. Biff agrees with his mother and insists only that he must have a talk with his father before leaving for good. Willy is in the yard planting seeds by flashlight. He imagines a visit from Ben, with whom he discusses the feasibility of suicide, to provide Biff with twenty thousand dollars in insurance money. Biff tries to tell his father that both of them are ordinary men driven by the wrong dreams and a mistaken image of themselves. He points out that the theft of the pen was like his other thefts, done out of a desire to get something without the necessary work and ability. Willy, hardly rational, interprets all of Biff's statements as mere spite against his father. Utterly frustrated by his failure to communicate and racked by his grief for his father, Biff weeps. The tears restore Willy's faith in his son's magnificent sensitivity and devotion. He goes out to his car, drives away, and crashes.

At Willy's funeral, Biff insists his father had the wrong ideals. Charley justifies Willy's ideals by explaining that a salesman can only exist if he has a grand belief in himself. Linda is held by the bitter irony of a life ended just when all the bills are paid; the mortgage-free house will now be empty.

Critical Opinion

Arthur Miller says his original idea for what became *Death of a Salesman* started out as a play which would begin with a picture of a face occupying the whole of the proscenium arch. This was to open up and the story would be acted as if it were taking place inside the mind of his hero. The play was to be called *A Man's Head.* For the finished work, Miller used far more subtle techniques, but he kept Willy's mental disintegration at the center of the action. The play covers barely twenty-four hours, and in that time Willy moves from mental and physical fatigue through increasingly painful memories to hallucination and suicide. Since the audience's understanding of background and motive depends on the information provided by Willy's inner turmoil, we are drawn relentlessly into his mind. However we may evaluate Willy's life, his suffering is immediate and overwhelming. We are for most of the play inside the man's head.

The story of Willy Loman embodies a number of American themes. As a father, Willy thinks always of his son's success. His son must surpass him. For this Willy will sacrifice himself through back-breaking work and, when insanity takes over, with his life. The failure of the sons, particularly the favored son, is therefore a double failure, for the father fails in the son, and his whole life becomes worthless. When Biff says to his father that they are both "a dime a dozen," this is something Willy cannot accept, for what has given his life meaning is the illusion that he is great and his son even greater.

The father's dream is embedded in the even larger and more destructive dream of success. Willy measures success in terms of wealth and status, and as Charley warns him, he goes further and reverses the sequence. Popularity is for Willy the essential ingredient of success. Skill and hard work are nothing. In his mind's eye he always retains the image of Dave Singelman, the eighty-four-year-old salesman who stayed in his hotel room, wearing green velvet slippers and making splendid sales by phone. Dave's elegant success, glimpsed by Willy when he was a young man unsure of his future, is the ideal, and he cannot understand that times have changed, that personal attractiveness may not have been Dave's only attribute, and that, in any event, Willy's own personality may not fit the image of the popular, ever-cheerful salesman. Here lies the deepest of Willy's tragic mistakes, for he has all his life denied his real skills—farming and carpentry—because they brought none of the prestige and rewards of commerce. What then does the salesman do who must sell himself even before he sells his merchandise? He tries to convince himself that he is the success he is trying to attain—a vicious circle. He also tries to instill the same ideal into his sons. Happy swallows the idea whole and painlessly, since he has his father's charm but none of his self-awareness or self-doubt. Biff tries to reject the idea, but is always caught by the sense of self-justifying worth his father has impressed on him, so he steals to show his father he leads a charmed life and to show himself that the rewards of the world belong to him. And he hates himself for being a failure in his father's eyes and for his inability to find another set of values.

Few modern works so richly combine psychological and philosophical insights. At every point Willy's intensely personal dilemma, the sufferings of a specific, complex person, is also a wide-screen example of the American dream gone sour. Some critics have objected that the story of Willy Loman as a representative American tragedy is exaggerated and not always consistent. This is true if one tries to find a perfect parallel in each of Willy's experiences. However, it is the emotional texture which carries the burden of meaning. For example, few men were abandoned by their fathers under a wagon somewhere in the West, as Willy was, but a part of the American myth is of an open frontier somewhere in the past, and a sense of that lost opportunity makes the constrictions of urban life more desiccating than ever. It is also true that few people completely surrender to the salesman's dream of selling himself, but we all recognize the urgency in Willy's need to be not just liked, but well liked. *Death of a Salesman* may not fit the classical definitions of tragedy, but it is freighted with pity and terror in its depiction of one American life.

In addition to the relevance and power of its theme, *Death of a Salesman* ranks among the finest American plays because of its brilliant structure and style. The basic story is a search for the key moments in the past that can illuminate the tragic dilemmas of the present. In its assumptions about the development of personality and in its underlying pattern of exposition and revelation, the play owes much to Ibsen, a dramatist Miller acknowledges as one of his models. However, instead of unfolding the drama only through realistic dialogue, of which he is a master, Miller devised a complex mixture of present event, selective memory, and hallucination. In *Death of a Salesman,* the playwright drew skillfully on both the naturalistic and the expressionistic traditions of the modern theater and brought a new vitality and richness to the dramatization of contemporary subjects.

The Crucible

by

ARTHUR MILLER (1916–   )

The Characters

Mr. Miller says that "the fate of each character is exactly that of his historical model," though he admits to making some minor changes in such matters as age.

John Proctor—a farmer, in his 30s. A man of independent spirit who would normally prefer to stay out of public matters, he is suspicious of those who crave power or succumb to mob hysteria. He knows himself to be imperfect.

Elizabeth Proctor—his wife. Though she has a great capacity for love, her firm sense of duty and moral rectitude make her cold and unforgiving.

Reverend Samuel Parris—minister of the church in Salem, a harsh preacher constantly preoccupied with damnation; a petty man who measures his prestige in small material advances, suspicious, always suspecting conspiracies.

Betty—his daughter, about 10, a simple, malleable child.

Abigail Williams—his niece and ward, 17, a beautiful, sensual girl chafing at the limits of a Puritan society, keen-witted, and skillful at dissembling.

Thomas and Ann Putnam—the wealthiest couple in the village. He is greedy, vindictive, and feels he does not have the respect he deserves. Mrs. Putnam is jealous and superstitious.

Francis and Rebecca Nurse—an old, highly regarded couple. Rebecca is a warm, motherly woman, honored for her saintliness.

Giles Corey—a farmer, in his 80s, a hard-of-hearing, litigious man, a bit senile, but deeply honest.

Reverend John Hale—minister from Beverly. He is an expert in demonology, a scholar who has never doubted the existence of witches while reading about them in his fascinating books, and whose emotions have never been stirred.

Mary Warren—17, servant to the Proctors, a naïve, fearful girl.

Mercy Lewis and Susanna Walcott—girls involved in the crying out of witches.

Deputy Governor Danforth—presiding at the trials, an intelligent but narrow man, concerned above all about order.

Judge Hathorne—one of the trial judges, unquestioning in his desire to expose and punish the witches.

Tituba—Reverend Parris's Barbados slave.

The Setting

Salem in 1692 is still a small settlement. Its houses and public buildings are simple, sturdy, and unadorned, bespeaking the harshness both of the living conditions and of the Puritan creed.

The Story

Led by Abigail, some of the girls go to the woods with Tituba to dance and conjure up spirits. There they are surprised by Parris, whose daughter is so frightened that she falls into a catatonic coma. Rumors quickly spread through the village that witchcraft is abroad. Parris sends for Reverend Hale, hoping to forestall criticism of his ministery. Ann Putnam, who has lost eight children at birth, is particularly eager to find a sinister explanation. She and her husband press for an immediate investigation. Proctor comes looking for Mary Warren, and is briefly alone with Abigail. She pleads for his love (she was dismissed by John's wife when he confessed to adultery with the girl) and admits the girls were only playing in the woods.

Hale arrives, and though he tries to be precise in his investigations, is quickly drawn into the atmosphere of hysteria. Tituba is called in. Fearing punishment, she quickly confesses to acts of witchcraft. Abigail, realizing that the suspicion may turn on her, joins in accusing some of the town's eccentrics of being witches. The other girls follow her lead.

A week later, there is a full-fledged trial. Proctor is angered by the absense of Mary, who has become a star witness and must attend court every day. Elizabeth tells her husband he must go to the court and tell them of Abigail's admission, but when she discovers that he was alone with Abigail, she interprets his hesitation as proof that he is still in love with the girl. Mary returns, exhausted and frightened, for they have begun sentencing people to execution. She gives Elizabeth a rag doll she made while sitting in the court.

Hale comes to talk to the Proctors, for Elizabeth, like many others, including Rebecca Nurse, has been "somewhat mentioned." He is disturbed by John's poor church attendance and by the farmer's critical attitude toward Parris. He is still there when the court officers come to arrest Elizabeth. They find the rag doll with a needle in its belly, just as Abigail said it would be when she had a terrible attack of pain at dinner and "discovered" a needle in her stomach. John tries to prevent the arrest, but Hale assures him the court will be just. Proctor insists that Mary must go with him to tell the judges that Abigail put the needle into the doll. The girl is terrified.

Proctor brings Mary to the court. She tells Danforth and Hathorne that the girls have all been pretending. Proctor also brings a signed statement from many townspeople declaring their good opinion of Elizabeth, Rebecca, and others. Parris accuses Proctor of wanting to overthrow the court. Danforth tells John that, since Elizabeth is pregnant, she will not be executed for at least a year, but Proctor realizes he cannot stop with merely saving his wife. Hale is beginning to have doubts and speaks up for Proctor, but the judges are adamant in interpreting all opposition or criticism as contempt or rebellion.

The judges ask Mary to pretend for them now as she had done in court. She cannot. The other girls are brought in. Abigail pretends Mary is exercising a spell. In a desperate attempt to discredit Abigail, John admits his adultery with her. Danforth has Elizabeth brought in and asks her if her husband has ever committed the crime of lechery. Unaware of what he has said and hoping to save him, she lies, thus vindicating the girl. Mary realizes the danger to herself if she continues to accuse the others, and turns on John, accusing him of being in league with the devil and having cast a spell on her.

Some months later, the day of execution arrives. Reverend Parris has grown frantic with fear and dimly apprehended guilt. Abigail has stolen his money and run away, and the village is in a state of profound unrest. He pleads with Danforth to postpone the executions of Rebecca Nurse and John Proctor, two of the most respected members of the community. Hale has returned utterly disillusioned, and speaking very much like an atheist. He spends all his time with the prisoners, exhorting them to confess. If they confess they will not be killed. He cannot persuade Danforth that the condemned are innocent. Danforth agrees to let Proctor see his wife and Hale, and he hopes they can extract a confession before sunrise, the time of execution. Danforth is determined to exercise authority. If he weakens now, past executions will be called into question, and there have been rebellious movements in other towns.

Elizabeth tells her husband that Corey is dead, crushed by the great stones piled on his chest to force a statement from him. But he said nothing, thus saving his property for his sons. She is unable to counsel John, for she is torn, as he is, between living with a lie or dying for the truth. Proctor decides that he cannot sacrifice his life for a principle and agrees to confess. When Danforth insists that John must name others he has seen in the devil's company, Proctor balks, insists he can speak only for himself. Reluctantly, Danforth agrees to a confession that mentions no one else, and asks Proctor to sign the confession. John tries to avoid this commitment, then signs it but insists on keeping the paper. Danforth demands that the confession be made public. Recognizing that he is buying his life with public dishonor and disgrace for his family, Proctor savagely destroys the document. With Rebecca, he is led out to the scaffold and hanged. In an agony of grief, Elizabeth knows that her husband has achieved a transcendent nobility.

Critical Opinion

The Crucible was produced in 1953, when Senator Joseph McCarthy's power was at its peak, making sweeping accusations of communism against many people in public life and effectively gagging criticism by generating fear. Miller explicitly states that the play was written to attack McCarthyism by equating it with the hysteria of the Salem witch trials. The parallels he most strongly emphasizes are the power of the accusers, the difficulty of proving innocence, the danger of opposition, and guilt by association. Just as the testimony of ex-communists was often taken as sufficient evidence to damage a person's reputation and chance for employment, so the Salem girls and the frightened defendants gain power by admitting occult practices and fellowship with those they accuse. When Proctor comes to challenge the testimony, he is charged with wanting to overthrow the court, just as critics of McCarthy were accused of being in league with the enemy or at best dupes of communist forces. And throughout the play, as in many of the Senate hearings, simply to be mentioned in some way is tantamount to being accused. Finally, as with Proctor's attempted confession, the surest sign of good faith was to implicate others. (Miller himself was found guilty of contempt of Congress in 1957 for refusing to name people he knew to be communists. The conviction was later reversed.)

The very explicitness of the parallels was to a considerable extent damaging to the play when it first appeared. Even those most sympathetic to Miller's position found it difficult to ignore the differences between witch-hunting and Red-hunting. In the printed text, Miller tries to deal with some of these criticisms in his long, explanatory stage directions, but the parallels are still questionable. Puritan belief in the literal existence of the devil and of witches is not the same as knowledge of the existence of communists, whether Senator McCarthy had correctly identified them or not. To condemn the Puritans for murder in the name of a superstition is not the same as condemning McCarthy for distorting a real danger.

With the passing of McCarthyism, *The Crucible* has become a somewhat different play. It now ranks with Miller's best work, a largely successful attempt to dramatize a moment of American history. Miller's interest in his modern theme, combined with his careful research, kept the play from turning into an exercise in historical reconstruction. A full sense of the hard life of the Puritan settlers, its limitations, and its high standards comes through. The play is also a fascinating study of mass hysteria, and in that more general sense does parallel many contemporary events. Most of all, in John Proctor the author has created one of the few heroes of modern American drama. A blunt, honest man, but neither an exceptionally good nor a complicated one, Proctor grows with the pressure of circumstances. Like most of Miller's heroes, he asks only to preserve the honor of his name, his right to face himself and his children without apology. However, when a society has gone mad, such a simple, reasonable desire makes a man an enemy of the state.

A crucible is a vessel for heating and refining metals, hence, metaphorically, a severe test. Miller sees the witch trials as a crucible in which the Puritan colony tested and eventually rejected a theocratic state. For John Proctor, the trials became his test by fire, burning away all but the finest parts of his spirit.

The Author

There was little about Arthur Miller's youth to indicate the direction his life would take. He grew up in Brooklyn far more interested in football than in his studies. When he graduated from high school with an undistinguished record, he hoped to enter the University of Michigan because of its football team. But 1933 was a bad year for his father's clothing business, as it was for almost everyone, and Miller went to work instead. His job as a shipping clerk lasted for more than two years. During this time, he saved for his college expenses. He gives a vivid picture of that job in *A Memory of Two Mondays* (1955), a one-act play in which the central character's interest in literature grows into his determination to become a writer.

After he entered Michigan, Miller was stimulated and encouraged by Kenneth Rowe, who taught playwriting. Twice he won the Avery Hopwood award for original plays. After graduation, he wrote for the Federal Theatre Project and for radio. Miller first made his mark as a writer with *Situation Normal* (1944), a report on Army camps written in the course of doing research for a documentary film; and with *Focus* (1945), a novel about anti-Semitism. A play, *The Man Who Had All the Luck*, was produced in 1944, but it lasted only four performances.

Miller emerged as a playwright in 1947 with *All My Sons*. Though it is too dependent on coincidences and other transparent devices, this play about an airplane-parts manufacturer who sold defective equipment, and contrived to have another man take the blame, powerfully embodied postwar disillusion. The play also introduced one of Miller's most persistent motifs, the conflict between a father and his two sons.

Two years later, Miller's *Death of a Salesman* (1949) appeared, and four years after that, *The Crucible* (1953). In 1955 a double bill consisting of *A Memory of Two Mondays* and *A View from the Bridge* was coolly received by everyone. For a London production a few months later, however, Miller expanded the latter into a full-length drama. It has since been recognized as one of his most impressive works. The story of a longshoreman destroyed by his love for his niece, *A View from the Bridge* achieves a sense of tragic inevitability.

For almost a decade, Miller had no new plays produced. In 1956 he married Marilyn Monroe, the movie star, and primarily for her he wrote the script of the film *The Misfits* (1961), a story of rootless cowboys and a confused girl, all unable to exist in the competitive commercial world. He was also much in the public eye because of his legal battle over a charge of contempt of Congress, a case he finally won. His marriage ended in divorce in 1962. Miss Monroe committed suicide some months later. All of his confusion, his searching, and his grief during those years took form in *After the Fall* (1963), the drama of a lawyer who confides to the audience his guilt and pain. Much of the play is clearly, embarrassingly autobiographical, and the ending, in which the hero recognizes that all men share in the guilt of their era, seems oversimplified.

The theme of guilt and responsibility reappeared in *Incident at Vichy* (1964). Set in a Nazi detention room in 1942, the play deals with an Austrian nobleman who exchanges papers with a Jewish doctor. The aristocrat acknowledges how much he has been an accessory to evil by failing to oppose it. The motif of father and sons reappeared in *The Price* (1967), a confrontation between two brothers, each justifying the way he behaved after their father's bankruptcy.

In 1950 Arthur Miller adapted Ibsen's *An Enemy of the People*. He not only chose a play about an idealist who finds himself attacked by the greedy, corrupt majority, but he altered it to make the point even more relevant to modern America. In his own plays, the conflict has never been that simple, but the image of a common man transformed into a hero through his dedication to principle is implicit in all his work.

Arthur Miller is a writer of international stature, recognized as a master of theater and a penetrating explorer of contemporary problems. He has successfully used surrealistic and expressionistic techniques, and in *The Price* he has revealed a rich vein of comedy. Miller excels in the creation of solidly realistic scenes in which his characters struggle with profound moral and psychological questions. These crises are always very close to the consciousness of his audience, which recognizes in Miller's plays an immediate and serious relevance which few other modern playwrights approach. Arthur Miller has been in part a critical conscience for his times, but the skill and solidity of his plays, their universal dimensions, carry them beyond the concerns of the moment.

The Member of the Wedding

by

CARSON MCCULLERS (1917–1967)

The Characters

Frankie (Frances) Addams—a gawky, tall, 12-year-old girl, no
  longer a child and not yet an adolescent. She is lonely, restless, curious, and inventive, at odds with herself and the
  world around her.
Mr. Addams—her father, a jeweler. A widower whose wife
  died at Frankie's birth, he works hard and is too busy to
  pay much attention to his daughter.
Jarvis Addams—his son, 21, at present a soldier, a pleasant,
  rather quiet small-town boy.
Janice—his fiancée, 19, a sweet, pretty small-town girl.
Berenice Sadie Brown—the Addams' Negro cook, about 45,
  a calm, maternal woman whose life has given her a deep
  understanding of grief and loneliness.
John Henry West—Frankie's cousin and neighbor, about 7.
  He seems surprisingly adult, but his understanding of the
  world is still that of a child.
T. T. Williams—a friend of Berenice, a polite, quiet Negro of
  about 50.
Honey Camden Brown—Berenice's foster brother, about 20,

a high-strung, hot-tempered young man, resentful of the subservient role he is expected to play.

The Setting

In a small Southern town, the Addams family lives in a large, rambling old house. The kitchen, where Frankie and John Henry spend most of their time with Berenice, is a big, comfortable room. At its center is a table where the cook and the children eat, play cards, or just sit around talking. The walls are decorated with children's drawings. The kitchen opens onto a porch and the backyard. It is August, 1945.

The Story

The summer has been an unhappy one for Frankie. Her best friend has moved away, and the neighborhood girls are older and ignore her. She has cut her hair so short that she looks like a boy, and she worries about growing even taller and becoming a freak. In her loneliness, she spends most of her time in the kitchen listening to Berenice's tales of her four husbands, and dreaming of a glorious future. John Henry is happy to join them, to play cards or to wear the costumes Frankie creates for the plays she performs in the grape arbor.

Frankie's brother, who has just returned from a period of service in Alaska, brings his fiancée, a girl from a neighboring town, to meet his family two days before their wedding. Frankie is enraptured by the beauty and glamour her imagination endows the couple with. She can talk of nothing else. Berenice warmly and half-jokingly reproves Frankie for exaggerating the compliments people pay her; any suggestion that she is attractive or clever immediately becomes, in her mind, a suggestion that she go to Hollywood. Since Jarvis and Janice have such similar names, she decides to change hers to F. Jasmine. When Berenice laughs, Frankie is furious and even more determined to change her life. Suddenly she is inspired. She will leave with Jarvis and Janice after the wedding. She has realized that she has been too solitary, "just an 'I' person," but now she is ready to belong to a "we." Jarvis and Janice, she says, are "the *we* of me."

The next day, possessed by her dream, Frankie buys herself clothes for the wedding, a bright, cheap evening gown and silver shoes. She begins packing, giving away all her toys and costumes to John Henry. Berenice tries to dissuade Frankie from her foolishness, but the girl is adamant. Besides, Berenice has worries of her own. Honey has been smoking marijuana and getting more and more rebellious. Berenice is afraid he will get into trouble. Rapturously describing the exciting life of travel and celebrities she will live with Jarvis and Janice, Frankie is still child enough to crawl into Berenice's lap and join her in singing a spiritual.

At the wedding, held in the living room, Frankie is embarrassed about her clothes and her appearance, and she cannot find a way to tell her brother about going with the newly married couple. When the bride and groom prepare to leave, Frankie tries to go with them. There is a painful scene, and though her sister-in-law invites her for a long visit in the future, Frankie is inconsolable. When her father tries to comfort her, she angrily rushes out with her suitcase, determined to run away. John Henry tells Mr. Addams that the girl has stolen her father's pistol.

Hours later, Frankie comes back, exhausted and subdued. She has realized that her expectations of exotic adventure are foolish. She had contemplated suicide, but quickly changed her mind. Berenice meets her in the yard, where they are joined by Honey. Refused service in a bar, he has killed a white man. Berenice gives him what little money she has but has little hope that he will escape. Frankie wishes him good luck, seeing in him the rebellion and freedom she had dreamed of for herself. She learns that John Henry, whose complaints of a headache they had all been ignoring, is critically ill with meningitis.

In the following weeks, Honey is captured and hangs himself in jail. John Henry dies. Yet, by November, Frankie is in a cheerful mood. She has made a new friend and even begun to get a bit interested in boys. She and her father are moving with the Wests to a new suburb. Frankie promises to visit Berenice, who will not be coming along, but the cook tells the girl that their roads are different now. While Frankie runs out to greet her friends, Berenice softly sings the spiritual they all loved:

I sing because I'm happy,
I sing because I'm free,
For His eye is on the sparrow,
And I know He watches me.

Critical Opinion

The Member of the Wedding is a play which depends a
great deal more on mood than on plot. In the second act, for
example, virtually nothing happens to move the story forward
except that time passes and the wedding approaches. What
does happen is a series of scenes in which Frankie's longings
and fantasies intermingle with Berenice's memories and fears
to create something very close to music. Through much of the
act there is the sound of a piano being tuned in a house nearby, and the unfinished scales, the repeated notes, the bits and
pieces of melody all add to the dreaminess and melancholy, the
disconnected thoughts and the difficulties of communication.
John Henry also adds a special note to the whole, often acting
like an echo, solemnly repeating Frankie's "I never believed
in love" or repeating Berenice's idea that "gray eyes is glass."
Sometimes he cuts through the dreaming with a child's request
to play outside or make cookies.

"The we of me" is the refrain of the play. Everyone, Frankie
feels, can point to a group to which he belongs, and, by belonging, each person is able to define himself. Only she cannot,
for she has no strong family ties, is without friends, and has no
sense of her own identity. Is she a boy or a girl, a child or a
woman, Berenice's charge or confidante or mistress? Does she
merely tolerate John Henry as a little pest or need him to
assure herself that she does have a companion and a responsibility, a reason she cannot be out with the others? At the same
time, Frankie feels stifled, eager to get beyond her town to the
great world, where she can make her mark. The fact that her
brother was stationed in Alaska and plans to live in a town
called Winter Hill entrances her, for cold and snow are signs
of an exotic, different life. All these aspects of confusion and
frustration focus on the wedding, a ritual wherein a "we" is
formed, and Frankie desperately tries to become a member of
the wedding, a part of an intimate group.

Counterpointed in the play is the story of Honey, who also wants to break loose, though he knows all too well what group he belongs to and cannot accept the role of self-effacing black man. After he has killed the white man, he feels exuberant, free, for the act has released the anger and frustration he has felt most of his life, and his suicide again asserts his refusal to cooperate with the dominant white society. Though Honey's problems are racial and social while Frankie's are due to her age and family circumstances, the man and the young girl share a sense of frustration, of deep loneliness. So does Berenice, whose first husband, the only one she really loved, died young; she has tried to make do with the bits and pieces of him she has found in other men.

Although Mrs. McCullers was essentially a novelist, in dramatizing *The Member of the Wedding* she succeeded in improving on her original conception. A number of scenes were cut out, particularly a rather implausible sequence in which Frankie is picked up by a soldier, and the theme and mood were intensified. The author was also extremely fortunate in the director and cast who helped her shape the script. She was particularly lucky in Ethel Waters, who brought to the role of Berenice a depth and complexity which are only hinted at in the novel. A typical American theater story tells of the destruction of a fine idea by the conflicting demands of stars, producers, directors, etc. *The Member of the Wedding* demonstrates how successful a sensitive collaboration can be.

The Author

When Carson Smith left her home town of Columbus, Georgia, to come to New York, she was seventeen, and her destination was the Juilliard School of Music. She was planning a career as a concert pianist, but she lost her tuition money on the subway and had to look for work instead. She went to school at night and wrote whenever she could. Although she dropped the idea of a musical career, music is often an integral part of her stories, and her lyrical, evocative style also suggests her earlier interest. At twenty-three, she published her first novel, *The Heart Is a Lonely Hunter* (1940), to which sensitive readers immediately responded.

The play of *The Member of the Wedding* (1950) was

adapted from the novel published four years earlier. Mrs. McCullers wrote one other play, *The Square Root of Wonderful* (1957), which failed. In 1963 Edward Albee dramatized her novella *The Ballad of the Sad Café* (1951), a strange, grotesque love story, but her delicate, evocative approach was lost in the transition to the stage.

Mrs. McCullers' major novels were all written before she was thirty. *The Heart Is a Lonely Hunter,* like *The Member of the Wedding,* deals with loneliness and frustration. The central character, a deafmute, is the focus for others' dreams and despairs. Those who are attracted to him include a fourteen-year-old girl who might well be Frankie Addams still looking for an identity. *Reflections in a Golden Eye* (1941), set on an Army base, deals with twisted and disappointed love. No matter how ugly or sensational the subject, however, the author imbued all her works with a poetic intensity and a profound sympathy for the unhappy people she dealt with.

Her marriage to Reeves McCullers was an unhappy one. During the latter half of her life Mrs. McCullers was painfully ill. Except for some short stories, her only other important work after the stage version of *The Member of the Wedding* was *Clock Without Hands* (1961), a novel dealing sensitively with racial strife in the South.

Tea and Sympathy

by

ROBERT ANDERSON (1917–   )

The Characters

Bill Reynolds—about 40, master at an exclusive boys' school. A vigorous, athletic man, he is excessively dedicated to the values of manliness, which he defines in simple, locker-room terms. He is completely unsympathetic to any other values.

Laura Reynolds—his wife, in her late 20s. A beautiful, sensitive woman, eager to love someone who needs her.

Tom Lee—18, a gentle, awkward, and lonely boy, interested in music. Though he has spent most of his life in boarding schools and camps, he is naïve and shy.

Herbert Lee—his father, about 40, a businessman. Earnestly concerned that his son should be a "man," he is unable to talk to him.

Al—Tom's roommate, a successful and popular athlete.

Ralph, Steve, Phil, and *Paul*—other boys in Reynolds' house, boisterous, immature, and unaware of the pain they can cause.

David Harris—a young music teacher.

The Setting

A cross section of Reynolds' house at an exclusive boys' school in New England. On one side is the housemaster's study, used as a kind of living room by both Mr. and Mrs. Reynolds and the boys. On the other side is Tom Lee's room. Between is a hallway which the boys use to reach their rooms. The play takes place early in June.

The Story

Laura Reynolds is still unsure about her role as wife and housemother. She had met Bill and married him only a year before while he was on sabbatical in Italy. There she had sensed a loneliness and need to which she had responded, but once back at school he has become totally involved with his job. Even weekends are taken up with mountain climbing with a group of students or other activities which keep him away from home. Left much on her own, Laura is drawn to one of the house residents, Tom Lee, a boy who reminds her of her first husband; they had married at eighteen, and he was killed in World War II very soon afterward. Tom is clearly in love with Laura, but she does not at first realize the intensity of his feelings, and acts maternal.

Tom comes to invite her to the big weekend dance, for which he is a committee member, and she asks him to stay and try on the costume she is making for him. He is to play Lady Teazle in the spring production of *The School for Scandal*. This is the second time he has played a woman's role, and he is somewhat embarrassed about the jokes this produces. Also, the boys have nicknamed him "Grace," after he enthusiastically praised a Grace Moore film. Tom is afraid to mention the play to his father, who is always critical of his son's failure to act masculine. Tom tells Laura about his parents. After their divorce, he had stayed with his mother until he was five, but since then his father has placed him in schools and camps.

Tom returns to his room where he is met by Harris, who hysterically accuses the boy of telling the dean about their going swimming together. Tom denies telling anyone, and is

bewildered when Harris says he will be dismissed. The boys
returning to the house gossip about the latest scandal, that
Harris and Tom had been seen swimming in the nude, and
they strongly suspect that both are homosexuals. Bill Reynolds
is quick to draw the same inference. Laura argues about lack
of evidence, but he will not listen. She is appalled by the
ferocity of his feelings. For Bill, Tom is an "off horse," an
unconventional personality, and therefore immediately suspect
and unwelcome.

Tom's father arrives and confides to Reynolds his concern
about his son. A conversation with Tom, in which the boy for
the first time understands and vehemently denies the accusa-
tion of homosexuality, still leaves the father unhappy. Mr. Lee
suggests a "manlier" haircut, and insists that Tom withdraw
from the school play.

A few days later, Tom's roommate announces his decision
to move in the fall. He realizes this is unjust, but the pressures
on him from the other boys and his father are too strong. Tom
has spent a miserable day being ignored or taunted by his
classmates. Later, he is released from the dance committee. Al
suggests that a visit to Ellie Martin, the town tart, would solve
the problem by demonstrating Tom's masculinity. Laura tries
to get Bill to help, but he is unresponsive. When she suggests
that their marriage is growing colder because Bill draws away,
unwilling to admit any need for love or comforting, he grows
furious and storms out of the house. Laura overhears Tom
make a date with Ellie.

On the evening of the dance, Laura stays in the study,
waiting to catch Tom before he can leave for Ellie's. Bill has
gone off mountain climbing with some boys. Laura invites Tom
in for coffee. She talks to him about herself, asks him more
about his past, teaches him to dance—in every way tries to
keep him with her. He is so entranced that he kisses her and is
immediately, desperately confused. He rushes out, but before
Laura can go to him, Bill and the boys return.

The next afternoon, the gossip is that Tom went to Ellie's
but was unable to go through with it. To the boys, and to Bill
and Herb, this is conclusive evidence of Tom's deviance. Laura
argues that Tom is a sensitive, poetic boy who can understand
sex only when it is united with love. Alone with Bill, Laura
tells him that she knew of Tom's plan and that her "goodness"
prevented her from giving Tom the comfort he needed in his

loneliness, perhaps also finding some comfort for herself. Bill does not understand and wants to postpone the discussion, but Laura says she is leaving. Bill accuses her of failing to understand him, and of being attracted always to boys like her first husband. She is driven to tell him that he persecutes Tom for the weaknesses he fears to recognize in himself. This truth he cannot face, and he leaves.

Laura goes to Tom's room. He is in deepest despair, for he, too, thinks the failure with Ellie represents a lack of manliness. Laura tries to convince him that he is more of a man than her husband, but he cannot follow her logic. After hesitating a moment, Laura locks the door, unbuttons the top of her blouse, and gently offers herself to Tom, asking only that "Years from now . . . when you talk about this . . . you will . . . be kind."

Critical Opinion

> BILL: When the headmaster's wife gave you this teapot, she told you what she tells all the new masters' wives. You have to be an interested bystander . . . all you're supposed to do is every once in a while give the boys a little tea and sympathy.

As Bill and the school administration see it, there must be little or no involvement in the personal lives of the boys. That would become too much of a burden on the wives and would interfere with the boys' growth to manly maturity. *Tea and Sympathy* is a refutation of both claims. Both Laura Reynolds and Tom Lee need more than a coolly impersonal relationship. The Spartan toughness that Bill preaches is not a sure sign of masculinity.

Anderson builds his play carefully with strong contrasts. Tom's love of music, his poetic idealism, his somewhat girlish looks, and his surprising (though carefully accounted for) shyness and innocence are in direct opposition to the muscular heartiness of Bill Reynolds, Mr. Lee, and the other boys. Beneath the surface, there is a different contrast; Bill's masculinity is a facade for an unadmitted but not unrecognized homosexuality, while Tom's gentleness misleads almost everyone, for a time even Tom himself, into doubting his healthy sexuality. The broader theme of the deadening force of conformity grows out of similar roots. For example, Tom's father is more concerned about the country club members' opinions than he is about understanding and helping his boy.

The neatness of the playwright's pattern ultimately works against him. The arrangement is too symmetrical; everything is too thoroughly explained. The characters lack complexity; the moral confrontation is black and white. At every point the cards are stacked in favor of Tom and Laura. *Tea and Sympathy* is similar to Shaw's *Candida* (to which Anderson refers early in the play), in which a sensitive woman gives her love to the man who needs it most. Shaw, in his resolutely unsentimental way, has the heroine settle for her weak husband rather than the resilient poet. What is more important is that Shaw typically uses his story as a frame for a wide-ranging discussion of many issues, while Anderson focuses on his single problem, which he solves melodramatically.

When the play first appeared, its subject matter was fresh and the resolution startling in its explicitness. However, with today's lifting of taboos, the play no longer has as much substance. Unlike *Candida,* which retains much of its intellectual sparkle, *Tea and Sympathy* remains merely a skillful dramatic exercise.

The Author

The world of expensive boys' schools was no mystery to Robert Anderson when he came to write *Tea and Sympathy* (1953). The son of a successful New York businessman, he attended Phillips Exeter Academy, then earned a B.A. and an M.A. from Harvard. As a college undergraduate, he produced his first play, a musical comedy, *Hour Town* (1938), for which he wrote the script, music, and lyrics, and for which he served as director and actor. In the years preceding his immediately successful Broadway debut with *Tea and Sympathy,* he had plays produced at the University of Iowa and at the Arena Stage, Washington, D.C. He has worked for many years as a radio, film, and television writer.

Anderson's plays focus on problems of isolation and loneliness. Like *Tea and Sympathy, All Summer Long* (Washington, 1952; New York, 1954) concerns a lonely adolescent. He builds a retaining wall to prevent flood waters from undermining his family's summerhouse; the eroding waters symbolize the emotional failures within the family. In *Silent Night, Lonely Night* (1959), a man and a woman, both unhappy in their marriages, meet and make love on a Christmas Eve at a New England inn, learning to understand themselves and to return to their families with renewed courage. The theme of isolation is developed further in *I Never Sang for My Father* (1967). The protagonist is a middle-aged man who, when his mother dies, makes a futile attempt to build an emotional bridge to his sarcastic, despotic father.

A major exception to Anderson's preoccupation with such melancholy themes is *You Know I Can't Hear You When the Water's Running* (1966), a group of four short plays. The title comes from the first play, which deals with the casting of an actor in a play where he will be expected to come onto the stage naked to tell his wife he could not hear her while he was under the shower. The other three one-acters deal with domestic problems. Although treated lightly and humorously, the three domestic situations involve the basic human problems of misunderstanding and separation central to all of Anderson's plays.

Home of the Brave

by

ARTHUR LAURENTS (1918–   )

The Characters

Private First Class Peter Coen (Coney)—about 23. He is a
  bright young man with a talent for joking, but he is very
  sensitive to slights and insults he receives as a Jew. He is
  looking for a friend he can trust, but he is suspicious, self-
  conscious, on the defensive.
Finch—his buddy, a little younger, a warmhearted, naïve
  Arizonan.
Technical Sergeant Carl Mingo—27, a calm, self-possessed, intelligent man whom others respect almost instinctively.
Corporal T. J. Everitt (T. J.)—about 35, a successful businessman in civilian life who resents being in the Army and
  having an unimportant rank. He is a bigoted man who never
  understands why he irritates most of the men around him.
Major Robinson—26. He maintains a cold, businesslike attitude to conceal his inexperience.
Captain Harold Bittenger—a psychiatrist, about 43, a sensitive, fatherly man, dedicated to the hurt young men he tries
  to help.

The Setting

The play takes place during World War II at an American Army base in the Pacific and on a small, Japanese-held island.

The Story

Coney is suffering from amnesia and paralysis as a result of a traumatic shock which the doctor cannot fathom. It happened at the end of a dangerous mission, but none of the information Captain Bittenger has gathered explains the soldier's condition. He decides to use narcosynthesis, psychotherapy under sedation that helps the patient relive crucial experiences and release whatever is creating his mental state. As the drug begins to work, Coney is able to remember names and situations. He is rather ambivalent about Finch, first saying he hates him, then talking about him as his buddy, praising him warmly. As Coney remembers, the sequence of past events is reenacted in a flashback.

The Major had called together Coney, Finch, T. J., and Mingo, asking them to volunteer for a hazardous assignment. They will need to spend four days mapping a Japanese-held island in preparation for invasion. The men are reluctant, but realize they must accept or refuse as a group, and no one wants to make the decision. When the Major asks for their answer, they silently turn to Coney. He hesitates but says yes.

Near the end of the fourth day, the map team prepares to leave the island. The work has gone well, but all are tense after the nerve-racking time, always expecting to be detected. T. J. is particularly bad-tempered, and focuses his enmity on Coney, calling him "kike," "lousy Jew bastard," and other insulting names. Finch defends his friend Coney and Mingo manages to stop them from fighting. Coney tries to explain to the others what it was like as a boy being persecuted by anti-Semitic schoolmates.

Suddenly there is a shot. The Americans have been spotted by a sniper. Mingo is shot in the arm, but Coney gets the sniper. Finch must go into the jungle with a knife to make sure the enemy is dead. He returns retching. When they prepare to leave, he cannot find the map case. Coney stays with him to look, and both become panicky with fear. They insult each other, and Finch begins to call Coney a "lousy yellow Jew," but catches himself before the last word, changing it to "jerk." Coney is hurt and angry. Just then, Finch spots the case, and as he picks it up is shot in the belly and falls. Coney rushes to him, but Finch insists the other man must take the case and go to join the rest of the party. Reluctantly, Coney leaves his friend.

Near the beach, the Major, T. J., Mingo (his arm badly hurt), and Coney wait for sunset so they can get out the hidden canoes they will row out to a seaplane expected after dark. Coney is in despair about abandoning Finch, but the Major and Mingo both argue that he did the right thing, since the mission had to be completed. They hear Finch screaming and realize the Japanese soldiers are torturing him in an effort to flush out his comrades. Coney is ready to rush to him, but the others convince him that would only mean death to all. When the screams stop, they go to get the boats ready. Coney stays to guard their gear.

Finch, in frightful pain, comes crawling out of the jungle. Coney tries to comfort him, but his friend dies in his arms. His first reaction is to thrust the body from him brutally. Then he begins cradling it as he might a child. When the Japanese soldiers begin shouting threats from the darkness, Coney frantically begins digging a grave. Mingo and the Major return and try to get him to come with them, but he finds he cannot walk. They must drag him to safety.

In the hospital, Coney finally remembers everything but is still paralyzed. The doctor explains that the soldier had lost the use of his legs because subconsciously he did not want to abandon his friend as he thought he had done before. Coney accepts the explanation, but cannot walk until the doctor angers and challenges him by calling him a "lousy, yellow Jew bastard."

Two weeks later, Coney is considerably improved but still in a highly depressed state. The news that the invasion for which they worked was a success does not move him. In another session with the doctor, the soldier recognizes that his guilt comes from his feeling of gladness when Finch was shot just when his friend was about to insult him. The doctor insists that all soldiers have this initial feeling of joy when a buddy is shot and they have survived. Coney cannot accept the idea that his reaction was a normal one.

Mingo, who has had his right arm amputated, and Coney visit the Major just before their return to the States. T. J. is packing up, because the company is moving. Coney and Mingo are drawn together by their dislike of the corporal, whose taunts upset Coney. To calm the younger man, Mingo tells about his own experiences, mentioning in one of his stories how often he had felt glad when others got shot. Coney realizes the doctor was right, that he is not so different from others.

Critical Opinion

The title, *Home of the Brave,* is ironic in two ways. The phrase from "The Star-Spangled Banner" calls attention to the failure of Americans to live up to their democratic principles. Not only is anti-Semitism out of keeping with the ideals of American life, but in the Second World War the Nazi extermination of the Jews was an issue. Laurents never refers to Nazis but the parallels between German and American anti-Semitism are amply clear. In T. J. he has embodied the Rotarian bigot, envious, looking for a scapegoat to blame for his failures—in short, the ordinary, middle-class citizen who can all too easily become the tool of demagoguery.

The second irony in the title lies in the theme of bravery. Laurents presents the idea that heroism involves some kind of cowardice. Mingo's wife writes poetry, and when Mingo tries to take Coney's mind off Finch's screams, he recites one of her poems. It ends:

> And frightened, we are everyone.
> Someone must take a stand.
> Coward, take my coward's hand.

At the end, the awareness of a common element of cowardice brings Coney and Mingo together, providing each with reassurance and hope.

Coming so soon after the end of the war, *Home of the Brave* was one of the earliest reactions to the inflated ideas of patriotism and heroism that are part of all wars. Also, by building his play around psychiatry and narcosynthesis, Laurents dramatized some other unfamiliar aspects of war, particularly the heavy psychological damage so often ignored in flag-waving films and plays. These elements combined to give the play its tremendous impact. Time has since weakened some of its thrust, but its relevance remains.

The Author

Home of the Brave (1945) was Arthur Laurents' first play, and like so many first works it drew on the author's own background. The son of a lawyer and a schoolteacher, Laurents grew up in Brooklyn, where he no doubt experienced the kind of anti-Semitic taunts Coney describes in the play. He served in the U.S. Army from 1940 to 1945, and his play was begun while he was still in the service.

Laurents has shown in all his plays a serious concern with contemporary life, particularly with the loneliness and inhibitions of nice but relatively unimportant people. *The Time of the Cuckoo* (1952) is about an American schoolteacher, no longer young, who comes to Venice on a holiday, secretly hoping for a glamorous romance. However, her inhibitions and puritanism prevent her from accepting the opportunity when it arises. In *A Clearing in the Woods* (1957), through a series of fantasies and memories, his heroine comes to terms with herself and her imperfect world. *Invitation to a March* (1960) centers on a happy-go-lucky noncomformist who helps literally to awaken a girl whose reaction to her approaching marriage with a stuffy businessman is sleepiness.

In 1957 Laurents wrote the book for the musical *West Side Story*, changing Romeo and Juliet into residents of a Manhattan slum. In many ways, this marked his most successful dramatization of social issues since his first play. On the other hand, *Gypsy* (1959), a musical based on the life of Gypsy Rose Lee, was a far more conventional work. *Anyone Can Whistle* (1964), written with Stephen Sondheim, was an unsuccessful attempt to use a topical review as a medium for social criticism. *Hallelujah, Baby!* (1967) traced the stereotypes of the Negro entertainer from the turn of the century to the present.

Though he chooses very topical subjects, Laurents often

tends to skirt their deeper levels and end with an unwarranted optimism. Only *Home of the Brave, The Time of the Cuckoo,* and *West Side Story* avoid this pitfall and provide the sense of a problem confronted directly.

The Tenth Man

by

PADDY CHAYEFSKY (1923–   )

The Characters

Arthur Landau—an attorney, in his middle 30s. Intelligent and sensitive, he resists any involvement with others, convinced that life is meaningless.

Members of the congregation:
  Hirschman, the Cabalist—in his 70s, a pious Hasid (member of the most mystical Judaic sect) devoted to studying the occult.
  Bleyer, the sexton—about 50, the synagogue custodian.
  Schlissel—in his early 70s. A Marxist and an atheist, he dismisses religious ideas though he is one of the most regular participants in the services.
  Zitorsky—about the same age, nervous and gossipy.
  Alper—about the same age, intelligent, and an excellent rationalizer whenever a difficult situation arises.
  Foreman—about the same age, terrified of trouble, but determined to save his granddaughter.
  Harris—in his 80s, a frighteningly feeble man.
Evelyn Foreman—18, Foreman's granddaughter. She is a schizophrenic who has spent many years in mental in-

stitutions, but when she is in touch with reality, she is a
sweet, ingenuous girl, alert and responsive to her surroundings.

The Rabbi—in his early 30s, more a social director and public-
relations man than a religious leader.

The Setting

Congregation Atereth-Tifereth Yisroel in Mineola, Long
Island, is housed in a converted store. The synagogue section
has some folding chairs and a simple platform-altar. The rabbi's office, created by a rough partition, is crowded with an
old desk and some worn chairs. It is a place where only the
old men, now retired and living uneasily with their children
in the suburbs, gather faithfully each morning, more in search
of companionship than of religion.

The Story

On this bitterly cold morning, the few loyal worshipers begin to arrive at six-thirty. They find that Hirschman has spent
the night in prayer, and Schlissel mocks what he considers
their pietistic foolishness. The sexton begins his usual phoning
in an attempt to round up enough men to form the minimum
of ten (a *minyan*) needed for services. This morning it will
be more difficult than usual because Foreman is not expected;
today his granddaughter will be sent back to the mental institution, perhaps permanently. After exhausting his list of
possibilities, the sexton leaves to see if he can find someone on
the street.

Foreman rushes in, bringing his granddaughter with him.
She has spoken to him in a strange voice, referring to herself
as Hannah Luchinsky, a girl he had seduced in Russia when
he was a young man. Convinced that she is possessed by a
dybbuk (a soul in limbo), he has brought her to the synagogue
for exorcism. The other men, with the exception of Schlissel,
are quickly persuaded that Foreman is right when the girl
behaves with them as her grandfather described. They decide
a wonder-working Hasidic rabbi is needed, finally selecting

the Korpotchniker Rabbi, who lives in the Williamsburg section of Brooklyn. Hirschman, a cousin of the rabbi, phones and makes an appointment for Foreman. They hide the girl in the office while Foreman leaves for his meeting.

Bleyer returns with Arthur Landau, whom he has found wandering in the streets, sobering up from a long drinking bout. Scowling and embarrassed, Arthur agrees to stay the fifteen minutes for the service, though he knows no Hebrew and none of the rites. He asks if he may first make a phone call, and in the rabbi's office he calls his psychiatrist to arrange for an appointment, explaining that he has been drinking and wandering about for three days. The girl speaks to him with her dybbuk voice, which startles but also intrigues him. When one of the other men decides to take her home, she screams. The men explain to Arthur who she is. Their rabbi arrives, and they hurriedly begin the service, so that he cannot go to his office.

During the reading of the Torah, the midpoint in the service, the girl begins talking to Arthur, quite rationally. She explains her mental condition, a strong tendency to hallucinate unless firmly recalled to reality, and tells how much she dreads returning to the institution. Arthur also begins to talk of his past, particularly his many attempts at suicide. Evelyn is convinced he is a mystic with a great capacity for understanding and helping others, and she promises to give him a book that will explain his true personality. When he returns to participate in the service, she slips out and leaves.

Foreman returns in a panic. He has not been able to find the railroad station. Schlissel leaves with him to find the way. It is only after they are gone and Arthur tries to tell the rabbi about the girl that they discover she is gone. Reluctant to get more deeply involved, they hesitate to call either her father or the police, and are relieved when she returns. She had only gone home to get the book she promised. Arthur, who had left to go and see his analyst, also returns, to assure himself that the girl is all right. She clings to him, saying she loves him.

Several hours pass while they wait for Foreman to return. Hirschman tells them of a wonderful dream in which his father appeared to him, explaining that the son's spirit is cleansed. The older men join him in an exultant dance to celebrate. Suddenly the girl also begins a dance, but her movements are fiercely lascivious, ending in a faint. The cabalist warns that she will die if the dybbuk is not immediately exorcised, while Arthur insists she must be taken home. A call to her family, however, gets no answer, and before Arthur can do more, Foreman and Schlissel return, exhausted and unsuccessful. They never made the right connections, and have been riding trains and subways for hours without getting to Williamsburg. All agree that Hirschman will have to perform the exorcism.

The search for ten men begins once more. While they wait, Arthur and the girl talk. He has called his psychiatrist, who suggests that the exorcism may well provide excellent shock therapy. Evelyn, when not in the grip of the Hannah Luchinsky personality, tells the young man that he is also possessed by some kind of dybbuk, which prevents him from loving. She insists they must marry, and she will save him from his suicidal despair. He violently objects, saying that love is a fantasy and a delusion.

After gathering only nine men, the congregation decides to proceed. As they begin, however, a policeman enters in search of Evelyn. He turns out to be Jewish, and they enveigle him into staying as the tenth man to complete the *minyan*.

The ceremony of exorcism is solemn, but the girl remains unmoved. At the climax, it is Arthur who is suddenly struck by some inexplicable force, and he screams and falls into a faint. Alper calls out that they have exorcised the wrong dybbuk. They revive the young man, who awakes with a sense of rebirth, with a hunger for life. Vitalized by his experience, he announces that he will take the girl with him, love and cherish her, help her to fight her dybbuk. Briskly he rushes Foreman and the girl off to get her father's consent.

Critical Opinion

The Tenth Man derives from Salomon Ansky's play *The Dybbuk* (1914), which is set in a Hasidic Polish community where the cabala and tales of wandering, unhoused spirits were taken literally. Ansky's story ends tragically, with the death of the maiden possessed by the spirit of the man who had loved her in vain. In introducing elements of this earlier tale into a play that otherwise follows the pattern of prosaic realism, Paddy Chayefsky took a considerable risk. His problem was very similar to that of Graham Greene in such a play as *The Potting Shed,* but it was even more difficult because the occult and miraculous are relatively unimportant in contemporary Judaism. Also, Chayefsky wrote not as a pious Hasid but as a skeptical modern man for whom the notion of the dybbuk falls somewhere between a very faint possibility and a provocative metaphor. Therefore, he scrupulously provided a rational psychological explanation for the key events without entirely closing the route to an alternative explanation. Finally, and disappointingly, Chayefsky simplistically reduced all the problems in the play to an inability to love, and sentimentally brushed aside the deeper religious questions he had raised.

There is ground for arguing, as many critics have, that the author has done little more than hint at religious questions while actually he was interested only in the sensational, theatrical possibilities of his subject. He strains the limits of coincidence to bring together the disparate believers and nonbelievers who constitute the cast, and he resorts to ingenious manipulation of plot to keep the action moving. (The most obvious example is Foreman's repeated failure to reach the wonder-working rabbi.)

Despite these weaknesses, *The Tenth Man* is one of Chayefsky's best works. His greatest talent has always been the creation of solid, real, believable characters. They make the unlikely plots seem almost credible.

Even more important is the skill with which Chayefsky develops the theatrical elements of his play. The dance sequence beginning with the old men celebrating Hirschman's beatific dream and ending with Evelyn's frenzied, Gypsy-like movements is very powerful. The exorcism ceremony in the third act is overwhelming.

Nowhere is Chayefsky's skill more apparent than in his creation of Arthur and Evelyn. These are far more complex characters than the author had ever drawn before. In his earlier plays, such as *Marty* or *The Middle of the Night,* simple, half-articulate people were his heroes, and they spoke in banalities carefully selected to suggest the characters' hidden feelings. However, in *The Tenth Man* the cynical alcoholic and the sensitive girl wavering between two worlds achieve a poetic intensity as each discovers something of his own need and reaches out to the other to offer and to ask for help.

The Author

Paddy Chayefsky was born in New York City and graduated from De Witt Clinton High School and the City College of New York. In the Army during World War II, he wrote a musical, *To T. O. for Love,* and worked with Garson Kanin on the documentary film *The True Glory.* After the war, he began writing for radio and television. He rapidly became one of the most prominent television dramatists during the early fifties and played an important role in the development of a school of video drama.

Chayefsky's first important TV play was *Marty* (1953), the story of a self-conscious, unattractive butcher trying to find romance. The first television script to be made into a film, it won the Academy Award (1955). Other successful video plays were *The Bachelor Party* (1953) and *The Catered Affair* (1955), both expanded into successful films, and *The Middle of the Night* (1954; 1956), first converted into a popular Broadway play, then into a film. In all of these early works, the author dealt with domestic events in middle-class life, the kind of subject matter that is ideally adapted to the special physical and time limitations of television production. In his first original screenplay, *The Goddess* (1958), he explored a more complex subject, the contrast between the public and private life of a movie star.

The Tenth Man (1959), the author's first play written specifically for the theater, had a much greater range. Two years later, he produced *Gideon* (1961), an even more ambitious work. Like Archibald MacLeish's *J. B., Gideon* deals with man's struggle to understand his God. A simple farmer, Gideon is chosen by God to lead the Israelites, but he refuses to grant God unquestioning obedience or undeserved love. At the end, Chayefsky asserts man's independent and superior morality.

The Passion of Joseph D (1964) was Chayefsky's attempt to present the story of the Russian Revolution and of Stalin's seizure of power after Lenin's death. He used an episodic structure, combining a wide variety of styles, somewhat in the fashion of Brecht. However, the play lacks a clear point of view or a unifying theme.

The Latent Heterosexual (1968) is a satirical comedy about sexual deviation, income-tax evasion, and other contemporary subjects.

The Zoo Story

by

EDWARD ALBEE (1928–   )

The Characters

Peter—in his early 40s, an executive of a small textbook-pub-
lishing company. He is a polite, amiable, unadventurous
man who considers himself knowledgeable and sophisticated
but has been sheltered from the uglier side of life.

Jerry—in his late 30s, carelessly dressed and physically slack.
He is nervous and compulsively talkative but sharply aware
of his failure to say what he means. Desperately reaching
out for understanding, he still uses irony and insult defen-
sively.

The Setting

It is a pleasant Sunday afternoon in a secluded section of
Central Park.

The Story

Peter has come to this quiet section of the park to read, his favorite pastime for a mild afternoon. Jerry enters and announces he has just been to the zoo. Interrupted in his reading but always the gentleman, Peter helps Jerry to determine that he has been walking "northerly" from the zoo. Jerry suggests they talk, and Peter somewhat reluctantly agrees. Jerry holds him with the promise of interesting details about something that happened at the zoo.

Under Jerry's questioning, Peter explains that he is married, has two daughters, two cats, and two parakeets. He is quick to defend himself when Jerry suggests that his household lacks manhood, but Peter then sadly agrees that he had wanted a son. Jerry keeps pressing for information, explaining that he rarely gets to talk with anyone. Peter gives Jerry his address on the East Side, his occupation, and his comfortable income. He thinks Jerry is a bohemian when the younger man says he walked up Fifth Avenue from Washington Square.

Jerry angrily rejects Peter's simple categorizing of people according to where he believes they live. Instead, he tells of his life as a roomer in a shabby brownstone on the West Side. His fellow tenants include a Negro transvestite, a poor Puerto Rican family, and a woman who cries behind her closed door. His parents, alcoholic and irresponsible, died when he was young, and he now lives without ties to anyone. To explain his difficulty in forming meaningful relationships, he tells how he dealt with his landlady's dog. The old, sickly beast had always tried to bite Jerry. To win the dog's affection, Jerry bought it hamburgers, which the dog loved, but when he finished eating them, he promptly tried once more to bite him. Determined to force a change, Jerry tried to poison the dog, mixing rat poison with the meat. After a severe illness, the dog recovered, and now both man and dog carefully ignore each other. Jerry is tormented by this failure to achieve a link with another being, wondering whether the dog's urge to bite him had not been a kind of love which he had destroyed. Somehow, this had led to his visit to the zoo, to understand how animals and men can exist with each other.

Almost hypnotized by Jerry's storytelling, Peter is left bewildered by the ending of the narrative and by Jerry's abrupt shift to irony. The younger man wryly agrees that they live in different worlds, Peter the conservative married man, Jerry a "permanent transient." Suddenly, Jerry turns playful, joking and tickling Peter, then once more announces that he will tell what happened at the zoo. After each sentence or two, he angrily demands that Peter move over, until the older man is crowded onto an edge of the bench.

Peter becomes angrily possessive. He even calls for the police, but there are none around. Jerry demands that he fight for his honor, defending the bench. When they face each other, Jerry produces a knife, then tosses it at Peter's feet, insisting that the older man pick it up. He insults Peter, slaps him, finally goads him into taking the knife and holding it out in self-defense. With a sigh of resignation, Jerry throws himself forward, impaling himself on the knife.

Staggering to the bench, Jerry explains that this is what happened at the zoo. Peter can only repeat "Oh, my God!" over and over, while Jerry instructs him to take his book and leave the scene. Jerry himself wipes the fingerprints from the knife handle, then dies murmuring, "Oh . . . my . . . God."

Critical Opinion

The Zoo Story (1958) was Albee's first play, written swiftly in a burst of inspiration and enthusiasm, and it remains the author's most fully achieved work. In his other plays, he has gone on to more complex subjects and more demanding forms, but in *The Zoo Story* much of the power derives from its simple structure and thrust. Instead of an elaborate plot, Albee found a dramatic metaphor that could carry a heavy burden of emotion and intellectual suggestion without becoming a one-dimensional allegory or symbolic exercise.

The meeting between Jerry and Peter operates on many levels. On the most realistic plane, the two represent socio-economic poles, the successful, settled family man living comfortably on the East Side as opposed to the drifter from the West Side. Central Park acts as a buffer, shielding the secure from the poor and stateless. Until this confrontation, Peter's middle-class world is logical and predictable; Jerry's world is chaotic. The two also represent an emotional contrast; Peter is content with the vicarious, civilized pleasures of reading, while Jerry demands a deeper, immediate experience. Driving Peter to irrational anger, Jerry uncovers the visceral response that makes the two men one.

From another point of view, Jerry seems to have a mission: to awaken Peter to a great truth, though the prophet must, indeed wants to, destroy himself in the process. By the end of the play, the religious overtones have become very obvious, strongly suggesting parallels to Jesus and a reluctant disciple.

There are other themes and patterns in the play, ranging from Jerry's assertion that he is crazy to the many animal images and references. There are also frequent indications of Albee's misogyny and, as in *Who's Afraid of Virginia Woolf?*, his concern about sterility. No one interpretation completely covers the play, but all interpretations consistently point to the acrid sense of loneliness and broken communication which give the play its unifying tone. In a mysterious, only partially explained confrontation between two very different men, Albee evokes an awareness of the many polarities in our society, and provides a disturbing insight into the complexities and difficulties of human relationships.

Who's Afraid of Virginia Woolf?

by

EDWARD ALBEE (1928–   )

The Characters

Martha—52, daughter of the president of New Carthage College. Healthy and full-bodied, she looks younger than she is and radiates considerable sexual appeal. Her coarse, boisterous, often savage manner conceals pain and fear.

George—46, her husband, a member of the History Department. On the surface a faded, unassertive, donnish type, he can be sharply sardonic and even brutal.

Nick—30, a new member of the Biology Department. Good-looking, athletic, and polite, he is ambitious and not above making considerable compromises to get ahead.

Honey—26, his wife. She is blonde, thin, rather plain. During most of the play brandy makes her silly, but she is not very perceptive even at her best.

The Setting

New Carthage College is a small New England school. George and Martha live in a large old house on campus. Their living room is comfortably furnished, but Martha is not a very good housekeeper.

The action of the play covers about three hours, from 2:00 to 5:00 A.M. of a morning early in September.

The Story

George and Martha return from one of her father's annual parties welcoming new faculty members. Both are quite drunk, and Martha is in a surly mood. As usual, her husband has let her down, because he just sat around talking instead of being a sparkling center of attention. When George tries to go to bed, she tells him they are expecting guests, a young couple her father has suggested they be particularly nice to. They are quarreling and shouting obscenities when Nick and Honey arrive.

The young couple do not know how to react in the supercharged atmosphere but they try to joke about their hosts' rudeness. As Martha and Honey go out, George warns his wife not to talk about a certain, unspecified subject. George attacks Nick as a biologist who wants to control human heredity and as an opportunist who no doubt plans to move up in the academic hierarchy. He sardonically presents himself as a failure, only a member of his department, not its head.

When the women return, Martha begins alternately insulting her husband and flirting with Nick. George is furious because Martha has mentioned their son to Honey. Everyone keeps drinking, and Nick joins in the sport of mocking George, who responds to most sallies with jokes or obscure threats. He adds the information that their son is expected home the next day for his twenty-first birthday. Martha gets angrier and tells of marrying George because she thought he might be the next college president, but instead he turned out to be a "a great . . . big . . . fat . . . *flop!*" Before George can respond, Honey rushes to the bathroom to vomit.

Martha goes out to make coffee for the girl. Nick is angered but fascinated by the show his hosts are putting on. Embarrassed by his wife's sickness and general silliness, he admits that he married her because he thought she was pregnant. It was, however, an hysterical pregnancy and they have no children. He also acknowledges George's guess that the girl had money. George shares confidences with Nick, telling of a high-school friend who accidentally shot his mother and then later killed his father in a freak automobile crash. Relaxed and convinced that George is just a talker, Nick admits his ambition to get power even if it means committing adultery with influential faculty wives, offering to start with Martha. George jollies him along.

With Honey somewhat sobered up, Martha returns to the attack. She tells stories about George as an inept father, of his attempt to publish a novel. The plot is identical with the story George told about his friend. Martha's father had stopped George from publishing the book, though the author had defended the story as autobiographical. George is so incensed that he starts to strangle his wife, but Nick stops him.

Recovering his composure, George announces that the game of Humiliate the Host is over. How about playing Hump the Hostess next? No, save that for later. Instead, he will play Get the Guests, and he summarizes the plot of his next novel, the story of Nick and Honey's marriage. Honey is furious because Nick has revealed their secret, and they go out of the room quarreling. Martha and George decide that it is time for total war between them. She claims that she is only providing the kind of pain he really wants, and that, anyway, at the party she had felt a loss of any affection she ever had for him. When Nick returns, Martha sets about trying to seduce him, while George pretends utter indifference. She and Nick go up to the bedroom. Honey wanders in in a state of nightmarish hysteria, shouting that she does not want children, does not want the pain of pregnancy and childbirth. George realizes she has been aborting her pregnancies. This suggests to him a plan for his revenge. He tells Honey that a telegram has come telling of his son's death.

In bed with Martha, Nick is impotent. She taunts him, ordering him about like a houseboy, telling him that only her husband has ever satisfied her both sexually and emotionally. George arrives with snapdragons from the college greenhouse. At first he playfully throws them at his wife, then asks her to tell about their son. As she talks about maternal reminiscences, George quietly recites a Latin requiem. He solemnly announces the death of the boy. Martha is enraged, insisting George cannot kill their child. Nick suddenly realizes that the son is imaginary. George admits that they invented the boy to talk and dream about when they discovered they could not have children.

The young couple leave. Martha and George talk quietly. He explains that Martha had broken the injunction never to mention their child to strangers, and, anyway, it was time to end the game. He tries to comfort his wife in her profound grief.

Critical Opinion

Albee's play is like a long psychiatric analysis in which layer after layer of everyone's disguise is stripped away in the search for a central, aching truth. "We all peel labels," George says late in the play.

Act I is subtitled "Fun and Games," and throughout the play Martha and George refer to games. The term encompasses all the stratagems they use to mask their true feelings and to avoid facing their hatreds and terrors. The tone is set at the very beginning, when Martha looks at the living room, says, "What a dump!," and immediately switches to an imitation of Bette Davis in a movie delivering the same line. The skill with which the couple convert their antagonism and aggression into jokes and role-playing is one reason the play is so immensely funny even though the overall effect is serious, even depressing. Even when they are telling the truth, they may quickly change directions and indicate to Nick and Honey that perhaps that truth has been an illusion or a lie. They can even abruptly become collaborators attacking the young couple. Their struggle to destroy each other is so obvious that Nick occasionally joins in the sport, but what is always clear is that the real point is not on the surface.

The core motif of the play is sterility. The most elaborate of all the games is the pretense of parenthood, and the fullest demonstration of the sadomasochism at the heart of this marriage appears in the destruction of that pretense. The destruction of the illusion is also the first step toward some salvation for George and Martha. At the end of the play, George and Martha, all passion spent, seem ready to move in a new but as yet undefined direction. Albee significantly subtitles Act II "Walpurgisnacht," the wild gathering of the witches, the next stage beyond mere games, and Act III, "The Exorcism," the driving out of the evil spirits.

The plot of the play raises a number of thorny questions. Can the conscious invention of a child carry the emotional weight which the playwright claims? The play does not deal with the exposing of an illusion, an idea mistakenly believed to be true; instead, we are asked to accept the notion that a deliberate fiction can have the same effect. Furthermore, are not the young couple too convenient? Honey's deliberate sterility is perfectly counterpointed to Martha's frustrated maternity, and Nick is endlessly cooperative in playing whatever role is thrust upon him. Most seriously, his confession about the circumstances of his marriage is unclearly motivated. Why should he, in this house of dragons, open himself to attack? Albee uses drunkenness as an all-purpose explanation throughout the play, but this is much too simplistic.

The play survives these weaknesses because of its overwhelming emotional thrust. The story itself is, in fact, the least vital part of the work. Albee uses the stage as an arena for a struggle between his characters, who are clever and articulate but desperately unhappy and terrified of losing the bits and pieces of power that give them a sense of their own importance. The experience of that struggle, during which each character is forced to come to terms with his motives and drives, is what gives the play its extraordinary power and immediacy.

The Author

Adopted son of Reed Albee, the heir to a theater fortune, Edward Albee, until he was twenty, lived in surroundings of great wealth or rebelliously attended expensive private schools. The family was dominated by his mother, a woman who alienated her son by her harshness. In 1948, after a bitter quarrel, Albee left home for good. For most of the next decade, he worked at a number of jobs while he tried to become a writer. *The Zoo Story* was first produced in Berlin in 1959 (after being rejected by numerous American producers). It was presented in New York the following year. Albee won immediate recognition as an important new voice in the contemporary drama.

Following the success of *The Zoo Story,* Albee had a number of other short works produced Off Broadway. *The Death of Bessie Smith* (1960) uses the death of the Negro blues singer as a background for the study of a savage, destructive Southern nurse, who embodies not only the bigotry of her society but the fury of a frustrated woman. *The Sandbox* (1960) and *The American Dream* (1961) are consciously absurdist plays. The latter is concerned with Mommy and Daddy ordering a new son to replace the adopted one Mommy had dismembered. The boy who arrives is a gloriously handsome athlete with no emotions, morals, or real virility—Albee's view of what American mothers dream of.

Who's Afraid of Virginia Woolf? (1962) was Albee's first full-length play and his first phenomenally successful Broadway production. Success has not, however, stopped him from experimenting with new materials and techniques. He has adapted two unusual novels—Carson McCullers' *The Ballad of the Sad Café* (1963) and James Purdy's *Malcolm* (1966). In *Tiny Alice* (1964) he indulged his taste for mystery and poetic writing, but under the layers of pseudoreligious symbolism, the issue is still the sensitive man sacrificed to the will of the emasculating woman. *A Delicate Balance* (1966) examines the irony of a situation where friends may remain friends and families may retain their unity so long as no great demands are made on personal relationships. Yet another adaptation, *Everything in the Garden* (1967), from a play by Giles Cooper, attacks American materialism by presenting well-to-do suburbanites as prostitutes. *Box-Mao-Box* (1968) experiments with such matters as an empty stage, language detached from story or consecutive argument, and deliberate repetitions.

Although none of Albee's more recent works succeeded as fully as did *The Zoo Story* and *Who's Afraid of Virginia Woolf?*, he remains one of the most important playwrights in contemporary America. He has explored a great variety of subjects, and he has been strikingly inventive in his experiments with form. His main concerns, however, have not changed. Complacency about human suffering, the destructive passion to dominate, loneliness, and the difficulties of communication—these are the themes he continues to dramatize. The picture he paints of marriage, with hypocrisy only thinly concealing the war between the sexes, and of society, with its dismal lack of understanding among people, owes much to such predecessors as August Strindberg and Tennessee Williams. Albee's distinctive contributions are abrasive dialogue, bitterly witty comedy, and the remarkably skillful use of one of drama's most fundamental elements, the battle of wits.

The Connection

by

JACK GELBER (1932–   )

The Characters

Jim Dunn—the producer. Worried and eager to make a success, he pretends to an optimism he does not feel, and keeps nervously explaining what the play is about.

Jaybird—the author, intelligent, tense, self-deprecating.

The addicts (age and color are determined in production):

   Leach—the action takes place in his apartment. He is a fastidious person, worried about such things as matches on the floor. He tends to be a whiner.

   Solly—well-educated, perceptive, and cynical.

   Sam—illiterate and garrulous.

   Ernie—an unemployed musician, always claiming that he has a job waiting for him.

   Cowboy—the connection, the man who brings the heroin. His nickname indicates the way he dresses and the role he assumes.

Two photographers—one lively, the other cloddish.

Sister Salvation—an elderly Salvation Army sister, pious and naïve.

Four jazz musicians—they play intermittently during the play; at other times they doze.

The Setting

Leach's room is shabby, with some dilapidated furniture, much of it homemade.

The Story

Jim explains to the audience that a group of addicts has been assembled to improvise along lines prepared by Jaybird. The musicians are to provide authentic jazz as a background. Jaybird is angered by Jim's determination to explain everything and to add novel touches for effect. When the action begins, it is almost immediately interrupted by the arrival of two photographers, hired by Jim to make a movie as the play progresses.

Leach cuts up a pineapple and tries to get the others to eat. However, their only concern is the arrival of Cowboy and Leonard the Locomotive, who are to bring a supply of heroin. As they wait, they complain about Leach, who gets his supply by providing them with a meeting place. Jaybird interrupts to insist that they stick to what he had planned, but they ignore him. To the photographers they explain that they know nothing of an international dope ring; they care only about the man who provides their supply. At times, Solly philosophizes or Sam provides rambling reminiscences. Ernie toots through his mouthpiece and talks about the music he should be playing. Sometimes the musicians play for five minutes or so while the junkies doze, look out the window, or merely stare into space. Through binoculars, Solly finally sees Cowboy approaching with a Salvation sister. Jim interrupts to tell the audience that some girls have been invited, and promises that the second half will be more interesting.

After intermission, the addicts and the musicians enter the toilet one at a time to get their "fix" from Cowboy. The others explain to Sister Salvation that Cowboy is using the bath for baptisms. Cowboy tells them that he and Leonard the Locomotive had met the woman near the police station and had been tremendously impressed with her preaching. Later he explains that he had brought her along to fool the police, who had followed Leonard instead. Sister Salvation is sure they are not telling her the truth, but cannot figure out what is going on. One of the photographers asks if he can also have a dose of heroin, and the addicts persuade Jaybird to try, too, so he can really understand them.

When they have finished taking their shots of heroin, Sister goes into the bathroom and discovers many empty wine bottles. Convinced that she has uncovered the secret the men have been concealing, she delivers an impassioned temperance lecture and leaves.

The men begin to respond to the narcotic. Some fall asleep or talk in a garbled fashion. Jaybird becomes violently nauseated and then euphoric. Leach complains that the stuff is having no effect on him. A man from the audience insists that Sam tell a story, and he tells a long, confused tale about outsmarting the police.

Leach demands more heroin, and Cowboy gives him another packet. All the men realize that Leach has taken an overdose. The musicians and Ernie leave quickly. The rest watch Leach in his coma and talk about addiction. Jim and Jaybird discuss how to end the play. Neither as addicts nor as actors can they find a reasonable solution, for neither law nor medicine provides a way out. The resolution is left to the audience.

Critical Opinion

In *The Connection* Gelber combines two of the strongest currents of modern drama: naturalism and anti-illusionism. He builds his drama out of the unresolved tension between the two.

Naturalism attempts to put on the stage a setting and characters that may well deceive the audience into believing that it is not a play they are seeing, but true life. Gorki's *The Lower Depths* (1902) is an excellent example of naturalistic drama and one which has parallels in *The Connection*. In Gorki's play, a group of vagrants, many of them sick or alcoholic, huddle in a cellar lodging, the last shelter available to them. Though a number of interrelated plots unfold, the overall impression is of experience presented without editing, a slice of life. Gelber carries this approach even further, for Jaybird claims not to be using actors at all, but real addicts. The heroin doses administered in the second act are, we are told, real, and represent payment for the performers. Leach shoots the second dose into his arm in full view of the audience, while such scenes as Jaybird's nausea were done so convincingly in the original production that at almost every performance there were spectators who became ill. The final irony of the work is that Jaybird, the putative playwright, becomes an addict, drawn into the unstructured reality which he has attempted to shape into a work of art.

Herein lies the complete paradox, for, of course, these are not real addicts, nor is anyone improvising. Gelber and his producers stand in the wings directing both "addicts" and "squares," all of whom are carefully rehearsed actors. As in Pirandello's *Six Characters in Search of an Author*, Gelber seems to say that invented characters have more substance than the actors who try to play them. And the play ends, as does Pirandello's, with a failure to resolve the contradictions between life and art.

Gelber's achievement has the two approaches illuminate and intensify each other. Each of Jim Dunn's interruptions as producer and commentator is startling. Yet, when he leaves the stage, the naturalistic effect is again established. Jim's appearances provide a semicomic relief, a way of carrying off some of the tension, thus making it easier to suspend disbelief when the addicts reassert themselves. However, though the grimy life in Leach's room is almost intolerably real, *The Connection* is essentially a work of art, not merely a slice of life.

The Connection was very successful when it was produced Off Broadway in a small, grimy theater that added to the grim mood of the play. The vividly realistic details of behavior and language were fascinating to the audience, for such things had never before been presented so nakedly on a stage. Gelber's more subtle and complex concern with the theme of reality and illusion was ignored by many, who saw the work as a morbid study of derelicts. Many writers, however, responded enthusiastically to Gelber's combination of new, shocking subject matter and unconventional form. Many recent developments Off Broadway, where the most extreme and fascinating experiments in theater take place, have their genesis at least in part in *The Connection* and Gelber's other plays.

The Author

Jack Gelber is one of the most important and representative playwrights produced by the Off Broadway theater in the fifties and sixties. A native of Chicago, he grew up in that city and studied journalism at the University of Illinois. *The Connection* (1959) was his first play, and its production brought notoriety both to the author and to the Living Theater, the acting company directed by Judith Malina and Julian Beck. The film version of the play, directed by Shirley Clarke, captured much of the impact of that first production and also added to the author's reputation. Gelber's welding of fresh and different subject matter with unconventional forms has had a tremendous influence on the writers working in Off Broadway theaters and in the cafés, coffeehouses, and clubs that constitute the new Off Off Broadway.

In his next play, *The Apple* (1961), Gelber carried his experimental approach much further. The stage is set to suggest a coffeehouse, but the actors, who retain their own names, use it as a stage to improvise some kind of play or ritual. However, right from the beginning, they are interrupted by a foulmouthed, bigoted drunk who later turns out also to be an actor who has been pretending. No coherent plot emerges; there is rather a series of confused improvisations and confrontations suggesting the chaos of life, and the artist's difficulties in shaping it. *Square in the Eye* (1965) is relatively more conventional. It concerns a schoolteacher who wants to be a painter but feels constricted by family and friends. His wife's death releases him. The story is not, however, told directly. The first half is fairly realistic, though films and tape recordings help to underscore the action, and the protagonist frequently speaks directly to the audience. The second half begins with the hero's second marriage, and moves backward to the scene of his first wife's death, growing progressively more stylized.

On Ice (1964) is Gelber's single attempt so far at writing a novel. It deals with a cool, detached young man drawn into the business world. Compared with Gelber's experiments with drama, the novel is quite conventional in form and content.

In 1968 Gelber had his first Broadway production, *The Cuban Thing*. Dealing with a middle-class Cuban family's adjustment to the Castro revolution and the new Marxist state, the play aroused an impassioned protest from anti-Castro refugees. As a theatrical event, however, it proved to be very disappointing, and closed after only one performance.

A Raisin in the Sun

by

LORRAINE HANSBERRY (1930–1965)

The Characters

Lena Younger (Mama)—in her early 60s, still a healthy, strong woman who carries herself with dignity and inner serenity; conscientious, concerned, pious, quiet, and forceful, and somewhat domineering.

Walter Younger—her son, in his middle 30s. He works as a chauffeur. High-strung, deeply frustrated, and furious about his poverty and empty future, he daydreams about great financial triumphs.

Ruth—his wife. Bone tired and discouraged, she is something of a shrew.

Travis—their child, a high-spirited 10-year-old.

Beneatha—Walter's sister, about 20, a college student planning to become a doctor. She is sarcastic, intellectual, militant, but less mature than her brash air suggests.

Asagai—a Nigerian student. He is certain of his African identity and dedicated to preparing himself for a revolutionary role when he returns home.

George Murchison—a well-to-do college student, whose behavior is imitative of white bourgeois society.

Carl Lindner—a white man, representing Clybourne Park Improvement Association.

The Setting

The Youngers share a crowded, shabby flat on Chicago's South Side. Walter and Ruth have one small bedroom, Mama and Beneatha another. Travis sleeps on a couch in the living-dining room. The kitchen is little more than an alcove. One small window provides a little daylight but no sun.

The Story

It is Friday morning, and the daily routine begins with the usual shouting and bad tempers. Everyone is particularly excited by the thought of a check expected the next day, Papa's ten-thousand-dollar insurance. Walter is eager to invest in a liquor store. His wife is cool to the idea because she distrusts the men who would be his partners, and she discounts his ability to manage a business. His sister also scorns his plans, and they quarrel bitterly when he belittles her desire to become a doctor. Mama, who will not allow liquor in her home, is also opposed to Walter's scheme. Her own dream is of a little house with a garden.

The next morning, Ruth returns from the doctor with the news that she is pregnant. She is depressed by the thought of adding another person to these overcrowded rooms, and lets slip the fact that she has already seen an abortionist and made a down payment for a future operation.

Beneatha receives a visit from Asagai, who brings her native Nigerian robes. She is entranced but resists his amorous approaches. He calls her an assimilationist and laughs at her sophisticated pose.

The check arrives, and Walter comes rushing home soon afterward, more eager than ever to use the money for the liquor store. His mother absolutely refuses to finance such a move. He lashes out savagely, picturing his empty future, bitterly unable to accept his mother's goal of a happy family as a meaningful alternative to financial success. She tells him his wife is pregnant and intends to have an abortion. Mama wants Walter to order his wife to drop this plan, but he cannot.

Later that day, Walter comes home drunk. He and Beneatha, in her Nigerian outfit, play African roles, parodying movie stereotypes. However, when George Murchison, in his conservative, Ivy League clothes, comes to take Beneatha out on a date, Walter turns belligerent and insulting. His outburst increases in vehemence when he is alone with Ruth, but after he has deeply insulted her he grows calm and explains his confusion, his fear of softness.

Walter and Ruth are interrupted by Mama's return. After some tantalizing hints, she announces that she has made a down payment on a house. Ruth is jubilant, but she is taken aback by the address in Clybourne Park, an area in which there are no Negroes. Mama explains that houses in Negro areas are less desirable and more expensive. Walter quietly accuses her of running all their lives and butchering all their dreams.

A few weeks later, shortly before moving day, Ruth discovers that her husband has not been going to work and will probably be fired. Walter calmly explains that he might as well become a loafer. His mother tries to justify her actions. She tells Walter to take the $6,500 left after her down payment; he is to put $3,000 in a savings account for Beneatha's education, but the remainder he can use any way he wants. His confidence and enthusiasm are restored, and he paints a brilliantly colored future for his son.

On moving day, the younger people are busy packing. They receive a caller, Mr. Lindner, representing the neighborhood they are moving into. At first, he presents himself as a kind of welcoming committee, but soon reveals his real purpose, an offer to buy their house back from them at a profit. Walter orders him out.

Walter tells Mama about Mr. Lindner's visit when she returns. They all laugh it away and gaily continue with their preparations for the move. Her children give Mama a set of gardening tools, and her grandson gives her a big, fancy gardening hat. All their joy is ended when one of Walter's partners arrives with the news that Wally, who was to arrange to get their liquor license, has run off with all the money. As Mama instantly realizes, Beneatha's money is gone, too. Hysterically, she beats her son.

After brooding on what he has done, Walter decides to call Lindner. To his family he explains that he will make the white man pay enough to cover their losses. For once, he says, they will not be in the class of the "tooken," and only joining the "takers" can get them out of this slum. He prepares to abase himself before the white man.

The women are appalled, but Mama recognizes the pain of failure and the desperation in the man and fiercely upbraids her daughter for acting so superior. When Lindner arrives, Mama insists that Walter talk to the white man in front of Travis and the whole family. With growing strength, Walter tells the man that they intend to be good neighbors but have no intention of backing down.

The movers begin carrying out the furniture. Walter starts ordering his sister about once more. Mama, with mingled sadness and joy, looks about the flat once more, takes her treasured plant, and leaves.

Critical Opinion

The title of the play is drawn from "Harlem," in "Lenox Avenue Mural," by Langston Hughes. In the poem, the author asks, "What happens to a dream deferred?/ Does it dry up/ Like a raisin in the sun?/ . . . *Or does it explode?*" The dreams of the Younger family move between these two extremes, but the crises that could lead to disaster instead test the mettle of all and create greater self-awareness and maturity. Mama discovers that by doing what she thinks is right for her family she may be inadvertently keeping them in the position of dependent children. Beneatha comes to recognize that despite her humanitarian dedication to medicine, her judgments of others lack compassion. Most important, Walter struggles through various roles, all united by a fantasy of monetary glory and sullen resentment at being treated like a child, until he finds pride in himself as a father, a man, and a Negro.

A Raisin in the Sun (1959) was written before Black Power became a battle cry. Its picture of slum life now seems rather mild, and its conclusions somewhat oversimplified and unjustifiably optimistic. By focusing on Walter Younger's personal growth to maturity Miss Hansberry's work comes close to being a conventional problem play in which all difficulties are resolved by love. The play was welcomed by white reviewers as a splendid demonstration of the basic humanity of men of all races. They missed or minimized the play's stress on the emasculating effects of the matriarchy of the ghetto on the man who dreams not merely of affluence but of power. Miss Hansberry did, however, achieve another purpose, the demonstration of the various options open to the Negro, from the utter aimlessness that tempts Walter to the fierce black nationalism that appeals to Beneatha.

One major stream of American drama has consisted of plays that show elements of society which have not before been treated honestly and seriously. Sidney Howard's picture of an Italian immigrant in *They Knew What They Wanted;* Clifford Odets' picture of a Jewish family in the Bronx in *Awake and Sing!;* William Inge's picture of a small-town alcoholic in *Come Back, Little Sheba*—these are only a few examples. *A Raisin in the Sun* does much the same for Negroes. Such plays are rarely impressive in their plotting or profound in their themes, but they come and stay alive in the vivid details of speech and gesture which reveal essential character. Like Odets, with whom her work has most in common, Miss Hansberry drew partially on her own observation and experience.

The number of plays by and about Negroes has increased greatly since Miss Hansberry's first drama helped to introduce a more honest approach to racial issues. The changing political and intellectual climate has also contributed to greater self-awareness for the black writer and performer. The new Negro drama has tended to deal, usually in vividly detailed naturalistic terms, with the theme Miss Hansberry had developed—the black man's eagerness to define and his determination to assert his identity. Among the Negro playwrights to appear in the early sixties were Ossie Davis, with *Purlie Victorious* (1961); James Baldwin, with *Blues for Mister Charlie* (1963); and LeRoi Jones, with a number of one-act plays, the most effective of which was *Dutchman* (1964). More recent work includes Douglas Turner Ward's *Day of Absence* (1965), Ron Milner's *Who's Got His Own* (1966), and Ed Bullins' *The Electronic Nigger* (1968). Ward was one of the founders in 1967 of the Negro Ensemble Company, a group devoted to creating a repertoire of plays dealing with Negro subjects; they have produced such notable works as *Ceremonies in Dark Old Men* (1969) by Lonne Elder III. White writers have also been deeply concerned with the need to understand the pains and aspirations of the Negro. *Big Time Buck White,* by Joseph Tuotti, was first produced in Los Angeles in 1965 and reflected the attempts of the Watts community to come to terms with its own frustration and violence. Howard Sackler's *The Great White Hope* (1967) is a slightly fictionalized account of the career of Jack Johnson, the Negro boxer who won the heavyweight championship in 1910.

The Author

Lorraine Hansberry was the daughter of a prosperous Negro real-estate broker and banker in Chicago, but this did not completely spare her the pains of ghetto life. She attended overcrowded, segregated schools and was familiar with the world of the poor. She went on to the University of Wisconsin where she became seriously interested in the theater and playwriting, being particularly impressed by the dramas of Sean O'Casey, with their portraits of poor but noble people. After two years, she left college and moved to New York, hoping to become a painter. She soon abandoned this goal for a career as a writer.

A few short stories preceded the composition of *A Raisin in the Sun* (1959), which reached the Broadway stage only after considerable difficulty in finding financial backing. It was a great success and not only brought fame to the author, but also marked a major change in the status of the Negro in the theater. Among other things, it was the first time a Broadway production had used a Negro director.

One of the most promising playwrights to appear in the 1950s, Miss Hansberry was able to complete only one other work before her death at thirty-five. In *The Sign of Sidney Brustein's Window* (1965) Miss Hansberry attempted a serio-comic treatment of a white intellectual and the world he moves in. She was working on the play while in the hospital during the last, painful weeks of her life.

Appendix

50 American Plays, arranged by date of first production

ONE-THIRD OF A NATION   1938

THE LITTLE FOXES   1939

YOU CAN'T TAKE IT WITH YOU   1939

LIFE WITH FATHER   1939

THE TIME OF YOUR LIFE   1939

THE MALE ANIMAL   1940

THE SKIN OF OUR TEETH   1942

I REMEMBER MAMA   1944

THE GLASS MENAGERIE   1945

HOME OF THE BRAVE   1945

BORN YESTERDAY   1946

THE ICEMAN COMETH   1946 (written in 1940)

A STREETCAR NAMED DESIRE   1947

DEATH OF A SALESMAN   1949

THE MEMBER OF THE WEDDING   1950

COME BACK, LITTLE SHEBA   1950

TEA AND SYMPATHY   1953

THE CRUCIBLE   1953

INHERIT THE WIND   1955

LONG DAY'S JOURNEY INTO NIGHT   1956
(written in 1941)

J. B.   1958

THE TENTH MAN   1959

RAISIN IN THE SUN   1959

THE CONNECTION   1959

THE ZOO STORY   1959

WHO'S AFRAID OF VIRGINIA WOOLF?   1962

Bibliography

Bentley, Eric. *The Dramatic Event*. New York: Horizon Press, 1954.

———. *In Search of Theater*. New York: Alfred A. Knopf, 1953.

Brustein, Robert. *The Theatre of Revolt*. Boston: Little, Brown, 1964.

Clurman, Harold. *The Fervent Years*. New York: Alfred A. Knopf, 1950.

Downer, Alan. *Fifty Years of American Drama: 1900–1950*. Chicago: H. Regnery, 1951.

———. *Recent American Drama*. Minneapolis: University of Minnesota Press, 1961.

Flexner, Eleanor. *American Playwrights: 1918–1938*. New York: Simon and Schuster, 1938.

Gagey, Edmond M. *Revolution in the American Drama*. New York: Columbia University Press, 1947.

Gassner, John. *Form and Idea in Modern Theatre*. New York: Dryden Press, 1956.

———. *Masters of the Drama*. New York: Dover Publications, 1954.

———. *Theatre at the Crossroads*. New York: Holt, Rinehart and Winston, 1960.

Hewitt, Barnard. *Theatre U.S.A., 1668 to 1957*. New York: McGraw-Hill, 1959.

Hughes, Glenn. *A History of the American Theatre, 1700–1950*. New York: S. French, 1951.

Krutch, Joseph Wood. *The American Drama Since 1918*. New York: Random House, 1939. Revised edition. New York: George Braziller, 1957.

———. *"Modernism" in Modern Drama*. Ithaca, N.Y.; Cornell University Press, 1953.

Lumley, Frederick. *New Trends in 20th Century Drama*. New York: Oxford University Press, 1967.

McCarthy, Mary. *Sight and Spectacles, 1937–1956* New York: Farrar, Straus and Cudahy, 1956.

Weales, Gerald. *American Drama Since World War II*. New York: Harcourt, Brace and World, 1962.

Young, Stark. *Immortal Shadows*. New York: Charles Scribner's Sons, 1948.

Index